W9-BCE-471

HQ
1426
.W637
1979

Women in Crisis Conference
(1st: 1979: New York, N.Y.)

Women in crisis

DATE DUE			
SEP 3 0 1988			
NOV 0 8 1988			
NOV 1 8 1988			
OCT 0 4 1994			

WOMEN IN CRISIS

WOMEN IN CRISIS

Edited by

Penelope Russianoff, Ph.D.

Sponsored by Women in Crisis, Inc.

 **HUMAN SCIENCES PRESS**

72 Fifth Avenue   3 Henrietta Street
NEW YORK, NY 10011 ● LONDON, WC2E 8LU

Printed in the United States of America
123456789   987654321

Library of Congress Cataloging in Publication Data

Women in Crisis Conference, 1st, New York, 1979.
  Women in crisis.

  Sponsored by the Project Return Foundation and the School of Social Welfare of the State University of New York at Stony Brook.
    1. Women—United States—Social conditions—Congresses.
2. Women's rights—United States—Congresses.
I. Russianoff, Penelope. II. Project Return Foundation.
III. New York (State). State University at Stony Brook.
School of Social Welfare. IV. Title.
HQ1426.W637   305.4'2   80-29492
ISBN 0-89885-051-7

To all women in crisis

CONTENTS

CONTRIBUTORS

THE HONORABLE BELLA S. ABZUG, President, WOMEN USA; Former U.S. Representative; Civil Rights and Civil Liberties Attorney

SEVERA AUSTIN, Director, Bureau of Alternate Care, Wisconsin Department of Health and Social Services

SHEILA B. BLUME, M.D., Director, New York State Division of Alcoholism and Alcohol Abuse

MILLICENT BUXTON, Information Coordinator, Haight-Ashbury Free Medical Clinic, San Francisco, CA

DENISE CAPELLI, Rehabilitation Counselor, Nassau County Department of Drug and Alcohol Addiction, New York

VIOLET PADAYACHI CHERRY, A.C.S.W., Director, Health Services, City of Englewood, New Jersey

NIKKI N. DUFFIÉ, Director, Women's Prescription Drug Misuse Program, Together, Glassboro State College, New Jersey

MAJ FANT, Director, RFSU, Sweden's Association for Sex Education

NORMA FINKELSTEIN, M.S.W., Director, The Women's Alcoholism Program of CASPAR, Inc., Cambridge, MA

DAVID FOGEL, PH.D., Professor and Director of Graduate Studies, Department of Criminal Justice, University of Illinois

HERBERT J. FREUDENBERGER, PH.D., Psychoanalyst, Independent Practice; Training Consultant to the New York Archdiocese and Phoenix House, Inc.

EDITH S. LISANSKY GOMBERG, PH.D., Research Scientist, Institute of Gerontology; Professor, The University of Michigan School of Social Work and the Center of Alcohol Studies, Rutgers University

MARILEE GRYGELKO, Senior Budget Advisor, New York State Division of the Budget

JACQUELYN H. HALL, PH.D., Chief, Mental Health Education Branch, National Institute of Mental Health

SUSAN HALPERN, Author, *Rape: Treating the Victim;* consultant

JENNIFER JAMES, PH.D., Associate Professor, Department of Psychiatry, University of Washington

FLORA KOPPEL, Director of Social Services, Bedford Stuyvestant Alcoholism Treatment Center, Brooklyn, New York

JOYCE B. LAZAR, Chief, Social Science Section and Special Assistant to the Division Director—Research on Women, National Institute of Mental Health

ROSE LEONE, C.S.W., C.R.C., Psychotherapist, New York City

BARBARA A. LEWIS, PH.D., Feminist Psychotherapist, New York City

STEPHEN J. LEVY, PH.D., Director, Alcoholism Treatment Center, Beth Israel Medical Center, New York City

MARLENE CROSBY MAINKER, President, Womanpower Projects, Inc., Chatham, New Jersey

PEGGY ANN MCGARRY, Women Against Abuse, Philadelphia, PA

DENNIS MCGRATH, PH.D., Social Science Department, Community College of Philadelphia, PA

RUTH W. MESSINGER, Member of the New York City Council

CATHERINE MILTON, Special Assistant to the Assistant Secretary (Enforcement & Operations), U.S. Department of the Treasury

ELEANOR HOLMES NORTON, Commissioner, U.S. Equal Employment Opportunity Commission

CAROL PEACOCK, M.S.W., Assistant Commissioner for Girl's Services, Department of Youth Services, Boston, MA

LUCY BARRY ROBE, Author, *Just So It's Healthy*

PENELOPE RUSSIANOFF, PH.D., Clinical Psychologist; Faculty Member, New School, New York

MARGUERITE SAUNDERS, Deputy Commissioner, New York State Division of Substance Abuse Services

JUDITH SEIXAS, Alcoholism Services, Hastings-on-Hudson, New York

DAVID E. SMITH, M.D., Founder and Medical Director, Haight-Ashbury Free Medical Clinic, San Francisco, CA

BARBARA TAYLOR, Consultant, The American Red Cross; Principal, Huggins-Taylor Associates

JANE VELEZ, Conference Administrator, Women in Crisis, Inc.

JOAN WEITZEL, Coordinator, Maple Manor Residential Treatment Facility, Coudersport, PA

FOREWORD

Conclusion

In May 1979, 1,500 women and men from 46 states and 5 foreign countries convened in New York City at the first Women In Crisis Conference. The basic assumption of the conference was that there are thousands of women in America who are the victims of double discrimination. These women not only suffer all the traditional indignities of sexual discrimination inherent in our society, but have the added burden of drug abuse, alcoholism, mental illness, or involvement in the criminal justice system. For the most part, they receive no help because our laws, our institutions, and our attitudes in mental health, alcohol, drugs, and justice all but ignore the differences between male and female victims.

Realizing that human service providers working within any one of these disciplines too often functioned in a vacuum, the convenors of Women In Crisis created a conference format that promoted dialogue among the various problem components. Plenary sessions and integrated panels were carefully structured to include speakers from two or more of the areas of specialization. In addition, a limited number of special issue sessions and modular workshops were included to address issues of particular and timely concern to each discipline. Overwhelmingly, the total thrust of the conference was "making change," reaching and presenting alternative solutions for women.

The Women In Crisis Conference, funded initially by the Project Return Foundation and cosponsored by the School of Social Welfare of the State University of New York at Stony Brook, received additional support from the New York State Division of Substance Abuse Services, New York State Division of Alcoholism & Alcohol Abuse, Exxon Corporation, and the New Jersey State Division of Narcotic and Drug Abuse Control. Over 30 national organizations including the American Red Cross, the Fortune Society, The Girls Clubs of America, The National Council on Alcoholism, The National Women's Political Caucus, and the Salvation Army actively endorsed, supported, and participated in making the first year's conference the overwhelming success that it proved to be. Similarly, our National Advisory Board included some of the most distinguished women and men in American professional life; a number of their actual conference presentations appear in this compendium.

The total conference program included over 300 separate presentations, a listing of which appears in this volume. Papers included here represent a sample of the extraordinary range of issues addressed and perspectives represented from clients, academicians, service providers, and governmental officials. What cannot be reflected here is the atmosphere of excitement generated during the three days in New York, and the networking among women that grew out of "Women In Crisis" 1979.

Women In Crisis, Inc., and the Project Return Foundation would like to express sincere gratitude to the many women and men who planned for and implemented this conference. Their contribution of inordinate amounts of time and professional insight made this overwhelmingly successful effort possible.

Jane Velez
Conference Administrator

Barbara Taylor
Chairperson, Justice Task Force

INTRODUCTION

Penelope Russianoff

Suffering. Struggling. Hundreds of women in America live in constant
crisis. They are the twin victims of sexual discrimination and poverty:
the battered wives, the teenage prostitutes, the rape and incest victims,
the women offenders, the female drug abusers and alcoholics, the
women whose lives have been devastated by emotional starvation and
neglect.

From their desperate experience has emerged a desperate need.
From that need we have begun to build the means to end the tragedy
of WOMEN IN CRISIS.

So read the opening two paragraphs of the program for the first
"Women in Crisis" conference. On Thursday, May 17, 1979 the
conference opened in the Sheraton Center in New York City with
participants from all over the country. The atmosphere was charged
with the expectation and excitement that somehow this conference
was going to give a giant shove forward to women at all levels.
Women in desperate situations would see themselves in a new light,
that the liberation trail blazed primarily by middle class, intellectual
women would now have meaning for them. Vast numbers of frustrated, hopeless women who had passively accepted their depressing
lot would find inspiration and guidance to move from desperation

and victimization to awareness of their problems, and hopefully the ability to take charge of their lives.

Listening to the programs and reading the papers from this conference, the most striking message is women's ignorance of the forces that keep so many of them in poverty, psychological deadening, and passive acceptance of their assigned social roles. The participants in this conference included agency and media personnel as well as housewives. All of us, including those well-schooled in women's liberation, had our consciousness raised. Many of the professional women came away from the conference with greatly increased knowledge of the problems that cut across all socioeconomic levels. I learned with emotional impact how ghettoes compound the discrimination against, and exploitation of, women. For example, I suddenly became much more sharply aware of the plight of the battered woman, particularly the psychologically battered woman.

From the moment they are born, women are subtly taught that they are the inferior sex. Acceptance of inferiority, fear of thinking for themselves, and fear of taking charge of their lives lead to depression, which leads to "escape" attempts. Women have been made so powerless by our culture that when they are told that rape is their own fault, they begin to believe it. The worst travesty forced upon women has been to indoctrinate them with the belief that men and authority figures know more about them than they know about themselves. Women's feelings of inferiority make them sitting ducks for manipulation and exploitation. They con themselves into believing what they are told is negative about themselves. In addition to the entrapments that all women face, there are additional obstacles to face when born in the ghetto.

In their socially assigned role, women, much more than men, are taught to seek others to define their lives; to tell them how and what to think. They are taught to accept emotional isolation and to love giving to others. Very few women and even fewer men have had their consciousness raised in terms of the pressure on women to deny their feelings and their right to be themselves.

One myth perpetrated on women is that "motherhood is wonderful and mothers are to be deified." The truth is that motherhood can be awful when one is not prepared psychologically or physically. A young unwed mother with several children, living by necessity in a ghetto commune with shared kitchen facilities, and shared sleeping and living quarters is likely to live a life of permanent frustration. Substance abuse, prostitution, and crime are viewed as survival routes as well as escapes. I remember several years ago making a home visit to a mother in such circumstances, to discuss with her the problem of her 13-year-old son. He had become a member of an extensive male prostitution ring. She said with resignation, and perhaps wisdom, "At least he makes a living and probably won't make children."

Related to the "motherhood is wonderful" myth is the belief that "women and especially mothers love self-sacrifice." The myth continues that they *should* love self-sacrifice because it is a fine, womanly characteristic. On the basis of this myth, many women end up serving others at their own expense. Serving others *can* be self-fulfilling, but only when it is a choice, not mandated by a gender role. Otherwise, a self-sacrifice can become a partial psychological suicide.

Another myth fed to all women regardless of socioeconomic level is that "if you are a good girl, you'll be treated nicely and someone will take care of you." At the poverty level, this myth is a joke, and yet women will prostitute to support a man's drug habit, even join the habit to please him, while believing that he's "taking care." *She's* been thoroughly trained that she's more complete with a man, *any* man. Mutual support here is very limited, and there is almost no hope for continued interest, love, encouragement, or help. Even where good agency help is available, personnel frequently change. Commitment is rare, and yet commitment and consistency are important ingredients in mental health.

Two experiences told to me by colleagues illustrate the importance of consistent caring and interest. One was with a troubled third-grade child who was born to poverty and whose mother had enough problems trying to exist and find a mate. My friend, who was a school psychologist, felt that continuity, caring, and commitment would make the big difference in helping this child. He decided to test his theory by making a commitment, not financially, but psychologically. This young woman is now 39 years old, but still keeps in touch with my friend even though she now lives far away. She often calls him for emotional support when a crisis arises. She claims that his continuing commitment, just on an emotional basis, has prevented a potential delinquent and criminal. Continuity in our changing world *is* difficult, but it is a major issue that has been brushed aside as "impossible."

Another friend who is a psychologist received a phone call from a woman who had been a high school dropout more than two years after she had tried to run a therapy group for underacheiving high school girls. The girl, whom I will call Betty, was one of this group and practically nonverbal. Betty called to tell her that in the time since she had been in the group, she had married, had a child, and her husband was no longer interested in her sexually. Could she find someone to talk to? My colleague referred her to a local mental health clinic as a possibility. Later, when I realized the colossal effort Betty must have expended to find out the psychologist's new, married surname, where she now worked, and had the guts to track her down, realized strongly how sadly lacking are many institutions in continuity of interest, support, and encouragement. I would like to see female support systems with a strong direction toward providing permanent, consistent caring. Brainstorming the issue of developing "connecting threads"—especially at the poverty level—would undoubtably result in creative new solutions to the "lack of continuity" problem.

I would like to see our service organizations augment the educational possibilities demonstrated by the consciousness-raising movement. Education is a relatively inexpensive resource that could help women become much more aware of their problems and include their victimization, brainwashing, and exploitation. New goals for women *can* be taught. For example, in my course, "Risking Change," taught at the New School for Social Research in New York City, women learn that they can take charge of their own lives and they can make their own decisions. They learn that they do not have to have inferiority feelings about themselves if they are without a man. Freedom from defining themselves and their life's worth in terms of "catching" a man can be an enormous liberation for divorced or widowed women who are terrified of facing themselves alone. If the woman has children, she must still be prepared for the fact that they often do not become the hoped-for future baby sitters for lonely mothers.

One of the most neglected resources for women are good female friendships. I strongly believe that courses could spring up all over the country helping women to see other women as therapeutic resources rather than as competitors to be avoided or "second best." Women often feel awful about themselves, while at the same time thinking, "I never knew anyone else felt the way I do." This is all the more reason to learn the therapeutic value of good friendships, where one can find common problems, supportive listening, and challenge to the negative self-judgment that cripples psychological growth.

Society, and particularly men, have discouraged female friendships. Is jealousy the reason? Do men sense that there is an emotional
sharing, a closeness that women can experience with good female
friendships? Do men miss that closeness in male friendships? Often
women believe men when they say "all women's talk is silly gossip."
In reality, women listen to each other's feelings, exchange information, and assuage each other's isolation and loneliness. Are friendships a threat to men because the insecure man fears his possesion,
i.e., his woman, might be influenced by someone else? Do they suspect that women are talking with their female friends about what's
lacking in their marriage? Are they talking about *him?* Luckily, they
are, and often gain support for their own worth. They can ventilate
their frustration, while laughing with each other about their problems. Learning to have good female friendships can be one of the
greatest therapeutic resources available to women.

Fulfillment from male–female relationships has been held out as
the big "love promise"; female–female friendships have been considered inferior. All of us need to be educated on the topic of therapeutic, mutually fulfilling intimacy, with or without sex. We need to
learn to make requests (such as that for nonjudgmental listening)
from a friend. A great deal of awareness and help can be generated
through lecturing, demonstrative role-plays, and developing groups
for the purpose of exploring same-sex friendships.

We have done a good job in pin-pointing and diagnosing problems. There is actually very little material on "how to" change.
In our next *Women in Crisis* conference I'd like to see major emphasis on *what* to do. Having taught "Risking Change," "Motivation,"
and other courses at the New School for several years, I cannot emphasize enough that new self-attitudes—*healthy* self-attitudes—and
self-motivation can be taught to vast numbers of people.

I hope this book, which represents a wide range of thought and
experience, will not just end up on the desks of agency personnel. I
hope that women and men who are in any way involved in change
(through ERA, abortion rights, NOW, or other means) will read this
book and think of new, creative ways to apply their skills, and help
women whose lives are miserable and who are unwitting victims of
society, because of being born into poverty. I would also like to see
forums defining the woman's inferiority complex, formulating new
means for self-respect, and bringing a positive image for women, with
strong emphasis on the right to self-fulfillment.

Part I

WOMEN IN CRISIS: THE ISSUE

This conference is giving the seed of recognition to what ought to be obvious to Americans by now but sadly is not. Women all around us—women whom we see and women who are hidden from view—are in a period of unusual crisis.

It will help to understand this crisis, I believe, if we look at women in something approaching historical perspective. There have been, in my judgment, about four key periods for American women in our history, when their very roles have changed almost overnight. This is one of those periods.

The first of these periods was, of course, the period of the settler, women who came initially from other countries with long historic cultures into a rough, unchartered wilderness, prepared only to meet a fearsomely new terrain. Next there was the period of the frontier woman, who left settled parts of the country to follow new opportunities and extreme danger. Then there was the period of the postsuffrage woman, the women of the 1920s, with the right to vote, the beginning of modern woman. And finally, there is the period of the post-1960s woman, the women who have shaped and been shaped by the new feminism—you and I.

This new woman is in a period of crisis today brought on by the unusual change she is experiencing in her core identity. We see this crisis in the stress associated with rapidly changing female roles and with new demands on and by women. We see it in the HEW report of last month indicating that smoking has declined among male teenagers but increased among female teenagers. We see it in the escalated use of drugs and pills among women of all ages. We see it in the extraordinary increase in crime among women. And we see it in new levels of violence by and against women.

At the same time, for good reasons, this has been a period of the glorification of the change women are undergoing. But if change is for the better, one might ask, why all the problems?

The answers are not simple. The problems women encounter today are as inevitable as the pride they feel in their new status. There can be no change on this scale without problems. There can be no change of this magnitude without victims. The victims are women caught between the demise of the old institutions and values and the

Remarks of Eleanor Holmes Norton, Chair, Equal Employment Opportunity Commission, at First Annual Women in Crisis Conference, New York, New York, May 19, 1979.

development of new ones. We owe a special responsibility to those caught in this transition.

Women—both those in obvious crisis and those not so obviously so—are experiencing no less than a mass identity crisis. They are being asked to define themselves anew. In the process they are re-defining womenhood.

Yet we are only beginning to develop aids to cope with the stresses such weighty change brings. Your conference schedule reads like a catalog of what results when stress goes unattended: juvenile prostitution, prescription drug abuse, and all the rest.

Many of your sessions will address these problems in terms of the women known to be experiencing them. But for every one of these, there are hundreds of others in crisis. For every woman who walks into an alcohol treatment center, there are hundreds sitting at home drinking by themselves. The problems of identity and role are not confined to the obviously vulnerable.

Still our own history is against us. The "good girl" image lingers from schooldays in other periods when the girls did better in school than the boys, when the girls did their homework while the boys dallied. The girls did what they were supposed to do and were expected to do and then graduated to motherhood, selfless and self-contained, with time for everyone else's problems, but, as was expected of them, without problems of their own. This is who we have been taught we are; and this is who some of us are, but we come in many varieties. We are people who have problems like everybody else. But because women have often borne their problems with unusual strength or in concealment, much that affects them has gone unnoticed or unheeded.

But the almost dizzying change women face today has produced unprecedented and excessive demands for adaptation. In one generation, the American woman has converted from housewife to worker. The full-time housewife role is fast disappearing. Today the male single breadwinner exists in less than one-third of our families; a generation ago this was the model in 56 percent of American families. In 1948, only 26 percent of married women worked outside of the home; in 1976, 54 percent—the majority of them—were in full-time jobs. The most dramatic change has been the strong emergence in the labor force of women with preschoolage children, unthinkable a generation ago except for black women, of course, for whom the life-style of a housewife has never been a reality.

Women have not gone into the workforce only because of the desire to work or the lure of the values of the women's movement. They are working today because of pressures presented by the American standard of living. They are working even when their children are infants, although the prevailing wisdom has been and for many continues to be that it is wrong for a woman with pre-schoolage children to work.

It is certainly close to impossible for women with preschoolage children to work. Infant and day-care centers are still rare. Yet today 37 percent of women with children under 5 work, as compared with only 13 percent in 1948. This trend mounts even without an organized and careful system of child care that is considered a basic essential for working mothers and children all over the world. Women with older children of school age, from first grade to high school, on the average work today. Younger women today see themselves as workers as much as they see themselves as wives or mothers. Older women are joining the workforce in huge numbers despite an upbringing that inculcated the belief that women should remain at home.

We in the women's movement, of course, have pushed and greeted this change in role. Most of it is magnificent. We have urged it with pride and encouraged it as progress. And it is. We have argued that the emergence of women as workers is part of the emergence of women as complete and whole people. And it is. Yet even we have paid too little attention to the stress that accompanies this change. We in the great movement for women's freedom must say louder what we know and feel: that it is not all pleasure and pride. It is partly pain and stress.

Whatever were the problems of the male-headed household (and they were many) there was a woman at home taking care of the children and a man who went out to work, the kind of order and stability that results when everyone accepts his or her role. With the decline of this structure nothing has emerged to take its place. The society has created neither guidance nor support for women trying to work and raise children at the same time. Men have thus far failed to fill the breach adequately. Despite inevitable and abrupt shifts in traditional family roles, there is little help for men and women who are becoming different kinds of mothers and fathers than their own mothers and fathers were.

If we have neglected the burden on women, we have also done little about the stresses of complex role change on family life.

We say little of the real reasons for the 700 percent increase in divorce since the turn of the century. We accept almost callously the doubling of the divorce rate in a single generation. As a result, the emergence of special support for the single mothers and their children who are the chief victims when divorce occurs has been stunted.

The steep rise in female-headed households with young children is not a natural phenomenon but a cause for alarm. It has reached crisis proportions in the black community, where almost 40 percent of all families are female-headed, with poverty disproportionately attending the mothers and children.

Displaced homemakers is a new word in our vocabulary, but the condition is as old as time. Such women confront emotional stress often in midlife with the abandonment of the marriage or the death of the spouse. Then many must cope also with economic deprivation, even poverty, sometimes for the first time in their lives. Twenty-five percent of white women and 40 percent of black women who were *not* poor when they were married fall into poverty after they are no longer married.

Have we expected too much? Did we truly expect this massive dose of social change to take hold calmly and automatically? How much longer can we ignore the personal guilt and helplessness many modern women feel as they try to cope without help with new and often unfamiliar roles?

Crisis situations in work and in marriage are no longer associated with the marginal woman. The same problems now face large numbers of mainstream women caught up in irresistible change. Women should not have to encounter deep distress before their problems are recognized. Large numbers of women should not have to become alcoholics or drug abusers before we acknowledge that women face unusual crisis conditions today.

Even women who may appear to have the most fulfilling lives are often in trouble. Until recently, the highest suicide rate for women was among divorced women over 70. But a new report reveals that the highest suicide rate in the United States today is among female doctors, who have four times the average suicide rate of all women. One in every 15 deaths of a female doctor is a suicide, with the average age being 47. The majority of these premature deaths occur during what should be the high years of productive life. The crisis women are facing is not limited by race, sex, age, and not even by employment or wealth.

In my work I see the crisis coming into the workplace. Women are pouring into the labor force. They are taking whatever jobs are available. They are the largest new cheap labor supply in this country. In many ways, these new women workers meet greater discrimination in the workforce than their mothers did a generation ago. If the number of women going into the workforce has exploded, their opportunities in many ways have diminished. This is heralded as the age of the woman worker. But what do women find? They find that the gap in income between male and female wages has actually increased in the last generation. They find that sex stereotyping in jobs is rampant. They find that women still work in a few familiar categories of jobs while men work in dozens.

The statistics are gruesome. Women are lumped in basically three occupations: clericals, service workers, and private household workers. In 1958, 53 percent of all women worked in these three large female-dominated categories; by 1975, 58 percent of all women worked in these same categories, which is up 5 percentage points. In 1958, 30 percent of all women worked as clerks and secretaries; by 1975, 35 percent of all women worked as clerks and secretaries, also up 5 percentage points. This is what "freedom" in the workplace has brought. It is an acceleration of already hardened, patterns of discrimination against women.

Some of the stress in women's lives would not be there if this situation did not obtain at work. This makes the importance of the antidiscrimination laws impossible to overemphasize. For women still face awesome problems of discrimination, from the most complicated to the most basic. Two examples affecting millions of women will suffice to make the point.

Sex discrimination is perhaps the largest unresolved issue in antidiscrimination work today. It is the issue of equal pay for work of comparable value. Millions of women do work equal to or of higher value than that performed by men but receive a fraction of the male wage. Their wages have been set according to sex, not skill. This discrimination is more elaborate, more complicated, and more widespread than the traditional area of equal pay for equal work. The Equal Employment Opportunity Council (EEOC) is pressing this issue through hearings scheduled for February 1980, through cases now in court, and through an EEOC commissioned-study now being undertaken by the National Academy of Sciences. For many women workers, this issue is key to the frustration that comes from knowing you are working for less than you are worth. Even the most basic issues frustrate women who work. The pregnant woman (and younger women today are almost inevitably workers) or the woman of child-bearing age has found a basic conflict at work. For years, employers have provided disability benefits for people who become ill or temporarily disabled. Pregnant women have been the large exception. Pregnancy was treated as a special condition that, unlike all others, could not be supported during the period of temporary disability. The result was that a woman often lost her job when she left to have a child. She could not qualify for the disability benefits a man could get if he were recovering from an illness, such as a heart attack. Thus, pregnancy brought a special set of stresses to women who at best had to absorb the cost of the period of disability, and at worst faced the loss of their jobs when pregnancy came.

In 1972, EEOC issued guidelines requiring that women be given equal treatment by receiving disability for pregnancy if an employer granted disability for other conditions. The Supreme Court later struck down those guidelines. Fortunately, the women's movement, the labor unions, and the EEOC fought to overturn this decision, and new legislation was passed in 1979. EEOC has now issued new pregnancy disability guidelines. Today, employers who offer disability for other conditions must offer disability payments to pregnant and postpartum women as well. This will relieve one form of anxiety with large ramifications for many women who work.

Precisely because discrimination is at the root of much of the stress women are feeling, it is important that the government be in a position to cope with this important problem. This is why it has been critical for us to get the EEOC itself in shape. Its great backlog of cases had tragically limited the ability of the agency to seriously attack the mammoth issues of discrimination still facing women and minorities. But improvements in EEOC operations have led President Carter and the Congress to approve a large and unprecedented 30 percent increase in Title VII positions, the transfer of seven new functions to the Commission, and authority for enforcing two statutes, in addition to Title VII, which is the Equal Pay Act and the Age Discrimination in Employment Act. The backlog of the agency diminished 30 percent in the first year, the first permanent backlog reduction in the agency's history, with total backlog elimination targeted for 1982. New case-processing systems have been placed in all the Commission's field offices. Today, the average case in an EEOC office anywhere in the country is processed in under two months. And the efficiency of the process in getting to cases early, when the evidence is fresh, has resulted in a near quadrupling of dollar benefits to complainants.

With the backlog no longer draining all the agency's energies and new cases being resolved on a current basis, we have been able to move the priority of the EEOC at last to pattern and practice or class action work. It is long ingrained patterns and not individual acts of discrimination that are responsible for the fact that when a woman goes to look for work today she almost always will find herself in one of the stereotypic female jobs. The only way to get at sex stereotyping and the other patterns of discrimination that keep women where they are in the workplace is to devote more and more resources to pattern and practice cases. We are finally able to do so.

These improvements in the government's ability to pursue discrimination come at a critical time for women. They come when women are flooding the workforce but are still being absorbed into the traditional women's occupations, which are most readily available, thus compounding already severe discrimination based on sex. In these jobs or in jobs newly opened to women, this new generation of working women is encountering new stresses in employment that we are under an obligation to arrest.

Yet even the women's rights movement, with its clear and noble concern for all women, has not taken sufficient action in the face of this multifaceted crisis. We have too often expected that women would simply accommodate these massive changes, especially changes in marriage, family, and work roles. In this expectation, we have appeared to accept the old notion that girls always do well. Instead, we must lead the country in facing this crisis, not in profile but full front. This conference is a worthy contribution to that end.

As I leave you, I am reminded of a few lines I wrote almost unconsciously a few years ago when I was thinking about women and their new choices. As I was writing down the words, I do not believe I realized that I was writing a poem. As you enter your discussions of women in crisis, I leave you with these words of hope, to remind us that the crisis is, after all, part of one of the large advances in human development.

> A woman is a person who makes choices
> A woman is a dreamer
> A woman is a planner
> A woman is a maker and the moulder
> A woman is a person who makes choices

A woman heals others
A woman builds bridges
A woman makes children and makes cars
A woman writes poetry and songs
A woman is a person who makes choices

Chapter 1

LEARNED HELPLESSNESS

Penelope Russianoff

Women are taught helplessness, and they learn it well, usually from their mothers, who have also been taught helplessness. Until fairly recently it has been considered the earmark of an attractive woman to appear helpless. Of course, after years of practice, helplessness becomes a habit, and the female "knows" that she *is* helpless. She has also been taught that if she is nice, pretty, and helpless, she is going to inspire in some man the desire to take care of her. Helplessness or pseudo-helplessness is played out in many ways at different socioeconomic levels. In essence, the net result is that a woman says to herself, "I am nothing without a man," and she feels that her destiny in this respect is beyond her control. She *must* capture a man who will live and take care of her permanently. She will then be known as a successful *woman.*

Concomitantly, in the process of learning helplessness, she is also quashing her own creative impulse. She is trying hard to bend herself into a mold that will fit someone else's wishes. She will try to be someone that a man, and ultimately *her* man, will desire. She will try to please and appease. The need to get a man is often exemplified in prostituting to support her man's drug habit. Hopelessness emerges out of learned helplessness and is seen at all socioeconomic levels. In poverty areas, the woman may get her man. She may also lose him shortly thereafter, but only after she's had children by him, and her life continues to be a matter of servicing others. She lives in an environment in which her potential, resources, innate ability, and creativity must be stamped out, as her time is consumed in servicing and survival activities.

Hopelessness leads to feelings of futility, despair, and depression, the consequences of which are seen in escape activities, which are often blatant alcoholism or other types of substance abuse, including hard and soft drugs. She may become involved in prostitution, both for economic reasons and for self-gratification, the illusion being that she is attractive to men, that she is still able to turn men on sexually, and perhaps develop a permanent relationship with one, pursuing the notion that she is living a much better life if it includes a man.

The helpless-hopeless condition is seen very obviously in the battered-woman syndrome. By this time, she has lost any shred of self-esteem she might have had, feels helpless and hopeless, and unable to leave her situation. A woman may also escape into criminal acts that provide excitement and possible rewards.

The helpless-hopeless, depressed woman may also take flight into physical illness or a psychotic episode. She may turn to food abuse, which serves many complex psychological problems. The overweight helpless-hopeless woman feels in her obese condition that she is not a love object, and therefore does not have to deal with the complexities of love objectism. Her spouse, who may very likely be a dependent male, may also encourage the weight, so that he does not have to deal with the thought of losing her. The helpless-hopeless depressed woman can escape from her problems with all manner of compulsions, including cleanliness and washing, and work.

The consequence of all the helpless-hopeless depression symptoms is a kind of partial suicide. She is a victim of society's false messages and false promises, the supreme promise being that she will be fulfilled if she gives to and services others.

One of the worst problems that arises for women in the helpless-hopeless syndrome is in believing what others tell them about themselves. For example, if the husband says to his wife, "Look, you're lucky to be married to me. Nobody else would want a fat, complaining slob like you. You're lucky I love you and am willing to live with you," she believes him. Women who have learned helplessness are also available to any kind of manipulative ploy. They are particularly ready to feel guilty, often blaming themselves for their man's infidelity. Similarly, women are sitting ducks for "gaslighting." They will readily accept someone else's deliberately false interpretation of what's going on inside them, rather than listening to themselves or taking charge of their own lives. If someone they depend on tells them that they are stupid, or crazy, they are quite apt to believe it although they may make feeble protests. The supreme example is when a man calls a woman a "castrating bitch." Most women are so terrified of that label that they promptly knuckle under, cease rebelling against the man's wishes, and become putty in his hands.

The real issue is one of how to change the learned helpless-hopeless and depressed syndrome in women. It is my opinion that education, including the large-size courses I give at the New School, have a lot more impact in changing people than one might think. Such didactic-workshop courses seem to go a very long way towards changing attitudes, assumptions, and premises. Education includes awareness, the very same kind of awareness that has been inspired by consciousness-raising groups. There are several themes that women seem to gravitate toward and respond to in an educational setting.

A recent example is the New York City YWCA's "Talk Tenderly to Yourself." Forty women from all walks of life showed up for this short lecture series. The results indicate that this particular mini-course, a grand total of three hours, had a definite effect on the lives of some people. The course consisted of demonstrating to women how they could be aware of the negative messages that they were giving themselves. They were shown how to stop these messages, and with conscious awareness, replace them with messages that were descriptive of reality. If one is to learn how to talk tenderly then one has to learn how to talk with understanding. Instead of saying, "Look what you did, you stupid lout, you knocked the glass off the table and broke it. Now you've got to pick up all those pieces, you idiot," the same person might say to herself, "I was so interested and enthusiastic about what we were discussing, I paid no attention to the glass on the table. When I made a stretch with my hand, I brushed the glass, which fell on the floor and broke. Now let me clean it up." Notice there's not a word of self-put-down in that statement. It is mainly descriptive of the actual event. Learning to talk objectively and understandingly to oneself, rather than putting oneself down, was the basic purpose of the "Talk Tenderly" course. The course moved on to the issue of letting in tender talk, and students learned to talk tenderly to others. The response to this theme was enormous. Many people have given feedback as to their ability to grasp this rather simple notion and put it into action. There are numerous other themes about relating to self and to others that can be successfully taught to women in an educational, workshop, or consciousness-raising setting.

Because of their helpless feelings, most women avoid situations where they might be rejected. They can be taught, rather quickly, to purposely set up rejection situations so they can practice coping, instead of perpetuating terror and anxiety about the possibility of rejection, which leads to a life of avoidance. Feelings of inferiority diminish with the increase of coping capacities, particularly in the areas of failure and rejection.

Self-motivation can be enhanced in a course situation. Most women caught in the helplessness syndrome do not know how to kick their own starter, so they wait and wait and wait for someone else to rev up their motors. Helpless women can be taught a great deal in an educational format about making decisions. Because they are so afraid of making the wrong decision, many women are afraid to make decisions, and thus accrue the wrath of someone on whom they are dependent.

Assertiveness training is a discipline that can be very effectively taught, and in the process of learning assertiveness women can learn rights that they have as human beings. Assertiveness training helps women to define and stick to their goals, even in the face of other people's attempts to distract them. They can learn to respect themselves, and above all, learn effective techniques of communication, an area in which most helpless women feel totally inadequate.

The whole area of communication is wide open for teaching. Take such a simple thing as manipulation through sentences that begin, "If you really loved me you would." Women can be taught to challenge such sentences. Questions such as, "Don't you trust me?" tend to frighten insecure women who know the question is really a statement: "Of course, you should trust me, and there's something wrong with *you* if you don't." The irrationality of such an assumption is easily demonstrated in a class. Women can also be taught a great deal about female sexuality, and handling put-downs in relationship to sex. There is a great need for information on communication in sexual situations. Women are just beginning to understand their rights as humans in sexual relationships.

There is a whole new world for women (and hence automatically for men) as women unlearn helplessness and begin to feel exhilaration by taking charge of their own lives, instead of accepting a dependent position. This paper has touched on just a few of the topics that could be easily taught to women as a leverage away from learned helplessness. Often women in these classes will say, "It seemed as if you're speaking personally to me about *my* problems." or "This class has changed me, because I began to see myself differently, and to act differently." Good education is therapeutic, and can move many women away from helpless-hopeless depression into feeling that they have a right to be themselves, to program their *own* lives, and to fight for changes that will bring them fulfillment.

Chapter 2

LEARNED HELPLESSNESS, DEPRESSION, AND ALCOHOL PROBLEMS OF WOMEN

Edith S. Lisansky Gomberg

Learned helplessness, as a concept used by psychologists and other social scientists, refers to a particular explanation of the origin of depression. As an explanatory concept, it is very appealing and it has been applied in many ways and in many situations that have little to do with the experiments and theory from which it is derived. The concept of learned helplessness has been overextended, e.g., to explain the psychology of women, the affect of hopelessness, and both individual behaviors and the response of oppressed groups to stress. Those who originated learned helplessness as an explanatory concept for depression are acutely aware of the problems of its overextension. A 1978 issue of the American Psychological Association *Journal of Abnormal Psychology* was devoted to articles dealing with learned helplessness as a model of depression. The originators of the concept point out that as presently defined, it fails to distinguish between universal and personal helplessness, between general or specific helplessness, between chronic or acute helplessness, and so on (Abramson, Seligman, & Teasdale, 1978).

There are three major theories of depression (Akiskal & McKinney, 1973). One explains depression with a biogenic amine model that posits biochemical imbalances in neurotransmitters. The second, a psychoanalytic model described by Freud and by Karl

Abraham, explains depression as hostility turned inward; this occurs in response to loss of a love object or to disruption of an attachment bond. The third model is a behavioristic or reinforcement model:

> Depression is equated with chronic frustration stemming from environmental stresses that are beyond the coping ability of the individual, who views himself as being helpless and finds relief in the rewards of the "sick role." (Akiskal and McKinney, p. 21).

It is from this third model, the behaviorist one, from which the concept of learned helplessness is derived.

The basic experiment is an animal experiment, one in which helplessness is induced. The animal can no longer cope with the frustrations in its environment and it therefore gives up the attempt. In the original experiments by Seligman and his colleagues (1972, 1976), dogs were given electric shock repeatedly while strapped so that they could not escape. Later, when the dogs are put into a box from which they *can* escape, *they do not.* Animals who have not been subjected to the same learning experience immediately jump the barrier and escape the shock. Learned helplessness, we think, parallels the effect and behavior of depression: The individual feels helpless, hopeless, and powerless, and negatively about expecting her efforts to be effective. These feelings lead to psychomotor retardation, to passivity, and the other clinical symptoms we use to diagnose depression.

THE EPIDEMIOLOGY OF DEPRESSION

We have no data about depression rates among young boys and girls, but starting with adolescence, it appears that depression associated with failure to meet adult expectations is characteristically reported by more females than males (Locksley & Douvan, 1979). The epidemiologists elaborate the picture: During the adult years, if married men and married women are compared, married women have higher depression rates than married men (Gove, 1979). If we look at the nonmarried, rates are highest for single men and for divorced women. Significantly, the group of women who appear at high risk for the development of alcohol problems, a disorder closely linked to depression, are women under the age of 35, working, and recently divorced or separated (Johnson, Armor, Polich, & Stambul, 1977).

Learned Helplessness, Disordered Behavior, Gender and Class

The concept of learned helplessness may be applied to women and their psychology in two different ways: 1) *all* women are socialized from birth to produce passive-dependent behaviors, to perceive themselves as incompetent, and unable to control their own lives; or 2) *some* women are socialized from birth to produce passive-dependent behaviors, to perceive themselves as incompetent, and unable to control their own lives.

That such socialization is more true probably in women's upbringing than in men's, we will set aside. We will argue that the second statement above is the more likely one. If we were all in a state of learned helplessness, there would be no one at this meeting. *Some* women are indeed socialized to perceive themselves as helpless and dependent and lacking in coping skills. It would appear, furthermore, that such women are a group *highly vulnerable to depression and to other forms of disordered behavior.* They constitute a psychopathology-prone group. A number of recent research reports have indicated that women who get high test scores in "femininity" are indeed reporting themselves as dependent, noncompetent, and low in survival skills. These same women who score high in test-defined "femininity" also tend to show more symptomatic behaviors, e.g., depression, high anxiety, low self-esteem, etc. One example of learned helplessness applied is the inability of some physically abused women to make the decision to leave the relationship in which they are abused (Walker, 1978).

Obviously an infant is helpless and dependent and it makes sense to assume that there are some patterns of childrearing that encourage the growing person to see himself or herself as helpless and passive and incompetent, just as there are patterns of childrearing that encourage the growing person to see himself or herself as independent, brave, and competent. Some patterns of childrearing encourage self-confidence and risk-taking behaviors, some patterns do not. But it should be stated that there are *men,* too, who are socialized to feelings of helplessness and dependence and lack of autonomy, and it is further complicated by the socialization of the male to cover over such feelings. Women, we think, are more often socialized to passive dependency, and it is also true that it is more permissible for women than for men to report such feelings and behaviors.

We also need to distinguish between the *perceived* dependence and feelings of helplessness and *objective reality.* Some grow up in groups relatively powerful in American society and some grow up with far less access to the opportunity, in groups which are relatively powerless in American society. Issues of social class and poverty, race and ethnicity, and perceived feelings of power and powerlessness needed exploration.

LEARNED HELPLESSNESS AND DEPRESSION

Learned helplessness or learned lack of control over one's own life or learned lack of autonomy are useful concepts but quite inadequate standing by themselves to explain depression in women. For one thing, the perceived lack of autonomy, the perceived lack of control over the circumstances of one's life is the core of clinical depression for both *men and women.* If we are seeking to account for the greater incidence of depression among women than among men, there are other factors besides *learned helplessness* to consider. The response of turning anger inward, or bottling up hostilities that are then directed toward the self is more acceptable for women than for men. Men may be belligerent and aggressive; women are reinforced for turning anger inward more. Furthermore, women receive a conflicting double message in adolescent years: It is good to achieve and do not compete with males. And, finally, it may well be that women are more vulnerable to disruption of attachment bonds (Weissman & Klerman, 1979).

DEPRESSION AND ALCOHOL PROBLEMS OF WOMEN

There is no question about the link between depression and alcohol problems. We know that virtually every alcoholic we see, young or old, male or female, early middle or late alcoholism manifests signs of depression. It is more difficult to clarify whether the depression is antecedent and causal of the heavy drinking or whether it is a consequence of the merry-go-round of drinking, disapproval, guilt, and more drinking that characterizes the alcoholic person. It is probably both; causes and effects are interwoven.

Among women, the linkage between depression and alcohol problems is even clearer than it is for men. Women, much more frequently than men, appear to develop alcohol problems because they turn to alcohol as medication, a search for mood change, and an analgesic for psychological pain. Men more frequently drink with buddies, in bars, and are more likely to drift into alcoholism from the social and recreational use of alcohol. Furthermore, the one finding that appears consistently among women alcoholics is their low self-esteem, their feelings of inadequacy, and their depressed mood.

One group of researchers on women and alcohol (Schuckit et al., 1969) have suggested that there are two kinds of alcoholism among women: primary alcoholism and alcoholism that is a complication, secondary to effective disorder.

I am also inclined to believe that while depressed feelings characterize all the women alcoholics we see clinically, there is more depression and more antecedent depression among women alcoholics in their forties than the younger, more stormy, more acting-out ones. We propose to study this, among other things, in a survey of younger and older women alcoholics.

I am also inclined to believe that alcoholic women are angry women and that their alcoholic acting-out is a splendid way to express anger at the world (at least significant others in the world) and at themselves at one and the same time.

Finally, I would like to report about some experiments done by Noel and Lisman (1977), not on female alcoholism per se but on the relationship between learned helplessness, depression, and consumption of alcohol. They studied women undergraduates and gave them a series of unsolvable problems, presumably an analog to the electric shock in the animal experiments. The unsolvable problems were apparently anxiety provoking and frustrating, and as the young women show increases in the depression scores, they drink more alcoholic beverage, and they show more anger and hostility. While this is one small step in studying the relationships involved, it is clear that even in this simple experiment, the "electric shock" has led to a variety of responses: depression (learned helplessness?) and stress responses, such as drinking, hostility, and aggressiveness. So let us end with this: the concept of learned helplessness may be useful but only in a limited way. It is quite insufficient, standing by itself, to explain depression in women.

REFERENCES

Abramson, L. Y., Seligman, M. E. P., & Teasdale, J. D. Learned helplessness in humans: critique and reformulation. *Journal of Abnormal Psychology,* 1978, *8,* 49–74.

Akiskal, H. S., & McKinney, W. T. Depressive disorders: toward a unified hypothesis. *Science,* 1973, *182,* 20–29.

Gove, W. R., Sex differences in the epidemiology of mental disorder: Evidence and explanations. In E. S. Gomberg & V. Franks (Eds.), *Gender and disordered behavior: sex differences in psychopathology.* New York: Brunner/Mazel, 1979.

Johnson, P., Armor, D. J., Polich, S., & Stambul, H. *U.S. adult drinking practices: time trends, social correlates and sex roles.* A Working Note Prepared for the National Institute on Alcohol Abuse and Alcoholism, Rand/WN-9923-NIAAA, November 1977.

Locksley, A., & Douvan, E., Problem behavior in adolescents. In E. S. Gomberg & V. Franks (Eds.), *Gender and disordered behavior: sex differences in psychopathology.* New York: Brunner/Mazel, 1979.

Noel, N. R., & Lisman, S. A., Effects of learned helplessness on alcohol consumption. *Paper presented at the Eastern Psychological Association Meeting,* Boston, April 1977. Alcohol, Depression and Learned Helplessness in Females. Paper presented at *A.A.B.T.,* Atlanta, December 1977.

Schuckit, M., et al. Alcoholism. I. Two types of alcoholism in women. *Archives of General Psychiatry,* 1969, *20,* 301–306.

Seligman, M. E. P. Learned helplessness. *Annual Review of Medicine,* 1972, *23,* 407–412.

Seligman, M. E. P., Klein, D. C., & Miller, W. R. Depression. In H. Leitenberg, (Ed.), *Handbook of behavior modification and behavior therapy.* Englewood Cliffs, N.J. Prentice-Hall, 1976.

Walker, L. E. Battered women and learned helplessness. *Victimology,* 1977–78, *2* (3–4), 525–534.

Weissman, M. M., & Klerman, G. L., Sex differences and the epidemiology of depression. In E. S. Gomberg & V. Franks (Eds.), Gender and disordered behavior: sex differences in psychopathology. New York: Brunner/Mazel, 1979.

Chapter 3

THE STIGMATIZED WOMAN

Rose Leone

A woman is first stigmatized at birth by virtue of being born female, as inferior to males, and therefore dominated by them and society. If she is to be viewed as an acceptable woman, knowing her role and place, passivity and conformity may appear to be the only course open to her. A woman may not simply submit to this subtle coercion, however, but struggle to become independent and to establish an identity other than that which has been ascribed to her by others. She may even dare to rebel against societal and familial constraints. If she dares to be different or to be sexual as an adolescent, she can be labeled by family, teachers, etc., as a delinquent.

Frustrated, feeling impotent or unlovable, she may resort to alcohol or drugs as an anesthetic to minimize her depression, rage, or anxiety. She often behaves in ways that further confirm her negative identity. She may also be a school dropout, be untrained and unable to earn a decent living. She may then resort to prostitution and become caught up in the spiral of drugs and prostitution until one day she is arrested on drug or morals charges. She then experiences degradation that she may feel will never be washed away. She is imprisoned, fingerprinted, and "mugged," which includes having a number hung around her neck like an albatross. She is violated by probing fingers in every bodily orifice and scrutinized for venereal diseases. She is treated with indifference, if not outright contempt, by the medical staff assigned to service her needs. These activities naturally reinforce her lowered self-esteem.

She has now effectively been separated from "decent" people and marked for life as a social deviant and criminal. She must remain with other social outcasts who, although they accept her as one of their own, prey upon her until she is completely bitter, filled with self-hate and hatred for the world around her and everyone within it. If her loneliness or need for tenderness forces her to risk an emotional affiliation, her vulnerability and her accessibility to companions with little ability to maintain adequate, close relationships ultimately results in total hopelessness and despair, continuing the need for the depression-relieving drug or alcohol cycle.

If she is very fortunate, one day she accepts that she is dying and that if she does not stop now, her life will be over and have counted for naught. Often terrified of death yet afraid of facing life without chemicals, she comprehends slowly that she must now relinquish every familiar aspect of her existence and begin a new way of life.

If she enters a treatment system, she is expected to exhibit "impulse control" by not showing an angry response to any treatment personnel's judgment of her sexuality or the individual pace at which her behavior changes occur. Clinician's attitudes often reflect the individual's need to achieve successful rehabilitation outcome, personal or cultural feelings about the addicted woman, or the misuse of power over the client. Male and female staff members may exhibit biases and overreactions to the woman's seeming inability to accept program values and behavior standards. Males in the environment often bring their own stereotypes into the treatment arena. They label and treat women accordingly. A woman, therefore, is expected to become independent, responsible, and her own person yet conform to these authoritarian standards or be called "unmotivated for rehabilitation." She may be provided with a new set of rules and "guilt" mechanisms to ensure change. She is given new "parents and family" or authority figures who demand conformity in the interests of the community. If she remains in care, the ultimate desired goal appears to be a conforming woman who has sex "responsibly," does not manipulate others, and who can survive in her community with these new skills and philosophy.

Economic independence demands that she gain some skill to earn a legal living; someone may suggest secretarial work: "There is always a need for good clerical workers." She may have to apply for public assistance to enable her to survive. The investigators ply her with countless questions, the details of which she has little memory and which make her want to run away and hide. She has no recent work history, has a police record, and is a confirmed substance abuser. The attitudes of civil servants reflect their disdain and judgment of this "fallen woman" who must be punished and reminded of her devalued position in society. If accepted for a training program, welfare funds are not available for clothing so she must daily face how different she looks to other students (or gratefully accept discarded clothing donated by the community or her family).

In my own experience, my caseworker suggested that I would never survive in an office after my "exciting" life and I would find it too confining and boring. I would soon quit and return to my former life-style. I was too ashamed and fearful to report him. I later applied for college and was accepted on the basis of a high school equivalency diploma earned while serving a sentence in a penal institution. After finishing two years of college, concentrating on secretarial skills, I was now ready to consider employment. Where could I go? How would I account for 15 years of unemployment? If the application requested information about arrests, (this was before the law was altered to include only convictions) should I lie? I knew instinctively that I would be rejected if I lied and was discovered and was also aware I could be rejected if I divulged the data. Therefore, I sought work in an antipoverty agency that employed community people. In filling out the application, I encountered the dreaded questions and was truthful. The girl accepting applications gulped, her eyes grew wide. She almost ran out of the chair into a rear office. In five minutes, three or four very important looking people emerged and ushered me into the Director's office. A half hour later they were finally convinced that I was neither a pathological liar nor a mental incompetent. Because of my history, I was hired for minimum wages although my skills were far above average.

Two years later, I expressed the desire to work as a vocational counselor and was trained to work with alcoholics, drug abusers, and parolees on an individual and group basis. By that time I had completed undergraduate work and switched to drug and alcohol counseling in a variety of modalities, including hospitals. When I worked at Lincoln Hospital, I was investigated closely because of my conviction record. At New York Medical College, the chief of security there probed so deeply into details of my background that I refused to divulge details of prostitution, which I stated had nothing to do with my current job nor presented a threat to security. I applied for graduate school at Rutgers and am convinced my record was responsible for the rejection, although the Admissions Department assured me otherwise. They could not provide me with any other sound reason but claimed they were oversubscribed. At New York University, some professors found my presentation disquieting and claimed I acted as though I knew better than they did about working with substance abusers. Again I felt stigmatized because I dared to question "experts" whose theories were less than contemporary. I had practical experience and competence and challenged teachers who had never worked with addicts or had no field experience in many years.

Concerned about greater professional competence, I acquired a second master's degree, this time in social work. I was treated with equality and respect throughout this experience by the faculty. I also registered for analytic training at a local institute. I have felt the professional distance throughout my association there. I still take courses although I am no longer concerned about certification.

Five years ago, I began a small private practice as a psychotherapist. Although some clients have substance abuse problems, most people coming to me for service experience daily living problems. When appropriate, a client may be informed of my personal background; others are completely unaware of it.

When I received my master's degree in social work, I applied for the licensing exam given by the State Education Department. As in the past, I revealed my conviction record. I was soon advised that I would be conditionally permitted to take the examination, pending final decision. I therefore submitted my fee and took the test. Although I passed the exam, I was denied licensing on the grounds that my character was considered morally unsuitable for licensing, but that I could request a hearing. Since it had been seventeen years since my last conviction, I applied for services at the Legal Action Center, a nonfee agency that provides legal representation for clients involved in licensing or employment discrimination litigation. In preparing for the hearing, I was requested to submit to a variety of necessary indignities. First, I had to apply for a Certificate of Relief from Disabilities. This procedure involved my going down to the courthouse and obtaining dispositions on each arrest and conviction. I then applied to Criminal Court and asked to be seen by the presiding judge. At that time, I presented my request for relief from disability, was taken by a police officer to be fingerprinted, sent to the Department of Parole for an interview and a full investigation. I was also assigned a court date and placed on the calendar. I appeared before the same judge who had received the investigation findings. I was then granted my request. During this time, I was advised by the State Education Department that I had to provide witnesses in my behalf who would testify about my "character." I contacted former employers, my grade advisor from NYU, and the Assistant Dean at Hunter College School of Social Work. Since I was still involved in personal psychotherapy, my therapist was subpoenaed to appear at the hearing.

The day of the hearing finally arrived. A board of social workers and the lawyer from the New York State Education Department presided over what turned out to be three hours of grueling cross-examination of my entire life, from its beginnings. I had to reveal painful family information and details of my childhood that should not have to be revealed. It included the most minute details of every arrest and conviction. My educational pursuits were scrutinized, my character assassinated and then demurred about. I was subjected to every verbal indignity and probed to the core of my being. At one point, the questioning about my childhood became so confrontational that I began to cry; I quickly regained my composure. I could not believe that arrests that did not result in convictions were introduced as evidence and then "stuck" out of the testimony, with the lawyer lamely apologizing after introducing it the second time. Finally, the ordeal was over. I quickly learned that I had been granted the license. The state lawyer assured me he had done his job and had not personally persecuted me. I remained silent.

I am sharing my experience with you today so that those of you involved in treatment or the penal system can better understand the obstacles one woman had to overcome when she attempted to rehabilitate herself. Society does not easily permit stigmatized women to leave their mistakes behind them or to become fully participating citizens on whatever level they exhibit the ability to function.

Chapter 4

THE DOUBLE BIND
Minority Women

Marguerite Saunders

It pleases me to be at a conference today of this scope which recognizes that women face unique and complex problems in the mental health, alcoholism, criminal justice, and substance abuse fields. I am certain that this conference could not have been held 10, or even 5 years ago, because of the prevailing sexism in these fields. The women involved in any of these systems in today's society faces far greater problems if she is black, hispanic, a lesbian, or any other minority. I will concentrate today on the black substance abuser, since she represents the greatest percentage of addicted women, but the problems she faces are common to other minorities.

I have been involved in the treatment of addicts for the past 12 years and spent most of those years as director of the Manhattan Treatment Center for Women, a New York State Division of Substance Abuse facility.

Twelve years ago the women with whom we worked were generally black heroin users in their mid-twenties, who had lengthy arrest records.

Over the years, the profile of the woman at Manhattan Treatment Center changed to include a large percentage of younger hispanic and white women of all socioeconomic classes who used substances other than heroin. Through our day-to-day work, it became evident that each of these groups of women although similar, had different backgrounds and different treatment needs arising from their backgrounds. I should point out here that although each ethnic group had needs different from each other, that there were just as pronounced differences among individuals within each group. I must further point out that studies conducted with hospital emergency room admissions shows that the quality of being both black and female appears to create greater risk of substance abuse than any other race-sex grouping (Dawn, 1976–1977, Petersen, 1974).

Twelve years ago the women entrusted to my care were mostly angry, aggressive, and street-wise. The client we thought was doing best was the one who echoed traditional ideal feminine characteristics, i.e., quiet, passive, and following the program. We all tried hard to imbue the rest with feminine virtues and rewarded them for controlling hostility and for not expressing anger. We worked to get them to wear skirts and had as our goal for them to be secretaries or teacher-aides, not imagining that they might want to be mechanics or mothers. This treatment thrust, I fear, was not confined to New York state in its treatment of women substance abusers, but was and is prevalent among drug treatment agencies, although I see some signs of change.

The last 15 to 20 years have seen substantial changes in society. Less than two decades ago, sex, familial, social, and occupational roles were well-defined; people knew what was expected of them and what they could expect from others. Social and legal sanctions for nonrole appropriate behaviors were usually severe. These role definitions have become increasingly vague and confusing over the past 20 years, and with deeply felt results. Although the women's movement has contributed much to the advancement of women, it has also created some real conflicts and problems. It may be that one of the underlying reasons for women in general to begin drug use may not be related at all to parental rejection or fear of becoming a woman or to group pressure. It may instead represent an inability to cope with a world that wants a girl to be something that she is not, frustration about the double messages she receives everyday through the media, or confusion regarding her identity.

The matter is further complicated if the woman is black, for the black woman generally has come from a matriarchal family structure, where her role model (mother or grandmother) was strong and competent. She was then thrust, at puberty, into a world where men relate to her in a sexual manner and squash her talk of women's liberation by attributing it to the cause of the white, middle-class woman. The hispanic women is in a different bind, for her sociocultural system demands that women be wives, mothers, submissive, and dependent on their macho men.

Let us look now at the background that the black woman brings into any treatment program. Although a good many black women have always been in or have risen to the middle class, some generalizations are true when we talk about the black woman who uses drugs. Here we are speaking of a woman who has grown up in a depressed neighborhood, who has had little or no positive experience with men, and who has had poor educational and/or vocational experiences. She has been raised by her mother who is often the breadwinner or welfare recipient, or by her grandmother who must support herself in the same manner.

The child then is living in a neighborhood where violence and poverty are rife, whose family consists of mother or grandmother and siblings, and maybe a father who is an alcoholic and perhaps violent, or maybe instead an occasional man who comes to stay for awhile and then leaves. Where do this child's fantasies turn? She is confronted by television with its mostly white, intact nuclear families who have Cuisinarts and two cars, who smile out at her from the screen and speak to her of detergents and daddies. But that family is light years away from her reality. She is, however, exposed to the street where flashily dressed pimps with their foxy ladies and cocaine dealers who drive big cars and look good to her. These people may be the only pretty things in this little girl's life. But, on the other side, we have mama and grandma, one of whom has certainly seen the light and who fill her little ears with promises of fire and brimstone if she as much as thinks about an evil life. What's a little girl to do? What's she to do when she's 12 and her daddy or mamma's boyfriend beats her and the neighborhood boy who wants to feel her body gives her a taste of wine, or a puff of a joint and she feels good and the boy's hand feels good and grandma is telling her that she'd better be in by 7:00, and she failed another spelling test, and her mama's drunk?

Well, she could come in and study and excell in school and go on to college and become famous; that would be nice and some exceptional persons are able to do that. Most of us though, black, white, or Asian, would not be able to overcome these obstacles to freedom and would find, like the little girl, that the wine and the joint and the pills and the coke and heroin began to taste and feel better and better. Even more importantly, we are able to shut out the anger, tension, and the rats, the hunger, the fear and the failures by their use until one day we find that the stuff did not work any more and we have been arrested again and again and we wanted off and we wanted to stop, but how?

A treatment program would seem the best answer, but traditional treatment programs do not work for women, and especially do not work for the minority woman. The problem of getting and retaining the woman substance abuser into treatment is well documented, as is the higher recidivism rate of women as compared to men. What seems to have gone unrecognized in treatment is that many women are aggressive, have children, wish to be independent, and like excitement. The black woman is in a particular bind here for she has had a mother or grandmother as a role model who, by circumstance, has had to be strong and independent. Few treatment programs have reported attempts to structure treatment in such a way that these traits are seen as positive aspects of the personality that need to be strengthened and built upon. In how many therapeutic communities are female residents put in charge of the maintenance unit? Most treatment programs are run by and for men, and the black woman will find in them the same dilemmas provided by society in general.

Male counselors and administrators tend to misinterpret the needs of women in treatment. In one unpublished report, the male director of an institutional treatment facility for women suggests that male staff must "learn how to be relaxed and even manage a little low-key flirtation without misjudging the individual and annoying her." In fact, no matter what the key, flirtation by male staff members is likely to confuse institutionalized young girls. Unfortunately, flirtation is not uncommon, (and even more unfortunate is the likelihood that the flirtation will develop into frank sexual exploitation).

Women will find few role models in most treatment programs, for responsible positions are held by males, and female staff are handled with the same sexist attitudes prevalent towards female patients, thus reinforcing confusing sexual stereotypes.

In groups, women are confronted with their past prostitution and accused of being seductive. God help her, however, if she talks of placing her children and entering a training program, because then she is hit with the "bad mother" label. But yet few programs have day-care facilities to allow her to be with her children.

The women's movement has made it unthinkable for a woman to be "only a mother, or only a housewife." This is reflected in our treatment where the measure of success is a job. I wish the message of the woman's movement could be interpreted as it should: that women have choices about what they do with their lives and that it's okay to be a mother, a nuclear physicist, a housewife, a mechanic, or a secretary and that each of these things is *worthy*. What will a minority woman face when she leaves this treatment? (*If* she can stay to complete it!) She will be equipped with some minimal skills, or perhaps none, and she will enter an ever-tightening labor market in which the competition for the few unskilled and semiskilled jobs increases daily. In contrast to the market for men, who can obtain high paying manual labor jobs, these unskilled or semiskilled jobs can be best described as low paying and sometimes force the woman to use food stamps or partial welfare.

The minority woman is in a particular bind when applying for jobs, for she reinforces old stereotypes in the white, personnel officer's mind. When he hears, "drug use," he thinks, "black, drug using prostitute," and he *or she* is uncomfortable. When a white woman mentions that she used drugs, the tendency is to think that she has made a mistake, but when the black woman does, her application is viewed through different eyes. And if the minority woman should get through the interview and get a job, her adjustment to the workplace is made more difficult because of prevailing institutional and personal racism. The recovering substance abuser has a difficult enough time trying to relate effectively to straight people. This is greatly exacerbated for minority women. This woman will be further plagued if she has children, for child care is expensive and she is earning very little. In some cases, children make it impossible for a woman to work.

If the minority woman chooses not to work, she must face the welfare maze. A maze, I think, designed to produce substance abusers.

Minority women must probably return to their families in the same communities that spawned their original drug use. While a woman is institutionalized, she tends to forget the pain she felt on the outside. The drunken father or husband does not seem so bad and mother is remembered as an all-loving, good woman who is anxiously awaiting her return home. When she gets home, she soon finds that things are the same and made only worse by her thinking they would be different. All too soon, mother is accusing her of whoring, drinking, and stealing; and all too soon, our ex-addict is 'ex'' no more.

In treatment, we need to prepare a woman for these realities. Treatment that does not consider the special needs of women in general, and minority women in particular, is doomed to failure. I would suggest that women need treatment programs designed especially for them and that the special backgrounds and needs of each patient be carefully considered in designing treatment plans. I believe women need programs that teach her reality skills, and these can be outlined as skills in consumerism, health-related issues, parenting, and in negotiating community resources, such as welfare, schools, clinics, and job training. In addition, I believe that all women, and especially minority women, need to be put in touch with their sexuality, their sex role conflicts, and their relationships and feelings toward men. They need to have child-care facilities available, and they need to know that it's okay to be "just a housewife" or "just a mother," as long as they are good ones. Very importantly, women need to be clinically involved with their families while they are in treatment. The family must learn to relate differently *before* the woman completes treatment and if a new way of family communication is not possible, she must know that before she returns home. Women also need transitional living situations that can serve as support centers for them on their road to an independent life. Women need to know ways to relax, whether this be through meditation, dance, creative writing, art, yoga, or biofeedback. They need to be able to support themselves and their children in a way that will bring them dignity and some pleasure. It is up to us, as clinicians, administrators, and program planners to fill these needs.

I have spent a lot of time talking about the special problems of the black woman, and I'd now like to say a few words about her strengths. The black woman has a proud history to draw on, one of strength and endurance. She has learned, through the years to survive in the worst of situations. She has held her family together, and at times been their sole support, scrubbing floors and working the fields. She has the religious background to draw on that has given strength to generations of black women and she has as her role models a mother and grandmother who have been strong and who have survived. She, too, can survive.

REFERENCES

Petersen, D. M. Acute drug reactions (overdose) among females: a race comparison. *Addictive Disease,* 1974, *1*(2), 223–233.

DAWN, Phase V Report, DEA Contract #76–25, IMS America, Ltd. Ambler, PA., pp. 15–16, 1976–1977.

Chapter 5

THE SPARSE GHETTO
Service Delivery
in a Rural Area

Joan Weitzel

The Concept of the Sparse Ghetto

Dispelling the Myth

Originally the word *ghetto* is rooted in the Italian "borgo" meaning "outside the city walls," contrasting sharply with the word's contemporary meaning. And that is where we indeed exist: outside the city walls in rural America in the *sparse ghetto.*

We are a nation involved with bigness, inflation, and overpopulation. We associate social problems with crowded urban areas. Sparsity and deprivation seem to be mutually exclusive. Can it be that pocketed among those picturesque hills and valleys (blanketed with clean air and cleansed with sparkling, crystalline water) problems of abuse, addiction, mental illness, incest, discrimination, and sexism exist? Among the greatest challenges today to service providers in rural areas is to convince our urban counterparts that serious social problems *do* exist in sparsely populated areas. The rural residents themselves do much to perpetuate the myth of idyllic country life. Often pride prevents problems from being identified or treated. Much education is needed. Not only do problems exist, but rural populations can be far less accessible to help from "the outside" owing to the traditional rural stance of "solving problems at home, keeping it within the family." And that "family" may be a quarter of the county related by marriage.

The Sparse Ghetto versus the Urban Ghetto

How then, is the sparse ghetto analogous to it's urban counterpart? Rural populations face similar problems. There is a lack of representation in the legislatures. Rural areas are attended to in election years; much is promised to citizens only to be forgotten in forthcoming years. For example, in Pennsylvania we have been waiting for five years for federal funds for completion of a new interstate that would improve our accessibility to Buffalo and Pittsburgh. As on the urban scene, there is mistrust of outsiders (here, the flatlander) in our area. Change is seen as a divisive force, not a positive one. Breakdowns in traditional roles, methods, and mind sets are frightening. As in urban ghettos, education in rural areas tends to be poorly subsidized; teacher pay is lower and it continues to be difficult to attract quality instructors. Children in some very rural areas may not venture more than 30 miles from their birthplace in their entire life. Inbreeding continues to weaken the gene pools in isolated areas.

Seeing is Believing

Unfortunately, to the naked eye, which cannot take in a 30 mile area at a glance, problems seem distant, spread out, and therefore weakened in intensity. There is no five block concentrated area to point out. Rural poverty has become synonomous with an entire region, such as Appalchia. Certainly this exemplifies the remoteness of rural poverty in the mind's eye of the city dweller. Harlem is a place, but is Appalachia? It is similar to discussing the "poor" on Saturn.

SPECIAL NEEDS OF WOMEN IN RURAL AREAS

Oppression in the Sparse Ghetto

We are just beginning to recognize the effects of isolating women, sequestering them in their homes, and segregating them from wholesome interaction with other women. We see groups of women hampered around other women by jealousy and discomfort and anger. This problem is compounded by geographic isolation. This is a part of oppression in the sparse ghetto. It is this very separateness that keeps women in rural areas "behind the times" in terms of feminism. They are limited by lack of vocational opportunity in nontraditional roles. In our area, several factories have "opened up" to women only in the last five years, but reluctantly and under the hammer of compliance with federal standards. There is a great feeling (among men and women) that a woman does indeed belong in the home. Women continue in their passive role as the feeder and the mother. Self-image is often defined in terms of family, husband, and church affiliation. Obesity, depression, prescription abuse are common. Women nourish others then salve themselves. The cure becomes the affliction. There is little hope for rehabilitation of the displaced homemaker. Women are infrequently in leadership roles in local government or industry.

Women are trapped by a double standard that condemns them in public for aggressive behavior and attempts at the same time to keep them at home and hidden. I have heard from those in the criminal justice system that it is acceptable for a man to beat his wife for a "good" reason. Local police refuse to involve themselves in domestic violence cases. Often the arresting officer is a relative. Social stigma for women with problems that cannot be handled at home is high. A woman who does not "stand by her man" as the familiar Tammy Wynette song wails, is seen as untrue, no good, and basically defective.

Needs of Women

Women in rural areas need education. Outreach is often ineffective as it cannot get to the well-protected country woman. An effective outreach effort on the part of an agency is a massive task that must be taken on in small sections: a small church group one week, a local woman's club, then a ladies auxilliary the next. It can be enormously time consuming.

Early problem identification is a large problem. Doctors often do not refer for abuse, because they have known both their whole lives. Women are seldom referred from driving while intoxicated. I know of only four in my five years experience. One method that appears to be working is for other women to be working at the referral site. A woman physician and a well-trained (through in-service) staff of nurses have opened up referral channels at a small nearby community hospital. Child care for those entering treatment is not as much of a problem as in urban areas. Women needing treatment can often rely on relatives, as extended families are common. A greater problem exists in meeting the needs of women who must move with their children; for example, those in need of a shelter.

Vocational counseling is very much needed. Women in rural areas tend to accept traditional service roles. "Professional" women are employed as nurses, teachers, and social workers. Women managers are scarce. Sheltering facilities and resource centers are needed. More effort needs to be put into the area of educating women about their options.

PROBLEMS OF SERVICE DELIVERY

Attitudes

Attitudes in rural areas are ingrained, passed from generation to generation without question. Mistrust of outsiders hampers referral and information from being transmitted. Often mistrust is warranted for outsider's often lack respect for rural values and strengths. Innovative programs can face overwhelming public apprehension. Group homes for the mentally retarded have met with great disapproval, rooted in fear, from neighborhoods they are planned for. For the isolated rural resident, his or her "community" is small. Strong moralistic approaches by various churches can hamper enlightened attitudes. On occasion, I have felt we are trying to turn back the night with a flashlight. Optimistically there are positive attitudes—a willingness to help, to share to improve town life with a cooperative spirit. Self-help and volunteer groups can provide immense support and unlimited aftercare resources.

Getting There

Getting women to services and services to women continues to be the single most overriding problem of rural service delivery. With little or no public transportation and many women with cars or unable to drive how are we to provide care?

Fitting Square Pegs in Round Holes

Funding models and criteria for rural programs is not made to "exist outside the city walls." Treatment models all too frequently are watered down versions of urban models rather than specifically designed to meet the geographic (large transportation allocations) and philosophical (social workers must also be good neighbors) needs of rural areas. Methods of outreach and utilization requirements based on urban structures are often impractical. The rural resident needs to know that you will come to her. Social stigma toward being seen at the mental health clinic is high. From a practical standpoint, only so many people in a town of 2500 people will drop in for help, others are expected to get there from the next town —20 miles away—and there is no public transportation.

A classic example is that in our four county area there are only two Detox units. The local police were to bring prospective admissions in for detox, thus treating the sick alcoholic and clearing the jails for more appropriate tenants. Well, the single town cop on shift in his borough from midnight to 8 A.M. would be hard pressed to justify a 50-mile drive, leaving the town unsupervised to transport a public inebriate for help. This is simply and totally impractical. Naturally our detox units were closed due to underutilization. Here, a component enabling the unit to be transported would have been a prime survival feature for a rural program of this nature.

SERVICES AVAILABLE IN THE CAMERON, ELK, MCKEAN, AND POTTER COUNTY AREAS OF NORTHWESTERN PENNSYLVANIA

Comprehensive Services Available

For a four-county area with an extremely sparse population (Potter County has 15 persons per square mile), we have a large array of services available to residents. In each of the four counties outpatient counseling clinics or satellites exist. Consultation and education services, drug and alcohol abuse counseling, outreach, inpatient treatment and aftercare, field social services, prevention services, a family and child guidance center, futures rehabilitation center for retarded adults, and a SCAN PEP (Screening Children to Assess Needs/Prescriptive Education Program) are among services provided. A 24-hour hotline service is available for around the clock emergency care. There is now operating a voluntarily staffed rape crisis line in one county and a 72-hour shelter for victims of domestic violence has recently opened.

NETWORKING

Some Answers

These are the overall problems in providing care in rural areas. What then are the solutions? The very strengths of rural women have developed as a result of their problems, and there still exists a pioneer attitude. The very idea that keeps outsiders out, for instance, strengthens bonds. If women can be assisted in getting together, they can often unite to solve problems.

Networking is the key to rural service delivery. It attempts to tie into the pattern of sparsity and use it. It makes a whole from the sum of its parts and the network can strengthen and reinforce those parts to improve the entire system. An effective network can grow as part of a positive feedback loop.

Keeping problems at home, translated often in rural areas in self-help and volunteer efforts (as money and personnel are invariably lacking) can be a most valuable resource. Groups, such as Parents Anonymous, Families Anonymous, and local women's clubs can be used to network to provide more and more effective service. If a person in Town A can voluntarily transport a victim of domestic violence to a shelter in Town B, 50 miles away, by means of a voluntary network, then service can often be provided to the remote and isolated woman.

In Cameron, Elk, McKean, and Potter counties, the four-county area where I am employed, a remarkable network is developing: A group of approximately seven women, some involved in area self-help groups, and in working voluntarily or part-time at a local alcoholism rehabilitation center, participated in a week long awareness training seminar, "women in treatment."* This core group found the bonding and energy so revitalizing that they continued to meet and discuss their needs, both as women personally and as women in a rural area. This nucleus group decided it was past due

*Executive Director, Violet Plantz, Harrisburg, Pa.

to form a women's task force to inform, discuss, and help alleviate problems women were facing in our four-county area. Two area women, already involved in the State of Pennsylvania Task Force on Women, encouraged the group to become involved as a regional affiliate of that organization. Shortly after the Four County Rural Task Force for Women was founded, we heard of a group of persons who had begun plans to open a Rape Crisis Line and Women's Shelter in a town in the four county area. These two women were invited to inform the Task Force of their activity and enlist our support. As their shelter was limited by transporting women to the facility, the Four County Task Force has taken on the job of developing a volunteer network so that women from four counties may avail themselves of this service. The Rape Crisis Line and Shelter has a totally volunteer staff.

The Task Force has also undertaken a survey of the elderly to provide information to the local drug and alcohol center, and to the offices of aging. This group of women is providing strong role models for women, informing themselves and other women of available service and serving as an advocacy group in this area for women's concerns. The local Cameron, Elk, McKean, and Potter Hotline is staffed by a combination of volunteers and paid counseling staff. Certainly coverage could not be provided if it were not for volunteers.

The local Alcohol and Drug Abuse Center cooperates with local self-help groups in handling referrals and transporting persons for detoxification. An active alumni association provides recreational activities for former residents as well as volunteer support for the program. Recently, this body's letter writing efforts were instrumental in introducing legislation. Alumni have voluntarily discussed funding problems at local County Commissioner meetings. It's all a network, and I give it an 80 share. The ratings for our programs will soar if we can develop, use, and reinforce this very rural propensity to cooperate and network to provide service.

A Word of Caution

Remember social service is capitalizing on a system that has been operating in one way or another (e.g., the Grange) for several hundreds of years. Nothing can cancel a network "show" faster than an often well-intended suggestion to "re-invent the wheel." To preserve and expand the network, we must respect it for what it is. A fine method of solving problems in today's sparse ghetto developed at a time when all of America's population was sparse and there were no ghettos.

Chapter 6

REACHING THE
MIDDLE CLASS FEMALE

Nikki N. Duffié

The middle class dilemma is whether or not to buy the "happiness package" that has been put together by society and carefully wrapped by the economic power structure. For the middle class woman, the "package deal" is that happiness and dependency are connected. The myth says that a woman will be happy if she is dependent and if she acts according to the dictates of advertising, society, husband, children, parents, and doctor.

But what if she does not buy the package? Then her unhappiness is her own fault. In other words, *something is wrong with her.* If she would just pay attention to the doctor, the kids, her husband, and buy the right things, then she would be happy.

And what if she buys the package and it is the wrong size and it does not make her happy? Then, again, *something is wrong with her.* She must be sick, under the influence, depressed, and/or crazy. The message is that if she followed the rules correctly, she would be happy.

This is nothing new. Betty Friedan brought the "feminine mystique" out of the closet in the early 1960s. The issues, however, have remained much the same as when the book came out. The problems we see at Glassboro are concerned with relationships and lack of self-confidence. The crucial issue of the middle class woman is dependency. There is much pressure on her to follow rules, to make her self-worth be dependent on pleasing others. When she chooses to be dependent, the conflict between her submerged autonomy and her need to please others produces the rule-following behavior accompanied by *not* the promised happiness, but instead by the pain and symptoms of sickness, substance dependency, depression, and craziness. The rules say there must be something wrong with her, and so she takes the blame and is sick, drugged, depressed, or crazy in order to please the others on whom she believes herself to be dependent. Even when these symptoms appear, she is still buying the package and is still trying to please others by fitting into the myth of the package deal.

The myth has given her a formula to follow: "If you just_____, others will feel OK about you and then you'll be OK. If you just *take Valium,* you'll be OK. If you just *buy a new dress,* you'll be OK. If you just *act sexier with your husband,* then he'll love you and you'll be OK. If you just *do what we say,* you'll be OK."

The cruel part of the myth is, of course, that it is a myth. The woman keeps hoping that if she just does one more thing that someone wants her to do, she will finally be OK, but instead the pain and symptoms grow.

When does she stop buying the package? Often, it is when the pain has become great enough so that she wants relief, even if it means taking the risk of not pleasing others.

When she is ready to take that risk she is ready to be reached. Nothing that was supposed to make her feel good about herself has worked. She is struggling with disillusionment and she is ready to try something new.

Now the question is, Who can reach out and connect? For our purposes, it is important that it be someone who had bought the package, has taken it back to the store herself, and who can show someone else the way to the return counter.

We have a woman then who is ready to risk not pleasing others and to risk growing through her pain and we have a reacher who knows first hand what it means to take those risks and to shed the layers of dependency. How can these women meet each other?

The following suggestions answer the question: "What do you think are the necessary ingredients for a successful outreach program for middle class females?" I have based my suggestions on Together's five years of experimentation with outreach to and treatment of middle class female prescription drug misusers.

The program should have such a tone and reputation that there is no stigma attached to being a client. Personal growth and adult education are not stigmatized among middle class women; drug and alcohol treatment, however, carry stigmas as does mental health treatment for many women. The program with the stigma views the client as a "patient" with whom something is wrong which they can fix. This merely repackages the package deal and any woman who is really ready to dump the package will not do so in such a program. The stigma-free program views the client as a person who is capable of taking care of herself and feeling good about herself and wants to learn new ways to do so. The absence of stigma in a treatment program is in itself its most successful outreach. The program's view of the female client is much more important to both outreach and treatment than are specific methods or techniques. In the women's center model, outreach and treatment coexist in the form of workshops and open group sharing sessions. Again, the program does not do outreach with a certain style or line to "get 'em in" and *then* do the therapy. The women's center model is a consumer model. The client gets a taste of treatment *during* outreach and so makes the decision whether or not to return or whether she will refer other women to the center's services.

The program's outreach should address the symptoms of women's pain in the language the female uses to describe her own pain. Together has had the most response to workshop titles that include the words, *depression* and *anger* or *taking time for yourself.* It is important to continue to use the language of the women throughout the program in workshops and in counseling. Women talk about "my nerves" about using "medication" (not about "taking drugs") and about "feeling down."

To be successful, *treatment should provide mutual and self-help therapy* rather than therapy provided by "experts" operating in the traditional medical model. Together has found it to be an important step in achieving autonomy to be involved in therapy with peers, and other women, rather than just with men, or "experts." If someone very much like the client can be her therapist, then she is very close to trusting herself to be her own therapist and close to ending the dependency pattern.

Treatment should be provided free of charge or by donation. At Together, we have found that this eliminates the stress on women who might not have money or do not have access to money for workshops or counseling fees. Dependent women on the whole do not have access to money for their personal growth needs. There is often an argument about this philosophy, which states that fees charged provide commitment on the part of the client. Together has found that middle class women have made a higher commitment than money. They are in such pain that they commit themselves to its relief, and wherever they find relief, they are committed.

The program staff should provide permission and protection for women to experiment with new behaviors and attitudes, without adding the stress of new "other pleasing" role expectations. Women, experimenting with freedom from the need to please husband, doctor, and the myth sellers, are susceptible to new dependencies. The therapists need to be very clear on their own stake in achieving a dependency transference. Therapists need to examine whether or not they are subtly perpretrating new myths. New myths might be: *If you are just assertive, then you'll be happy.* Or, *If you just get a job, then you'll be OK.* The woman in treatment must be encouraged to decide for herself what will make her happy and proceed to carry out her own decisions in order to be truly free of the dependent role.

The program should provide some way for the clients to give back services to other women. At Together, women in treatment are encouraged to participate in the volunteer work of the agency or of other agencies. Together offers opportunities for clients to do hotline counseling, office work, and to be trained to cofacilitate peer groups.

Given that a program is ideal and has all the previously mentioned qualities and viewpoints toward treatment, what can the program do specifically to attract the middle class woman? One of Together's most successful outreach components has been its workshops and the other has been its regular weekly open sharing group.

The weekly open sharing group has been meeting for seven years. Every Wednesday evening, women come to share their pain and growth and to receive and give support to other women. The group is a first experience in therapy for most of the women who come: therefore, the turnover is considerable. The typical woman who comes to the group pours out her story the first night, listens to the other stories, and feels the recognition of "it's not just me, it's not that there's something wrong with just me; I'm not the only one." She comes back to the group three or four times before moving on to more in-depth therapy or attending other workshops.

The workshops are advertised through posters, the mailing list, "saturation" mailings, and press releases. Together has tried various types of workshops to attract its target population. We find there is a narrow spectrum of workshops that attract women who are just beginning to risk and grow. Among them are *Nurturing Night*, a workshop in which each participant, in turn, experiences positive feedback from the rest of the group; *Assertiveness Training*, which teaches and supports a behavior change from passive-dependent to assertive; *Depression* workshops, which present didactic information on depression, its physiologic and sociologic causes and the behavioral techniques that work to alleviate it, and facilitates experiential exercises that allow women to explore the feelings and situations that contribute to depression; *How to Survive a Loss*, a workshop that describes the stages of loss of relationship through death or separation and provides an opportunity for sharing feelings and coping techniques; and *Coping With Stress*, which teaches coping skills, relaxation techniques, and provides a peer support group for the duration of the workshop. Other workshops on such topics as yoga, sexuality, getting a job, medication, and time planning seem to attract women who are more advanced in their coping skills and further on the road to autonomy.

In conclusion, it seems that the process of reaching the middle class female has three interacting components:

1. A woman who is reachable, ready to risk, and to grow beyond dependency
2. A "reacher" or "helper" who has been through it and has the skills to share with others
3. A program with the philosophy that a client is capable of growing and evolving towards autonomy; that the only inequality between a helper and a client is one of skill level and transcended experience, not one of intrinsic ability

Such a program does its best to share life skills with clients so as to bring them to their own desired skill level in the shortest amount of time, with the least amount of financial outlay, and with no dependency strings attached.

Chapter 7

REACHING THE MIDDLE CLASS ALCOHOLIC

Judith Seixas

How can we get the middle class female client into treatment for her alcoholism when she, in fact, is doing everything in her power to cover up the problem and deny that it exists? She is subjected to pressures and expectations from family and society that women in other social settings may not feel so intensely. These pressures engender such guilt and such fear of loss that she is forever clinging to her status and the outward veneer of propriety and well-being no matter what is really happening to her life and her health.

The stigma attached to the female drinker is incredibly forceful. Historically, she is frowned upon. In fact, there are societies in which, until very recently, the female simply did not drink at all. For example, Irish pubs have been strictly male. But as women go to work, come out of their closets and their houses, and become more visible, hiding and denying become major concerns for them. The impact is probably greater on them than for any other group simply because of society's demand on women and, in turn, her demands on herself. Consequently, middle class women have more trouble coming to grips with alcoholism, overcoming denial, admitting to their problem, seeking help for it, and getting into treatment.

For the counselor, there is extra work required in order to pursuade her to seek treatment. The counselor must find special ways to reach her and to let her know that alcoholism is an illness and that she *deserves* help. We must look hard for avenues that will not make her feel so guilty and helpless.

The disease concept of alcoholism is tremendously helpful in dealing with the alcoholic woman. The woman who is drinking heavily, for whatever reason, however, has a great deal of trouble accepting that concept and continues to feel that she is doing something "wrong" and/or "bad." Those feelings are often so strong that she must be nearly coerced into accepting treatment before she "hits bottom." Many times, by way of special strategies, she can be persuaded to get that help before she loses her family, friends, health, car (if she has one), or job. But she will always need vigorous encouragement to seek and accept the help.

Here are some suggested strategies by which professionals can help the middle class woman accept help for herself. First, and probably the most successful, is the employee alcoholism program where confidentiality is insured and where the cost of treatment is covered to a great extent by the employers' medical policy or third-party payments. When such a program is effective, the employee, because of work performance problems is given the choice of entering into an appropriate rehabilitation milieu or placing her job in jeopardy. Because her job is linked with her identity, her economic survival, or her feelings of self-worth, she is most likely to accept a diagnosis of "alcoholism" from the alcoholism counselor and, in turn, recognize the many ways in which her drinking is getting in the way of her functioning. This route is limited by the fact that many middle class women are not employed, particularly those in the 40–60-year-old group. And they may be precisely the ones who are becoming alcoholic.

Therefore, we have to look further. Another effective path, though less coercive, by which the middle class female alcoholic may get into treatment is when family pressures build up so that she becomes aware of the fact that she may lose her husband or her children. The threats of a spouse, where he is perceived as *really* able to carry them out, may motivate a woman to seek help. For instance, one man, after his drinking wife drove into a ditch with their three children in the car, simply took the keys and sold the car. The recognition of the near-miss tragedy resulted in this woman seeking treatment.

A husband's resolve to leave or to cease support for the drinking wife, along with other recognizable consequences of the drinking, may persuade her to look for 'ways out." Certainly the threat of court action to remove children from a home is dramatically effective in pointing up the realities of dangerous situations and intensifying pressure to effect change. Therefore, a knowledgeable family court judge is an incredibly effective resource.

One more way in which middle class women may get into treatment is via a Driving While Intoxicated (DWI) Program where the police will arrest a drunken driver and suspend or revoke her license unless she attends a "class" on alcohol, alcohol abuse, and alcoholism. During such a course, which must be a learning experience, she may come to recognize her alcoholism and through counselors, who are physically present during the course on "driving and drinking," she has the opportunity to explore the possibilities for help. Also, the tuned-in alcoholism counselor will be able to identify the woman with alcoholism and be able to differentiate her from those women who have simply had too much to drink on one occasion.

This route into treatment is so rarely used for two reasons. One, in middle class families, the driver is most often the male. And, two, the police seem to have trouble actually issuing a summons to a woman. The stigma of the drinking woman must play a role here. The result is that the census of middle class women in DWI courses is extremely low. One sponsored by the Westchester Council on Alcoholism had two women in it and over 30 men. Training for the police, court personnel, and law-enforcement agencies is our mandate. They can be infinitely helpful in motivating women to get well.

Perhaps above all, the medical community has a heavy responsibility to reinforce and convey evidence to patients that drinking too much alcohol results in the medical complications that the physician is seeing and the female patient is feeling. In other words, when the doctor links up the symptoms with the overdrinking, education takes place and the patient may consider the alternatives. Certainly not all alcoholics will do something about their illness when the doctor says that the drinking is causing it, but the physician must help the patient overcome the denial by pointing out the physical consequences of the drinking. At least, then, the groundwork is set for change, and the middle class woman is generally interested in good health, feeling good, and looking good. That points toward another path that can sometimes be helpful in motivating the female alcoholic to move toward sobriety. Cosmetic concerns are usually tremendously important to her and if the consequences of drinking include overweight,

underweight, poor complexion, puffy tissue, and embarrassing vari-
cose veins, she may be interested in correcting some of these problems. A physician can point out that these conditions will change
with sobriety. It should be noted, however, improvement physically
or cosmetically usually only acts as reenforcement after the first step,
acknowledging the alcoholism, has been taken.

A physician's warning about the fetal alcohol syndrome or the
consequences of drinking during pregnancy is another road by which
one can persuade a pregnant woman to recognize her addictive
drinking behavior and help her to overcome her illness. The possibility of giving birth to an abnormal child is a mighty powerful deterrent, and the pregnant woman should know the risks that she takes
when she drinks. It behooves the wise physician to warn her.

Last, but certainly immensely important, is the fact that many
middle class women consult their clergyman first when they feel that
they are in trouble or need advice. In fact, this should be a sure route
toward recovery. It is of paramount importance, then, that the clergy
have training and be knowledgeable about alcoholism as a disease
and resources for its treatment.

So, there are a multitude of routes to sobriety for the middle
class woman. To get her to take a route is difficult. The skills of the
professional who points to the road will determine whether or not
the road is traveled.

BIBLIOGRAPHY

Alcohol abuse among women: Special Problems and Unmet Needs, 1976 Hearing
before the Subcommittee on Alcoholism and Narcotics of the Committee on
Labor and Public Welfare, U.S. Senate Ninety-fourth congress, second session.
Sept. 29, 1976.

Browne-Mayers, A. N., Hamilton, F. J., Seelye, E. E., & Sillman, L. *Psychosocial
study of hospitalized middle class alcoholic women in the U.S.* White Plains,
N.Y.: Bloomingdale, 1975 (mimeographed).

Estes & Heineman. Alcoholism: Development, consequences and interventions. In
E. Gomberg (Ed.), *Women with alcohol problems.* St. Louis: Mosby, 1977, pp.
178–85.

Fort, T., & Porterfield, A. L. Some backgrounds and types of alcoholism among
women. *Journal of Health and Human Behavior,* 1961, *2,* 283.

Robe, L. B. *Just so it's healthy.* Minneapolis, Minn.: CompCare Publications, 1977.

Schmidt, W., Smart, R., & Moss, M. *Social class and the treatment of alcoholism.*
Brookside Monograph of the Addiction Research Foundation No. 7. Toronto:
University of Toronto Press, 1968.

Tamerin, J. B., Neumann, C. P., & Marshall, M. H.: The Upperclass alcoholic: a syndrome in itself? *Psychosomatic Medicine,* 1971, *12,* 200.

Youcha, G., *A dangerous pleasure-alcohol from the woman's perspective-its effect on body, mind, and relationships.* New York: Hawthorn Books, 1978.

Part II

INTERVENTION: PROBLEMS
AND APPROACHES

Chapter 8

HOLISTIC APPROACHES FOR WOMEN

Catherine Milton

I have been involved in the criminal justice system for 11 years: most of this time has been focused on the police, also I directed a project on female offenders for the American Bar Association, on victims for the Urban Coalition, and now I'm working at the federal level in the Treasury Department.

When I first got involved in the system, I naively thought that my being a woman was irrelevant, and I worked on issues such as effectiveness of police patrol, pro's and con's of college education for police, and so on. It didn't take me long to realize the incredible discriminatory manner in which the criminal justice system treated minorities and women. The criminal justice system is largely run by men for men: over 97 percent of police employees are men; the vast majority of offenders are men; and the majority of victims are men.

These facts are not surprising when you consider that the criminal justice system reflects values of society. There are rules that govern training and promotions in police departments that are for men only. Crimes where women are predominently victims (i.e., family assaults and rape) are given low priority by prosecutors and therefore are underrated. The female offender is often protected by men in the system and therefore kept out of jails and prisons unless her crime is "morally" reprehensible, such as being a drug addict or prostitute.

What is new and hard to believe is that the system has re- sponded in the past few years to pressure. There are more women police officers (from less than 1 percent to 3 percent). Victim advo- cate projects have been setup for battered wife and rape victims. Innovative projects for female offenders have been started. This con- ference could not have happened even three years ago. We have power to change the system as it relates to women, but it is going to take a lot of hard work and the progress will be slow. It is not going to happen in five or even ten years.

There are several important principles at work that apply to female offenders and victims. First, there is the need to help women become economically and psychologically independent and strong. The "typical" female offender is poor, uneducated, with few job skills; is a minority member; a mother (80 percent), and a welfare recipient. You may also be aware that a number of female offenders have also been *victims* of family assaults and have serious problems of dependency, either on drugs, alcohol, or a "man" who got them to go along to help out in his crime and to go into prostitution. It is totally unrealistic to think that giving this kind of woman training as a beautician or seamstress will make her "ok."

When I first directed the ABA project on women, I thought it would be a good idea to hire a female offender living at a facility as an assistant. Of the twelve women, four were alcoholic, two were drug addicts, two had serious mental problems, one was senile, and the other three had not finished the eighth grade. I was foolish enough to think I could hire one of them as a secretary.

Most women offenders are arrested because of economically motivated crimes, such as larceny, forgery, and embezzlement. A multiapproach is needed to treat the whole woman. Their essential program needs are vocational rehabilitation, education (reading and writing), job readiness (what it is like going to work, what is expected of you), counseling in job placement, health, parenting, and indepen- dent living (helping with budget, credit, checkbook, rent, etc.). Child care must also be provided. These are essentials, not frills.

These approaches must be integrated into a system and not be approached on a project basis because otherwise it won't survive. The biggest problem of the projects has been funding. We found that majority of projects only lasted three years. Two of the best projects are programs that have to be integrated into the system, For exam- ple, in 1972, I visited women in police departments around the country. Forty cities would start projects and twenty other cities would if a foundation paid for it; only one city was willing to do this on its own. Several ways to integrate a program into a system are through law suits (women in policing, offenders, work release, education); publicizing bad situations (rape victims, battered wives, offenders, and fact that your police office has no women); organizing a task force; and getting women inside the system. Women may not treat women victims or offenders necessarily better but more women inside make it easier to carry out changes and support those who want to do more. Women are sensitive to the problems of the system.

Problems are so big with no one solution. Each of us is a resource for change. Change is only going to happen if we use our own resources to do what we can to support other women. We have to fight when we have to, but persevere. There is so much to do, but if you persevere your opportunity will come.

Chapter 9

THE WOMAN IN TREATMENT
Evaluation and Diagnostic Implications

Herbert J. Freudenberger

This paper will explore the many complex dynamics, issues, and problems that a woman faces upon entering a treatment environment. The author will focus on the conflicts that women grapple with and what he has found in working and talking with women in various institutions, independent practice, and crisis centers.

Let us begin our discussion by looking at the "typical" woman addict that enters a treatment facility. She is between the ages of 17 and 25, is either black, Latino, Chicano, or comes from a lower socioeconomic white group. If she is a minority woman, then she more than likely has had numerous abortions and has been sexually assaulted, most often by a male member of her immediate family. If she is or was married, then she is either divorced or was abandoned by her mate. The children were left for her to fend with as best as she was able. If she was lucky, then some family members helped her out; she may have tried to go to work, but it she was not fortunate as her other sisters, then she was and is on welfare or has had family court to take her children away from her.

Her drug abuse history was most likely initiated by a man who turned her on to it, and for whom she eventually hustled and whored to support both their habits. She is impoverished emotionally and economically, has had a poor education and is inadequately qualified vocationally.

She is suffering from feelings of depression, loneliness, emptiness, a sense of inadequacy, dependency, or has become callous to
the world, has a poor self-image and is involved with a variety of
bodily symptoms, most of which are psychosomatic. These are the
qualities with which a woman enters a treatment community.

Once she enters, what does she find? First, the induction program personnel are predominantly men. The induction interview is
conducted in such a manner that the woman feels subtly berated for
her life's activities, for being a whore who "sold her body." She is
given little understanding or sympathy about her problems as a
woman addict: there is a minimum discussion about her concerns for
her children and how misunderstood and alienated she feels having
to relate to a male staff member at the height of her personal anxi-
eties.

Once she has passed through the induction stage of the treatment facility she finds that most of the administrators, unit directors,
and counselors are men. A minimum possibility exists for her to
begin to relate to and talk of her inner fears and womanly conflicts.

Further implications for the woman are that the social and
psychological structure of the program is geared towards men, not
women. She notices that there are fewer women than men in treatment. She finds that it is difficult to relate in terms of her own
confused role change struggles. But, she also comes to recognize that
if she continues to use her street con and manipulate she might be
able to survive. What in turn this manipulation does to her chances
for change are of course not dealt with, nor discovered.

She learns that charm, being sexually seductive, being young
and attractive, and playing upon these qualities with the men can
enhance her chances for survival. As time goes on, she finds out that
there are a number of possibilities open to her in treatment. As the
author has indicated in a previous paper (1974), within the structure
of a therapeutic community, the resident has the option to let go and
regress to a more childlike position. This regression, if it is constructive, can serve a very valuable function of regrowth. This is usually
not the case with the woman, however. She will also regress but to
a more infantile, little girl position. This position will have the qualities of being pampered, catered to, and give the overall impression
of helplessness. This need for pampering is usually responded to by
male residents as well as staff members whose sexist attitudes are
already present and can easily be translated from earlier male-female
relationships that exist within our society.

At this point, some of the more independent seeking women leave the program and seek to strike out once again on their own. It is estimated that 15 to 20 percent more women than men leave treatment during the first month of their entrance into a program.

Further serious issues arise when we seek to diagnose and evaluate a client. Historically, diagnosis is rooted in a medical model. This means that the labels we use are derived from looking at a person from a "sickness" or disease frame of reference. We need to recognize that when we diagnose we do so from a social and professional structure of authority and responsibility, and we tend to look at the individual from a maladaptive perspective.

It is further essential that we recognize as previously indicated by the author (1970) that the illness diagnoses stem from a large amount of material based on middle class patients. This has real implications in terms of mislabeling when we are working with lower socioeconomic class individuals. It is so easy to label a Puerto Rican woman as hysteric or schizophrenic if she is suffering from what is viewed as hallucinations. Closer scrutiny may elicit the fact that she believes in magic, is superstitious, and is culturally inclined to "hallucinate." To diagnose requires an understanding of the specific background of the individual, her culture, her economic status, education as well as belief and value systems.

The evaluation procedure especially requires training and "know-how" by the professional. The professional and human services worker come from different perspectives in terms of motivation, value system, education, personal belief systems, and personalities (Freudenberger, 1976).

This, in turn, impacts on evaluations. The professional may, for example, have a sense of a woman suffering from minimal brain dysfunction, a learning disability, perceptual disorder, hypoglycemia, or hypothyrodism. Each of these conditions if not known to the paraprofessional, definitely impact on a woman's personality and functioning. Some of these conditions may cause acting-out behavior, depression, concentration difficulties, loss of memory, inability to be flexible, and adapt to required behavior. An inexperienced or poorly trained counselor may misjudge therapeutically, may verbally assault, or become frustrated by the lack of movement in the client. If there is no adequate training and education, as well as knowledge of the dynamics of a woman serious consequences occur. As previously indicated, women leave programs at a higher rate than do men, and the worker tends to feel disenchanted with their work. The all too common burn-out condition, on which the writer has spoken on many previous occasions (Freudenberger, 1975) may have come about because the worker is not sufficiently trained to know how to cope with a more complex and dynamically confused individual.

What Do We Need to Do?

1. We need to understand that women are different from men; thay they have needs and role changes to go through that require special attention.
2. We as professionals as well as paraprofessionals need to stop rationalizing our failures with women clients in terms of "they were not motivated for treatment."
3. We need to recognize that our DSM diagnostic classification system is sorely in need of further revision to make it relevant for the 1980s.
4. We must take a serious and honest look at ourselves. The human services worker needs all the training and education they can get. The complexities of our daily world, the severe psychic impoverishment that has impacted upon many women, has left long lasting emotional scars. The scars may be organic, emotional, or behavioral in their manifestation. They may also be very subtle, but they are there.
5. We must upgrade our understanding of and recognize the importance of treating the total person. We need to know about nutrition, economics, culture, religion, family lifestyles as well as value systems in order to adequately diagnose and evaluate a client. If we do not know these basic facts, then we are performing a disservice. We are cheating our clients as well as ourselves of their possibility of achieving a healthier life-style.

References

Freudenberger, H. J. How we can right what's wrong with our therapeutic communities. *Journal of Drug Issues,* Fall 1974, 381–392.
Freudenberger, H. J. Departure from "medical" model oriented psychotherapies. *Journal of Clinical Issues in Psychology,* 1970, *1* (2)

Freudenberger, H. J. The professional and the human services worker: Some solutions to the problems they face in working together. *Journal of Drug Issues.* *6* (3), 1976.

Freudenberger, H. J. The staff burn-out syndrome. *Drug Abuse Council,* Inc. SS-7, 1975, *Psychotherapy, 12*, 1975.

Chapter 10

SEXISM IN TREATMENT

Barbara A. Lewis

Sexism in treatment is a highly complicated phenomenon that is continually self-reinforced by the health care system, therapists, and clients (or patients). To begin with, 90 percent of psychiatrists and 67 percent of clinical psychologists are male and white, while 60 to 75 percent of all people in therapy are women (Levine, Kamin, & Levine).

The majority of health care workers (female and male) ascribe to the traditional stereotype that women should be soft, emotional, intuitive, sensitive, childlike, passive, submissive, giving, loving, sympathetic, and masochistic, in short, all qualities suited to being a homemaker, wife, and mother. Men, however, are supposed to be powerful, strong, directed, intellectual, assertive, aggressive, mechanical, and athletic. Society and then therapists such as Freud and others have reinforced these views. Theorists also have not paid attention to the roles that society has played in oppressing women.

The majority of therapists interpret behavior differently, depending on whether they are exhibited by men or women. The well-known Broverman study showed that therapists consider normal behavior as that typically considered desirable for men, and that behavior considered desirable for women as essentially unhealthy; that is, so-called healthy behavior for women is really neurotic. *Crazy* for a woman, for example, means one who does not want to live with her husband anymore. *Sane* is when she decides to wear a skirt and apply for a job at Bell Telephone (Levering, 1972).

Women are often held responsible for men's problems. For example, an assertive woman can be called castrating and holding her husband back (Mintz, 1974). Women are also held responsible for their own rape; that is, they are accused of provoking the man, as if men were weak, helpless, and impulse-ridden with no control. (Ironically, this is the way women are often seen.)

Traditionally, therapists have made women think that their unhappiness and discontent comes from their inability to fulfill their traditional role as a woman. Some basic assumptions commonly held about women are the following (Mintz, 1974):

1. It is natural for a woman to want to get married. If she doesn't, she is anxious about sex, unfeminine, or maladjusted.
2. It is natural for a woman to want children. If she doesn't, she is maladjusted.
3. Lack of ambition is normal in a woman.
4. It is natural for a man to take the initiative in relationships with women and a woman is usurping the male role if she does.

The main goal of traditional therapy has been to get women to "adjust" to home and family. This is the answer to depression and is in fact what has often made her depressed. Feminist therapy, however, is a nonadjustment model that recognizes that anger is real and not necessarily "sick" at all. It recognizes that the anger is directed against societal oppression and is very often quite appropriate. When a woman objects to a traditional therapist who is trying to get her to "adjust," she is frequently accused of resisting treatment and refusing to face her problems (Friedman et al, 1979). For example, a woman who enjoys the company of other women more than she does that of men is often accused of denying or repressing her fear of men. Or a woman may feel that she loves her husband and children very much but feels anxious being cooped up in the house all day. Some therapists would interpret this anxiety as a symptom of really hating her husband and children. A woman may feel discriminated against by her boss because she is a woman. This may be interpreted by her therapist as blaming her boss for her inability to function well.

The ultimate form of resistance of which a woman might be accused is her refusal to sleep with her therapist. In the traditional stereotyped view, women are supposed to be submissive to men. The male therapist can feel very threatened by the woman's assertion (and thereby disagreement with him), whereas in a male client this might be seen as healthy behavior, reflecting growth. The "bottom line" for most women, unfortunately, seems to be that "you're ok if you get approval from a man."

Some of our sexist values are deep-seated, unaware, and often well-intentioned. An example is the male therapist who suggests to the female client that she wear her hair down and wear skirts and makeup so she can catch a man. Female therapists also do this as if the most important thing in life for a woman is to have a man. Women therapists and authority figures have often unwittingly reinforced sexist norms, such as the female co-therapist who always makes the coffee for a group or defers to the male co-therapist's decisions. I have too frequently seen highly competent women professionals defer to males who were lower in the hierarchy, simply because they were men.

Other subtle examples are the woman who has successfully completed her analysis with the exception of what her analyst still considers to be too much aggression. The therapist to whom the client is referred sees this woman simply as a go-getter who successfully goes after what she wants (Mintz, 1974). The ambitious woman is considered to be competing with men and therefore denying her female role.

For a long time, I avoided being in therapy with a woman because I did not believe that I could find one who was strong enough for me. I finally had a very positive experience with a woman therapist and came to realize that what had kept me away were my negative attitudes toward the competence of women. It also made me question what I was communicating during that time to my own clients about women. Another curious form of sexism I encountered is what I would call a split attitude. I have seen male therapists treat their female colleagues and trainees with the utmost non-sexist respect, but when working with women in relation to men, for example, couple or family therapy, they exhibit the traditional sexist mode of trying to get the woman to "adjust" to the role of catering to her husband and putting him first always. Being treated with the utmost respect by these men, it has made me conjecture what my experience would have been had I encountered them as part of a couple.

Another common form of somewhat subtle sexism is the failure on the part of the therapist to invite the client to participate in the treatment process; the therapist does not request or discuss with the client about working together for her welfare. Another subtlety taken for granted is the common procedure of referring to the client by her first name while the therapist is called "Dr." or the equivalent.

Another way that sexism is fostered is in the undermining of female authority figures and the lack of awareness on the part of the women that their difficulty is not necessarily all of their own making. Neither women nor men very much accept or respect women as leaders or authority figures.

Sexism in treatment appears to be the worst in institutions where the patients are the most helpless. The situation for men here is not a great deal better, but for women it seems worse. By virtue of being a patient in a mental hospital, the patients are almost automatically seen as "crazy." The hospital has been used by husbands as a way to gain control over their wives, especially in getting sex. Abuses of women in institutions are many. If a woman is considered too loud or aggressive she can be medicated; the drugs make her sluggish and docile and more adjustable to the status quo. She can be given electroshock therapy, put into seclusion, given aversive therapy, a "token economy," subjected to sterilization, or, the worst of all, psychosurgery. With aversive therapy, she can receive painful shock for drugs, alcoholism, homosexuality, or whatever behavior the hospital personnel decide is deviant. In a "token economy," she can be rewarded for setting her hair and wearing skirts.

The most profound form of sexist abuse is lobotomy in which the part of the brain is destroyed that controls emotions diagnosed as undesirable and renders women somewhat like the *Stepford Wives,* that is, obedient, docile robots. Lobotomies are performed on the basis of what is assumed to be "sane" behavior. I would like to read to you from a report on lobotomies (Roberts, 1972):

> Dr. Freedman, the "dean of lobotomists," openly stated that loboto-
> mized women make good housekeepers.... In Canada, Dr. Earle
> Baker of the University of Toronto reports the case of a promiscuous
> housewife who ran away from home frequently and sometimes became
> suicidal. After her lobotomy, her doctors bragged that she was *cured*
> of her promiscuity and was now a model housewife. Dr. Breggin con-
> tends that the reason women respond "better" to lobotomies is their
> passive conditioning, and adds that it is more socially acceptable to
> lobotomize women because creativity, which the operation totally de-

stroys, is, to this society, an "expendable quality" in women. . . . Dr. Lindstrom, a prominent California neurosurgeon writing in 1964, said that 72 percent of psychotics and 80 percent of neurotics operated on are women. Seventy-one percent of the lobotomies performed by Drs. Brown and Lighthill in 1968 were on women. And Dr. R. F. Heatherton, at the Kingston Psychiatric Hospital in Ontario, admitted at a 1970 medical conference that the hospital administration refused to allow lobotomies on men because of the unfavorable publicity given to lobotomy in Canada; that publicity did not, however, deter the hospital from performing lobotomies on seventeen women. Repeatedly in the psychosurgical literature it is regarded as evidence of success if a previously distraught woman is able to return to housekeeping chores.

STRATEGIES TO ELIMINATE SEXIST PRACTICES

No matter how aware the therapist, the institution or the client may think she or he is, the best place to start is with the assumption that your consciousness is not as high as you think, no matter how well intentioned you may be. If you have not struggled with these issues, it is my belief that you have not become sufficiently aware of your unconscious beliefs. This has certainly been true for me. I thought I was quite aware and only after involvement with the woman's movement did I realize how unaware I was. Consciousness raising must go on many levels with institutions, therapists, and clients; but first the need for this must be acknowledged. Reading feminist literature also helps.

I believe that the process of change in institutions has to be very different from that of individuals. The power in institutions rests primarily with men because they hold the majority of the status positions. The women patients are too afraid to speak up, lest they be labeled crazy, or drugged, shocked, beaten, or lobotomized. But the issue is deeper than sexism. There is an overall resistance to giving patients (of either sex) any power at all, which naturally reinforces their feelings of helplessness. I tried in vain for years in the hospitals in which I worked to change this. That mental hospitals are "revolving doors" is no surprise to me. I have often wondered how hospital administrations expect patients to go from a helpless position as patients with no responsibilities for themselves to being instant useful responsible citizens without any practice. The support of male administrators has to be enlisted. It is important that they not be blamed and therefore threatened. They must be shown that it is to their advantage to help women to become more self-sufficient.

The men then would have some of their burdens lifted and fewer demands made on them. It is also important to remember that feminism and femininity are not mutually exclusive.

In reality, the changes in institutions will probably come in response to political pressure, both from the women's movement and from legislation with some sort of affirmative action program. For example, the Psychology Committee at the National Organization for Women (NOW) is undertaking a survey of sexist attitudes and clinics that we consider to be sexist and that we will not refer clients to. It is also important to change some insurance policies that only cover such things as shock therapy and not psychotherapy. It is on the private level and to some extent on the clinic level that the most can be done by the client. The most important thing a current or potential client can do is become as informed as possible of her rights, which is why my committee at NOW wrote this booklet, *A Consumer's Guide to Nonsexist Therapy* (1978). Because of the inherent inequities of the therapy relationship, it is that much harder for a woman to assert her rights as a client. It is important to be aware and stay attuned to sexist attitudes and values in the therapist. Above all it is important for women to learn they are not alone, that there is support available. They are not helpless as they have been taught to believe. The therapy process should actively involve both therapist and client and is not something which is done to a client. The client should be consulted about everything and no decisions should be made concerning her welfare without her involvement and consent. It is important that the client educate her therapist.

It is very important for the female client to not play the helpless victim role, waif, or fragile doll. These are all myths unconsciously calculated to reinforce dependence and helplessness. Consciousness raising groups also are invaluable. Above all it is important for the client to trust her feelings, use her own judgment, and ask questions.

From the therapist's perspective, it is very important to be aware of sexist attitudes and to support, encourage and reinforce women in assertiveness and self-sufficiency. It is important to be alert to the possibilities of subtle domination and the reinforcement of helplessness and self-hatred. It is important to involve the client in all decisions concerning medications, psychological testing, confidentiality, type of therapy, etc. It can be devastating for a woman to have her hopes crushed. It is very important for women to have some good role models in women who are in authority positions. Too often these women are cold and withholding, which often is how they got where they are. What is needed is women in authority who are strong, yet warm and nurturing.

It is important for everyone to be aware of the relative contributions from society, the family, and intrapsychic elements to women's problems but not to overstress them either. The real bottom line is the important awareness that women need to determine an identity, life-style, and sexual orientation that is centered in their own feelings and not in the dictates of society. With the exception of some private therapists and some feminist therapy collectives, our programs still mirror the mainstream traditional stereotyped sexist attitudes of society. While I have seen some feminist therapists in institutions, it is my impression that they have been largely rendered ineffective by the overpowering sexist administration. So far, I have not seen, unfortunately, any real feminism at the top, where the power lies.

REFERENCES

Broverman, I. K., Broverman, D., & Clarkson, F. E. Sex-role stereotypes and clinical judgments of mental health. *Journal of Consulting and Clinical Psychology, 34,* 1–7.

Friedman, S. S., et al. *A woman's guide to therapy.* Englewood Cliffs, N.J.: Prentice-Hall, 1979 pp. 40–41.

Levering, S. W. She must be some kind of nut. *Rough Times,* 1972, *3,* (First entitled *The Radical Therapist, Rough Times* is now published under the name *State and Mind.*)

Levine, S. V., Kamin, L. E., & Levine, E. L. Sexism and psychiatry. *American Journal of Orthopsychiatry,* 1974, *44,* 329–330.

Mintz, E. E. What do we owe today's woman? *International Journal of Group Psychotherapy,* 1974, *24.*

National Organization for Women Psychology Committee. *A consumer's guide to nonsexist therapy.* New York: NOW, 1978.

Roberts, B. Rough times. In *A woman's guide to therapy.*

Chapter 11

SEXISM IN DRUG ABUSE TREATMENT PROGRAMS

Stephen J. Levy

Sexism refers to those attitudes and practices that effectively discriminate against persons of one sex and are founded upon rigidly assigned beliefs and opinions concerning sex differences. These beliefs and opinions are the building blocks upon which so many sexist practices are founded. They persist despite the fact that little scientific evidence support them. For example, the exhaustive volume by Maccoby and Jacklin (1974) reviews some 1,400 studies on sex differences and conclude that very little definitive evidence exists to support contemporary beliefs about men and women. Two separate issues of the *Journal of Social Issues*—"Sex Roles: Persistence and Change" (1976) and "Male Roles and the Male Experience" (1978) —further document the social psychological "cement" that binds these sexist stances. Let's not kid ourselves; what we are really dealing with is a power struggle involving control of the marketplace, delivery of services (via government funding), control of our own bodies, the size of the world population, and other interrelated issues of great moment for all persons. Sexism goes to the heart of societal structure, which includes family size and constellation and religious beliefs, the proverbial battle for the hearts and minds of the populace (witness the struggle over the Equal Rights Amendment). With these thoughts in mind, let us turn to a consideration of how this drama is uniquely played out in the drug abuse treatment movement in America, now more than a decade in existence.

In my early work and writings with my coauthors (Levy & Doyle, 1974; Levy & Doyle, 1976; Levy & Broudy, 1975), we gathered the first empirical evidence of overt and covert sexist attitudes and practices in a drug-free therapeutic community and a large methadone maintenance treatment program. Doyle, Quinones, Young, and Hughes (1977) continued these explorations in the same therapeutic community detailing the failure of a women's program caught in a double bind of difficult clients and a nonsupportive male hierarchy. The results of the therapeutic community (TCS) and methadone study (MMS) are summarized here for the reader, who is referred to the original articles for more detail.

The overall findings indicate that attitudes and practices concerning women reflect the views of the general society more than those beliefs that are unique to the drug scene. It may be that researchers and clinicians have overemphasized the "deviant subculture" nature of drug abusers. Many of the attitudes of both staff and clients reflect differences between the sexes that can be found in many social settings in our society.

The TCS data indicate that men and women receive different treatment and that most of the staff believe that these differences are justified. What emerges is a portrait of male-female differences in terms of psychology, biology, and social behavior. Women are viewed, by both staff and clients, as more dependent, more "emotional," and "sicker" than men. Practices regarding job assignments and job training indicate a stereotyped view of the sexes. It was also found that male and female staff members do not differ substantially in their attitudes toward women with both groups having only a fairly liberal outlook. There is some evidence that female staff members (who are fewer in number and power to influence program policy) must meet implicit "male-oriented" criteria (such as "toughness") for employment as staff members.

The MMS data indicate that female clients complain of more problems than do male clients. Despite the fact that most staff members are female (and female staff score significantly higher on the Attitudes Toward Women Scale), the staff appears to be less perceptive in dealing with female clients than males. Indeed, staff ability to perceive client problems in both studies (regardless of sex) appears to be significantly different from the clients' own views.

MMS female clients report significantly greater concerns than male clients regarding a lack of job training and a lack of education, stating that the program favors males in these pursuits. When asked to indicate their problem areas, MMS clients point to more "outward-bound" considerations, such as school and work, while TCS clients point to more personal problem areas. (This is a function, in part, of differences in treatment philosophy and practice.) In both studies, however, males view their problems more readily in terms of competence and striving while females view their problems in more intrapsychic and interpersonal areas. Most of the differences noted were significant at the 0.05 level or higher.

In our paper on sex role differences in the therapeutic community, Marie Broudy and I (1975) issued a call for the introduction of the concept of androgyny, that is, a definition of human traits, behaviors, and attributes that is not limited by one's sex, as a means of righting some ancient wrongs.

In their comprehensive survey article entitled *Issues in the Treatment of Female Addiction: A Review and Critique of the Literature,* Cuskey, Berger, and Densen-Gerber (1978) points to the mounting evidence for which our early work had only broken the ice. They cite studies that have yielded further empirically derived evidence that the sad trend (originally only available as anecdotes) that women enter drug treatment programs in fewer numbers than men and leave (prematurely) in proportionately higher numbers than men still exists.

The therapeutic community movement itself points to the enormous service gap they have created for women in the proceedings of their 1976 planning conference. "As currently conceived, the therapeutic community has difficulty in providing services to, and holding, women residents" (p. 100). Even in their attempts to document their own shortcomings, they further expose their biased thinking. "Women should be oriented toward part-time work until their children reach school age, with an emphasis on the importance of the task of rearing children" (p. 102). This is simply not a viable alternative for some women. Why does the nurturant role fall exclusively to women?

The promulgation of government guidelines and funding cutbacks have rendered most methadone maintenance programs turnstile pharmacies without any of what are euphemistically called "ancillary services." If drug addiction, in great measure, represents a total life-style, does the shift from street drugs to blockading doses of methadone suffice to counteract that life-style? For all too many methadone clients the answer is of course not! In a study I conducted for the New Jersey Division of Narcotics and Drug Abuse Control (Levy, 1977) on three of their methadone maintenance clinics, it was revealed that while the staff believes they are working toward psychotherapeutic goals, the clients are mainly interested in the free government-sponsored medication and perceive little need for such psychologically oriented services.

Unfortunately, when we turn our attention to nondrug abuse treatment settings where women do enter and participate in greater numbers, we do not find encouraging practices regarding the female (or male) substance abuser. I (1975) conducted a survey of drug and alcohol use among patients at a suburban community mental health center in Bergen County, New Jersey in an effort to see if the report of only 1 percent admissions for drug and alcohol problems respectively was a real phenomenon. The results indicated several facts: 1) when staff consciousness is raised they reveal figures of 3 percent for drug admissions and 8 percent for alcohol admission (much closer to National Institute of Mental Health averages for the nation); 2) half the staff had never visited a drug or alcohol treatment program; 3) 30 percent of staff always or often avoid drug or alcohol problems as a primary diagnosis; 4) half the staff had little or no experience with substance abusers; and 5) more than half do not want drug abusers or addicts as part of their caseloads. If these findings are indicative of a more pervasive phenomenon, then it would seem that the female drug abuser and addict have few places indeed where they can turn for sensitive and informed helpers in their addictive plight.

Fortunately, quality programs that can meet the unique needs of female clients are beginning to surface. Family House in Pennsylvania, Interim House, Together Inc., Women's Resource and Survival Center in New Jersey, the Women's program at Project RETURN in New York City, Women Inc., in Massachusetts and others too numerous to mention here, are blazing the trails. In time, as such programs grow in size (not too big, we hope, no more empires please) and number the more traditional agencies may eventually find themselves competing to keep their beds filled as funds continue to shrink. They will truly have cut off their own noses to spite their faces. Tragically, for many of the women clients who have passed and will pass through their doors, they will encounter too little too late to meet their needs.

Finally, I would like to consider some strategies that the more traditional agencies can incorporate if they wish to make *genuine* change. Let me start with the obvious. In drug treatment programs, as in most bureaucracies, things fall from the top. The leadership (and here I mean senior management) must support efforts to upgrade programs. It this means that they must begin by checking out their own self and vestiges of sexism then so be it. Frankly I do not know any other human way to really begin. Feminists and traditionalists must first talk among themselves and staff to find their own level of comfort and willingness to work for change. Attitudinal skills training and consciousness raising, along with factual programs on sex differences in law, economics, and society can be useful tools. It is time to end hiring token "female providers" to go out and play the lone ranger so that agencies can say they are meeting women's needs. This is analogous to putting rice and beans on the menu (and nothing else) and then saying you are meeting the needs of Hispanic clients. There must be some attempt to integrate the number of male and female staff members, including in top management and clinical positions.

We have experimented with a variety of the above in our co-ed Halfway House at Beth Israel Medical Center's Alcoholism Treatment Program and raised our attraction and retention rates dramatically, so that now women represent a constant 25 percent of our house population, which was previously 8 percent. The women have formed a core group and are continuing in treatment together. We also have a significant number of recovering female providers on staff to act as role models for clients.

I believe that one of the single most important things that can be done to increase retention of female clients is to provide a women's support group in the early months of treatment. Our women are in group and individual counseling only with other women for the first two or three months of treatment. Women and men have enough issues to deal with in early abstinence without having to rejoin the battle of the sexes immediately. Men and women merge when they are ready (self-interest, sustained sobriety, movement in counseling, etc.).

The task force on sex bias and sex role stereotyping in psychotherapeutic practice of the American Psychological Association (1978) have provided some excellent guidelines for therapy with women that I believe we can all profit from. Each guideline is accompanied with a verbatim example drawn from complaints of female therapists who responded to a survey conducted by the task force.

1. The conduct of therapy should be free of constrictions based on gender-defined roles, and the options explored between client and practitioner should be free of sex role stereotypes. (I have had women report to me that they could not continue in therapy because the objective seemed to be for them to learn to adjust better to their roles as wives, mothers, daughters, or underlings of one kind or another, and they needed to become free persons.)

2. Psychologists should recognize the reality, variety, and implications of sex-discriminatory practices in society and should facilitate client examination of options in dealing with such practices. (The major source of my anxiety was my sense of self-worth as a psychologist. I want to do a good job and enjoy status, prestige, money, etc., that comes from being a productive worker. Situational factors that thwart these ends, such as sex discrimination, are thus highly threatening and frustrating.)

3. The therapist should be knowledgeable about current empirical findings on sex roles, sexism, and individual differences resulting from the client's gender-defined identity. (Surprisingly, many male and female colleagues still define maturity in women as the capacity for vaginal orgasm. My feeling is that women who do not experience or report this are seen and therefore subtly treated as emotionally limited.)

4. The theoretical concepts employed by the therapist should be free of sex bias and sex role stereotypes. (In personal psychotherapy, it is hard to separate out basic psychoanalytic bias from therapist attitude but certainly a focus on the "normal" woman as passive, nonassertive, homemaker, as a result of treatment free of "penis envy," competitiveness with men, etc.)

5. The psychologist should demonstrate acceptance of women as equal to men by using language free of derogatory labels. (As a graduate student, women patients were likely to be seen as "castrating" if they responded in an assertive, not necessarily hostile, manner. Men would be seen more as assertive, mature, or some other positive view.)

6. The psychologist should avoid establishing the source of personal problems within the client when they are more properly attributable to situational or cultural factors.

(Friends of mine in treatment experience the frustrations associated with therapists who interpret frustrations arising from the very real inequities that exist in our society as being nothing more than male or penis envy on the part of the female patient.)

7. The psychologist and a fully informed client mutually should agree upon aspects of the therapy relationship such as treatment modality, time factors, and fee arrangements. (Female psychiatrist asked me if I had my husband's agreement for me to see therapist twice a week. I earn more money than he, and am capable of making that decision with or without his agreement.)

8. While the importance of the availability of accurate information to a client's family is recognized, the privilege of communication about diagnosis, prognosis, and progress ultimately resides with the client, not with the therapist. (I have seen child therapists who were concerned that a mother is not appropriately handling her child, tell the husband about this concern, without confronting the mother herself.)

9. If authoritarian processes are employed as a technique, the therapy should not have the effect of maintaining or reinforcing stereotype dependence of women. (I have recently tried to work as a co-therapist with a male psychiatrist who believes that all females *need* to feel they are adjunct to the male; his idea of solving most marital problems is to manipulate the female into a subordinate position and convince her that she likes it.)

10. The client's assertive behaviors should be respected. (Tendency to label healthy assertive behavior as "castrating" or "phallic" in a derogatory manner.)

11. The psychologist whose female clients are subjected to violence in the form of physical abuse or rape should recognize and acknowledge that the client is the victim of a crime. (A psychoanalytically oriented male therapist, with some agreement from some of the other male therapists insisted that there was no such thing as rape, that the woman always "asked" for it in some way.)

12. The psychologist should recognize and encourage exploration of a woman client's sexuality and should recognize her right to define her own sexual preferences. (One pa-

tient said, "My male therapist told me I was too aggressive sexually, that I should put up a good show, every man likes a challenge, but go down gracefully in defeat.")
13. The psychologist should not have sexual relations with a woman client nor treat her has a sex object.

In my years as a psychotherapist, many women have come to me with stories of seduction and sexual intimacies with male therapists. In most instances, the patients were deeply disturbed by these relationships, saw them as exploitative (although sometimes they justified the therapists' role and protected them), and sometimes resulted in psychotic breaks. This is the ultimate of sex role bias: the rationalization of the therapist that his exploitation of the doctor-patient relationship for his gratification could be construed as therapeutic "for a woman."

I heartily subscribe to the idea that when men oppress women the oppressor is not free either. There are many obstacles to be overcome, not the least of which is men learning intimacy, dropping some of our destructive competitiveness, learning to show our feelings, learning to nurture our children, and last, the joyous discovery of a personhood free of sexist bias. To fail to do so will make us custodians instead of clinicians. Sexist walls not only keep them out; they keep *us* in!

REFERENCES

Cuskey, W. R., Berger, L. H., & Densen-Gerber, J. Issues in the treatment of female addiction: A review and critique of the literature. *Contemporary Drug Problems,* 1978.

DeLeon G., & Beschner, G. M. (Eds), *The therapeutic community.* Proceedings of Therapeutic Communities of America Planning Conference, January 29–30, 1976. Washington, D.C.; Alcohol, Drug Abuse and Mental Health Administration, 1976.

Doyle, K. M., Quinones, M. A., Young, D., & Hughes, J. Change by women for women: Analysis of a failure. Newark, N.J.: Division of Drug Abuse, Department of Preventive Medicine and Community Health, New Jersey Medical School, 1977.

Levy, S. J. *A survey of drug and alcohol use among patients at the community center for mental health.* Dumont, N.J., December, 1975.

Levy, S. J., Broudy, M. Sex role differences in the therapeutic community: Moving from sexism to adrogyny. *Journal of Psychedelic Drugs,* 1975, 7 (3).

Levy, S. J., & Doyle, K. M. Attitudes toward women in a drug abuse treatment program. *Journal of Drug Issues,* 1974, *4,* (4).

Levy, S. J., & Doyle, K. M. Treatment of women in a methadone maintenance program. In *Resource book, women in treatment, issues and approaches.* Arlington, Va.: National Drug Abuse Center for Training and Resource Development, Systems and Development Corporation, under contract to the National Institute on Drug Abuse, 1976.

Maccoby, E. E., & Jacklin, C. N., *The psychology of sex differences.* Stanford, Calif., Stanford University Press, 1974.

Male roles and the male experience. *Journal of Social Issues,* 1978, *34,* (1).

Sex roles: Persistence and change. *Journal of Social Issues,* 1976, *32,* (3).

Task Force on Sex Bias and Sex Role Stereotyping in Psychotherapeutic Practice, Guidelines for Therapy with Women. *American Psychologist,* 1978, *33,* (12).

Chapter 12

WOMEN AND SUBSTANCE ABUSE

Treatment Issues

David E. Smith
Millicent E. Buxton

We exist in what Dr. Andrew Malcolm has aptly called a "chemo-phillic" society in which chemists invent, pharmaceutical houses manufacture, advertisers advertise, doctors prescribe or overpre-scribe, druggists dispense, and the people eat, apply, swallow, insert, or inject a seemingly endless variety of psychoactive drugs. Of the millions of people in the United States who use psychoactive drugs, a significant percentage develop substance abuse problems in which their drug or drugs of choice produce impairment in their health, or economic or social functioning. It is estimated that there are approxi-mately 10 million alcoholics in the United States, 2 million nonnar-cotic drug abusers, and 500,000 opiate abusers. This abuse population of approximately 12½ million represents a major public health problem in the United States and it is estimated that approxi-mately one-half of this population are women.

Who is the woman with the alcohol and drug abuse problems? A young white middle class woman in suburbia struggling with the myth of fulfillment through marriage and babies; a young Chicano woman born and reared in East Los Angeles struggling to survive with her family; the wife of a United States senator; the former First Lady of the United States; the black prostitute hustling in the Ten-derloin for a fix; a young woman looking years beyond her age being picked up for being drunk in public for the umpteenth time; one of the world's leading female rock vocalists; your sister; or your mother. Any woman can potentially develop a substance abuse problem if the contributory physical, psychological, or environmental factors exist. The population of women substance abusers is diverse and hetero-geneous knowing no socioeconomic bounds, no cultural or ethnic bounds, and no bounds of sexual preference. Even though the popu-lation is heterogeneous, the same themes faced by all of these women include feelings of inadequacy, guilt, lack of self-worth, and low self-concepts. This intense feeling of low esteem, hopelessness, pow-erlessness, and despair, often prevent women with addictive disease from seeking the proper treatment. In the traditional role, women are seen as passive, fragile, dependent, noncompetetive, inner-oriented, sensitive, nurturing, yielding, unable to take risks, stupid, and lack-ing in intellectual capabilities. A woman's role is defined in terms of childbearing capacity and the relationship to men. Women were perceived not by their own achievements but by the basis of their relationships, particularly their husband or children. In the 1960s, the movement for redefinition of women's roles in western societies was mobilized. Some women were beginning to loosen the ties that bound them to their traditional wife-mother role and began the search to reach their full human potential. The search for self-fulfill-ment has not been one without conflict or pain, and often this conflict and identity crisis contributed to new drug problems. There have been many casualties as a result of this. For example, 60 percent of all drug-related emergency room visits involve women; of these two-thirds were suicide attempts by women with the remaining one-third a result of drug dependency; 43 percent of all drug-related deaths are women, and 94 percent of Valium-related deaths with alco-hol or another drug involved are women. In fact, there appears to be a greater problem with prescription drug abuse in women than in men.

Substance-abusing women may seek help in a variety of ways. They may be seen in an emergency room as a result of a drug crisis, they may seek help for medical help complications of their substance abuse including trauma; they may seek help for detoxification from physical or psychological drug dependence; or they may request long-term psychological counseling or self-participation in a group process in order to achieve a drug-free life. Unfortunately, despite the many avenues in which a woman may receive help for her substance abuse problem, there is still an underrepresentation of women in most alcohol and drug abuse treatment programs. What are the reasons that women fail to seek help through existing treatment efforts?

There are many, but one is the stigma that women feel about having an alcohol or drug abuse problem. It has greater impact for a woman to say, "I am an alcoholic, or I am an addict" than a male. Fortunately, more prominent women such as Betty Ford, Joan Kennedy, or Grace Slick have said, "I am an alcoholic or addict, and I need treatment." Some of this stigma has begun to fade. We view addictive disease like any other health problem. If a woman has an addictive disease, then she deserves treatment in a nonjudgmental, nonmoralistic fashion like she would if she had any other type of problem.

Approaching the woman with a substance abuse problem in a nonjudgmental, nonmoralistic way is particularly important early in the treatment contact, for, at that time the woman's self-esteem is at a very low ebb and a nonsupportive, inappropriate interaction may reduce the possibility of a long-term treatment interaction as well as drive the woman further into her substance abuse isolation. Once denial has been broken through, it is important that the approach be supportive and directive.

Another big issue is that many of the alcohol and drug abuse programs are male-oriented with relatively few specialized treatment programs for women. In the research that we have done, we found that when one moves from the street into a treatment program, many attitudes will change; attitudes towards drugs may change and their attitudes towards rehabilitation may change, but the attitudes of men towards women do not change. There are the same oppressive attitudes in treatment programs as there are on the street, and quite often, it is this particular type of male-oriented attitude that prevents women from either coming in for treatment, or when they are in treatment, finding that it is inappropriate for them.

We stress the importance of approaching the woman as an individual, and in making an evaluation and establishing a treatment plan based on her individual needs. You cannot treat all women with a substance abuse problem the same and the treatment plan must vary. One of our concerns is that, very often in treatment programs, there are generalizations made that are often counterproductive to treatment. For example, in our polydrug research where we studied various forms of drug abuse in women, we attempted to come up with some categorization that could be translated into a treatment

Table 12.1   Streetwise vs. Nonstreetwise Criteria*

Parameter	Streetwise	Nonstreetwise
Primary means of support	(+2) Dealing Drugs Prostitution Stealing Friends Spouse Welfare None	(−2) Legitimate employment Welfare Student Spouse None
Dress	(+1) Unconventional	(−1) Conventional
Personal appearance and grooming	(+1) Unconventional	(−1) Conventional
Knowledge of street jargon	(+1) Yes	(−1) No
Means of funding drug habit	(+2) Stealing Prostitution Dealing Drugs Welfare	(−2) Legitimate employment Welfare
Ability to purchase drugs from "street" drug dealers if drugs are not available thru usual channels	(+2) Yes	(−2) No
Living in a geographic area known as a youth drug subculture	(+1) Yes	(−1) No

*The distinction between streetwise and nonstreetwise is made by summing the values of parameters one through seven. A positive score indicates the individual is streetwise, a negative score indicates the individual is not streetwise. A zero score indicates an uncertain state which we indicate as "unable to classify." In using this schemata, if an individual falls into a category which appears on both the streetwise and nonstreetwise cells (such as welfare for parameter one) a zero is assigned for the value of that parameter. Wesson & Smith, 1975.

plan. One of the categories was the street polydrug abuser versus the nonstreetwise polydrug abuser (Table 12.1). This category came out of the situation in which we would see an adolescent or young woman from a higher socioeconomic background being viewed as someone who is in the mainstream of society and not involved in the drug culture versus an inner city black female welfare mother on Medi-Cal sitting right in the middle of the inner city drug culture, being perceived as streetwise. Actually, when we did a detailed evaluation, it would be just the opposite; the black welfare mother with children would in no way identify with the drug culture. It seems very repulsive and repelling to her and she would go to the doctor and obtain her psychoactive drugs, usually stimulants and depressants, via her Medi-Cal prescription. Whereas, the adolescent female from the suburbs would come into the inner city and acquire the drugs from the drug culture and abuse in that fashion. This is one categorization that helps move towards a specific evaluation and analysis because the woman that is involved in the drug culture has to be treated in a different fashion than a woman who is not involved with the drug culture.

For example, most of the women in the drug culture do not obtain their drugs from physicians; they obtain them on the street. The drugs they abuse are different and they prefer treatment in drug culture oriented facilities. The woman that is not involved with the drug culture (nonstreetwise polydrug abuser) obtains her drugs primarily from a physician and prefers treatment in a more traditional non-drug-culture facility.

We have also found that a large number of women who abuse multiple drugs have an underlying depression. It is important that they receive a psychological evaluation to determine if they are self-medicators. With this condition, the woman self-administers a psychoactive drug in an attemp to deal with this underlying psychopathology. Often when they are detoxified, the depression becomes worse rather than better and other types of medication such as a tricyclic antidepressant are needed in association with psychosocial counseling. Women that require such mixed modality therapy including the use of medication in conjunction with counseling, should not be referred to self-help, drug-free programs. In contrast, those women in which the depression is induced by the drug and there is no evidence of major underlying psychopathology do quite well in such drug-free, self-help programs whether they be outpatient treatment efforts such as Alcoholics Anonymous, Narcotics Anonymous, or inpatient residential therapeutic communities.

One of the most consistent aspects of the substance-abusing woman, in general, is poor self-image and low self-esteem. This is one of the most consistent findings and one of the biggest problems that has to be dealt with in treatment. If "I'm not worth anything, why not fill my body full of drugs? And, if you want me to stop, you'd better provide something for me that does a better job than the drug." In this context, we have found that the use of appropriate female role models can be particularly effective, especially when dealing with intimate emotional issues and skill development in the sociosexual area while the woman is attempting to lead a drug-free life (Smith & Buxton, 1979). Such female role models can range from a sensitive counselor to a recovered female addict or alcoholic, within the framework of a health care team approach to substance abuse to demonstrate and encourage the idea that recovery is possible (Smith & Buxton, 1979). Very often women that have substance-abuse problems have serious doubts as to whether they will ever be able to recover from their addictive disease and have particular need to share experience that can help them chart a drug-free existence. Early in the treatment process, however, there may be some conflict and controversy around this issue.

For example, some women we have found are resistant to seeing a female counselor, in part, because while they were actively using (particularly in the drug culture) they were in competition with other women. In initial contact, rather than propagating an ideological position that a female substance abuser should always see a female counselor, we should reemphasize the importance of respecting the woman's position and allowing her to see a male counselor initially, then evolving into an appropriate treatment plan utilizing a female counselor at a later time. In addition, many of these issues of antagonism towards other women which coincide with poor self-image and low self-esteem may also be dealt with in a group process including a consciousness raising women's group. Also, sociosexual counseling may be indicated in those women who have a primary sexual dysfunction such as dyspareunia or anorgasmia and are using psychoactive drugs to self-medicate this condition who are dealing with the concern and anxiety that arises out of such sexual dysfunction. Within the diverse population of substance-abusing women, we also see within the framework of the drug culture, individuals who have divorced their sociosexual interaction from their feelings in order to maintain their drug habits. Female prostitutes, for example, use sexual activity for nonsexual purposes in order to obtain money to support their heroin habit. Following detoxification, we have found that many women with this background describe a difficulty in establishing a feeling relationship that is satisfying to them. In addition, many women when they achieve their drug-free state have a substantial amount of guilt and concern relative to their relationships to current children or their concern about ability to bear children in the future. In this context, it is important to give factual information relative to the effects of drugs on pregnancy and deal with the concerns relative to reproduction, childbearing, and childrearing in an informative, nonjudgmental, and supportive context. In summary, we emphasize that the substance-abusing woman needs to be approached as a human being and representative of a diverse and heterogeneous population. The treatment plan has to be appropriate to her specific concerns and needs and be flexible enough to change as the woman's needs vary.

REFERENCES

Smith, D. E., Buxton, M. E., & Dammann, G. Amphetamine abuse and sexual dysfunction: Clinical and research considerations. In *Amphetamine use, misuse and abuse.* Boston: G. K. Hall, 1979.

Smith, D. E., & Buxton, M. E. An integrated medical and non-medical approach to the treatment of the substance abuser: A healthcare team approach utilizing professionals, paraprofessionals and self-help groups. In Kane, A. (Ed.) 1979.

Wesson, D. R., & Smith, D. E. Streetwise vs. nonstreetwise. *Journal of Psychedelic Drugs.* 1975.

Chapter 13

PLENARY SESSION: INTERVENTION/SERVICE DELIVERY SYSTEMS

Severa Austin

It's much more intimidating to look out from this perspective than to sit in the back row this morning. I am very pleased and very appreciative of being asked to be here. When I got a call a couple of months ago, or a month ago, I agreed happily to participate and hung up the phone and thought, "What does someone from Wisconsin have to say to someone in New York?" I suffer the, I guess not unusual inferiority complex of the midwesterner trying to talk to the easterner. So I sat this morning and listened to Governor Carey and I heard that there were people here from 46 states and that made me feel somewhat better. I heard Gov. Carey talk about all of the commissions relating to women, about all the task forces and programs related to women, and I realized that we have every one of those commissions and task forces in Wisconsin. I suspect that we have also in common the fact that we have done a great deal of problem identification but probably not a great deal of implementation of answers to those questions, so I'm only a little bit impressed with the fact that there are a number of task forces and commissions that I suspect you haven't implemented the solutions to those problems any better than we have in Wisconsin.

I got on a plane yesterday with a friend to come here who had been invited to go to the White House to have lunch with the Presi-

dent on the 25th anniversary of *Brown* v. *Board of Education* and
we talked unhappily about how little and how far we have not come
since the implementation of that decision 25 years ago. I would hope
that 25 years from now we're not all in a meeting discussing women
in crisis and have to look back and see and come no further than the
implementation of that same decision. I also think that the Supreme
Court must have heard that you had called this conference in New
York because the day before yesterday they of course come down
with three decisions that have a massive amount of impact on
women. As they say, there's some good news and some bad news.
The good news is that under Title IX, the education act, women or
an individual can now sue a state university or a university if there
is discrimination in their education program. The bad news appears
to be the antiabortion decision in Massachusetts where women cannot . . . receive state funds for abortions and another that raises my
concern which relates to strip searches in jails and that the Supreme
Court found in their wisdom that pre-trial prisoners have no more
rights than convicted felons and therefore strip searches are appropriate. Any of you who have worked in criminal justice know about
those strip searches and what can and does happen in our jails in this
country, particularly to women. Well, the Supreme Court has found
that that's okay. So, I don't know what that means or where, where
we are.

When I started writing and doing some reading for this speech
I try to give a title to things, I try and get people's attention because
I'll find that they'll read something if you have a title or something
that doesn't sound boring and what I originally thought to use was
a title called *In Your Own Best Interest* or *For Your Own Good.* In
my experience in about 10 years of working with women's services,
we seem always to give the service to a woman based on her needs
and in her best interest for her own good. Usually, however, that in
your own interest, for your own good, is something that we determine and something that she does not. So I guess that's what I'm
talking about, because I don't see that that generally in the history
of my experience and in my historical reading of women's services
issues, we have had a great deal of change. We are still talking about
"for her own good." As was stated earlier, my own career in this field
and in this so-called helping professions has been integrally tied to
women's service issue. My early direct experience has been primarily
and was primarily in institutions, whether it was a result of accident
or overt sexism, I always found myself assigned, in whatever institu-

tion I worked in, to work with women. I was not allowed in those days to work with men. I have been in children's institutions, mental hospitals, juvenile detention centers, and a city jail. In all those situations, I worked with and enjoyed working with women. I have moved from that to a policy making position on the state level and those early direct service experiences for a number of reasons were very important to me. I attempt to maintain my interest in a concern for women's service issues in the current policy-making position that I have. Some points are extremely difficult.

I think a story of my early experience is illustrative of the kinds of things I want to say briefly today, and that relates to how I think we make policy related to women. I call it anecdotal policy making. In a small jail in Wisconsin, a woman was incarcerated in a pretrial situation. She knocked on the cell of her jail cell and asked the sheriff to please come down, she wanted to talk to him. And the sheriff came down and asked what she wanted, and she had had her period, she wanted to have some Tampax. And the sheriff scratched his head, and said, "Well, I don't know, I don't think we have any of those things, but I'll go talk to my wife, who is the matron." And he went down the hall to talk to his wife the matron and ask whether they had something called Tampax, it was not many years ago, and the matron, his wife, said, "no, we use Kotex or Modess and that's good enough for me, so it's good enough for her." The sheriff went back to the woman and informed her that that was the policy of the jail; it was a policy that his wife had decided upon and therefore that was what she would get.

I call that anecdotal policy making and I think it's made all the time, as to what somebody's wife or daughter or sister-in-law happens to believe about what should happen to women frequently happens when men are in policy making positions. I'm removed from the social delivery system in a direct line, but I find that what I decide and what the decision makers of my level and the policy makers and legislators decided have a massive impact on women as clients and that the social delivery system is impacted upon by those kinds of decisions. What I'd like to do is try and relate the experience of all of you who are perhaps in that direct service line as well as policy making and how the one impacts on the other.

There's three primary service delivery processes that you all know about. Generally I define them as the mental health system, which includes the drug and alcohol services, the social service system, which includes economic assistance, and the criminal justice system. In both social service and mental health, it appears, and research now tells us that women comprise the majority of clients in these service systems. Thanks to a number of pieces of research done recently, we don't have to say any more that we don't know who's out there, or that we don't know what's happening to women because we do know. We know that over half the residents of psychiatric hospitals are women, we know that they also comprise over half of the outpatient psychotherapy clients now in this country. Women attempt suicide more often than men. They fail more often, but they attempt it more often. The presenting problems for one out of three women relate to mental health issues. For men it's one out of seven that bring a mental health issue to their doctor.

In the area of juveniles, we know that the rate of adolescent pregnancy is increasing in massive proportions. One researcher has estimated that four out of ten young women in this country will have been pregnant in their teenage years. One out of eight will have had an abortion and one out of four of those will have had a child. Juvenile girls are detained longer in our juvenile justice system than are their brothers. Some female crime is increasing, and incarceration rates, unfortunately, are higher now with our wonderful new prisons for women than they have been in the past and certainly were ten years ago.

We know rates of rape, sexual assault, sexual abuse, and child abuse are much higher than ever previously acknowledged. With the new interest in aging, we now have new terms in our human and social service system called the older and isolated woman; I find it interesting in some of the affirmative action guidelines now that, having come into my 40th year I now reach the cutoff line and am now elderly. I don't know if that's good or bad.

Our nursing home beds are filled with primarily women. What does all of that mean? How has the service delivery system changed if it has acknowledged all of those things? I think the value of a conference like this is to bring all of those facts together in one place, because the system does not acknowledge that these data are there. In terms of our mental health and social service system, I don't see that much has changed in the way we stereotype the role-related expectations, which remain much the same for the past centuries. I don't have time.

I have a wonderful historical list of descriptive phrases for women in the human services system. I'd only like to give you a couple of them that come, unfortunately, from this century. One of my favorites is, by a writer and researcher in the early twentieth century called Thomas, and he was talking about human service issues for women. He thought he was trying to defend women, and as many writers do in defending them, they identify us as basically an inadequately, innately inferior. But he said that modern woman plagued by "irregularity, pettiness, ill health," and my favorite term, "inserviceableness." I guess that means that services that were delivered were not and they didn't take. I don't know what it means, but I like it.

As recently as 1968, a group of sociologic researchers explained women's human service problem or our deviant behavior in terms of a chromosomal difference. They gave a small consideration to the fact that our socialization was different, but that really what it came down to was that our chromosomes were different and therefore women had problems in getting service that "took." We still have, unfortunately. I come from the state where Senator Proxmire continues to give awards for the most preposterous money research awards going out. We still have a great deal of research and I'm waiting for him to give one that finds the relationship between women's menstrual cycles and any problem you can name. So I don't feel out of hope there.

My favorite comes from the 1920s and I guess if I was to be described as having a problem in human services, I'd rather have this because I think the words are kind of interesting. Lombroso, good old Lombroso had explanations for everything based on some physiologic aspect, said that the problems of passivity and dependence in women related to "the immobility of the ovule compared to the zoo-sperm." I would rather have that as an explanation for my behavior than "inserviceability."

So where are we today? We still have prostitution as a crime in this country. Women are still the only ones prostituted. Wisconsin, which has the progressive tradition, had a case in the Supreme Court based on discrimination against women, which said that prostitution was, by definition, a female crime, that there was no such thing as a male prostitute, and therefore our laws that say women in the law was not unconstitutional. I've only been here one day, and I walked around a little bit last night, but I can tell you that I strongly do believe that there are male prostitutes. I've known that for years. We still have our young women in this country detained, as I said, for a longer period of time than their brothers for behavior called incorrigible or in need of supervision. The real reason for this attention, of course, is protection for her own good. We continue to identify delinquent behavior in young women as that which violates sexual norms, not that which violates legal norms. And sexual behavior continues to be a primary reason for our intervention.

I don't know about some of the states represented here, but I have done some research. In presentence reports, we still discuss a woman's sexual history so that the judge will be able to make a decision about what should happen to her in cases that have absolutely nothing to do with her sexual behavior. We do not discuss male sexual behavior in his presentence report, something that needs to be looked at in the system.

A favorite study that I found in mental health comes from only three or four years ago. They were trying to find out in the psychiatric and psychiatric social work professions what clinicians thought about the differences between men and women these days. Was it really as sexist as it appeared? And they asked these clinicians to define the healthy male, the healthy female, and the healthy adult. What were the characteristics of all of those groups? Well, guess what. The concept of a healthy male correlated perfectly with that of a healthy adult. Did I say that right? Healthy male equals healthy adult. The characteristics of a healthy female included the characteristics of passivity, dependence, and submissiveness, but those same clinicians rated all those three characteristics as socially undesirable in the general population. While it appears, at least in the literature that psychiatrically related programs appear to agree that Freudian concepts of women are erroneous in many of their implementation aspects, it appears that we continue in many cases to attribute the low self-esteem, the passive-anxious female client as inherently endowed with these characteristics rather than them being a result of our social conditioning.

I was told I had 15 minutes to give a 30-minute speech, so I'm going to try to cut some things out. In criminal justice, which is my background primarily, I used to say we were moving rapidly into the 14th century; I'm now convinced we're moving into the 13th. I see that we've lost some ground. It is interesting to note, and it concerns me that reform for women's institutions historically has come about largely as a result of women's efforts. If you read correctional history, by in the 19th century, we started to take women out of men's institutions and build women's prisons. That was a result of women's effort and what they called reform. Or, as one writer stated, a return to true womanhood. From my reading these days, I don't see a great deal of difference between what they refer to as true womanhood and what now we refer to as fascinating womanhood. The characteristics appear much the same. The movement perpetuates stereotypical views of the fallen, immoral woman, needing only to return to the accepted virtues. Female administrators of those institutions, and I think the same is frequently true today, continue maternal, "I know what's best for you," service delivery, and some industry sells a great deal of lace and chintz to make it look pleasant. That hasn't really changed in my experience with some very nice and notable but rare exceptions. We still act as though there is a husband at the gate when a woman walks out the door, instead of concentrating on the economic realities of her life. I take all of this and I put it into my direct experience and my current job which is policy making in attempting to try and translate that experience and my historical perspective on what it is that I do now and what policymakers do.

I'd like to just list three policy concerns that I have: We have to do our homework, number one, and we have to present the homework that we all have done to those who need to listen. It is very clear when you look at the data (if we take the data from the entire system instead of a categorical approach) that women and women's crises and problems can make a major fiscal argument to policy makers in this country. The majority of the recipients of many of our services are women or their children. I believe that the rate of adolescent pregnancy that I cited before, if it's accurate, and I suspect that it is, is one of the most terrifying things that's happening today to young women. And I think we can make a case for the ultimate cost of that data if we present it in the right way.

I think we have to look at our categorical and disability programs. Where is the money going in your state or at your local level? Where are the Title XX funds going? What kinds of services are they providing? How many women are recipients of those services and how are they defined? Every state gets Title XX funds; they are the majority of the social service funds. Where are your Title XIX health funds going? And who is defining those services? What does it have to do with women? I also am concerned, and I think perhaps we're at the point where someone's offer to give us demonstration money to deal with women's services is a buy-off that we should consider rejecting. I think the issues have been identified. I think the problems have been identified. Demonstration funds are a nice buy-off to someone that you want to get rid of. If you don't want to identify the issues and you don't want to say that they've identified the problems sufficiently. You offer them a few thousand dollars or a few hundred thousand dollars, and they go away saying, "well at least someone listened to me for a while." I think it's dangerous to continue to say that we don't know enough about women's issues so that we'll continue to demonstrate that women have problems. I think that we know that, and that it is serious policy issue that should be considered.

I'm close to ending and I have a lot more to say. I just want to say that I think what comes across to women clients and to male policy makers in the women's movement gets us in difficulty. I think that talking about the unity of all women is fine, but I think that it's very difficult for many women to see that they are experiencing economic and social deprivation. I think that we have to be careful with the experiences that some of us have had in translating that into service needs or in policy making.

A favorite quote, which I will end with, is from a notable law professor, Charles Wright, who, in talking about general service systems, was not relating to women, but it's very pertinent to me, said, "Society cannot long be content in assisting. Soon enough it also wants to improve." I think that women's history in human services is the opposite. I think we started trying to improve women. What I think we have to do is move to assistance and not to improvement. Thank you.

Chapter 14

PLENARY SESSION: INTERVENTION/SERVICE DELIVERY SYSTEMS

Joyce Lazar

Due to the pressure of time, I'm going to read just one sentence from each page of the speech I've prepared. This should make about as much sense to you as the service delivery system in this country today. On the other hand, I think we should look for a minute at where we have been. Look at the conference agenda: ten years ago, there was no such thing as the theory of learned helplessness. Wife battering and rape were taboo topics. Alcoholism and drug abuse were well-kept secrets as they related to women. We have these topics out in the open now for discussion, and we also have developed a large number of woman's mutual-help groups around these areas. We had never even thought about these services 10 years ago. I'd like very very briefly to somewhat describe the magnitude of a portion of the mental health problem in this country for women, and then go on to talk about new directtions in service delivery.

At every age over 15, more women than men receive treatment in the mental health system. Schizophrenia affects approximately two million people at any given time in the United States. There is no difference in rates of schizophrenia between men and women. The situation is, however, very different when we look at rates of depression: 175 women to every 100 men are treated . . . admitted and treated to hospitals for depression each year; 238 women to every 100 men are treated in outpatient services. When we look then at the rates of depression they vary with age and with marital status. Community surveys indicate that rates are higher for women than men at every age up to age 55. After 55, they are similar. The highest rates for treatment in public facilities are among nonwhite women, among women between the ages of 25 and 44 who are separated or divorced, and among women of all ages whose children are living with them. The lowest rates of depression are among women who never married and among older women whose children have left home. The data should tell us something and I hear that they do.

For one thing, the data show that involutional melancholia, or, as it is commonly known, menopausal depression, and the empty nest syndrome are myths. The data also belie the popular belief that women who do not marry and have children are likely to find the condition depressing. Psychological depression is not the only emotional disturbance that affect more women than men. Just for one, agoraphobia, . . . or fear of public places, affects one million women in the United States, but only a fourth as many men. Anorexia nervosa is almost entirely a women's disease. And then there are all kinds of other life conditions that bear more heavily on women than on men. We then have to ask, why are more women depressed than men? The data tell us about the magnitude of the problem, but they don't really tell us why more women experience more depression. And there are a variety of explanatory theories that contribute to our understanding of the etiology of depression. It is important to talk about etiology because how one defines the problem affects what one does about the problem. And let us look at this—and I'm going to pass very quickly over some of the theories of depression—the first is, that there is no difference, that the rates really are the same, it's just that women go to doctors more often and more readily report their symptoms. A second theory is the traditional psychoanalytic model. Then there is the loss model which holds that women are affected more deeply by the loss of a loved one. There is also biologic, genetic, and endocrine explanations. And I realize that these kinds of explanations are not popular in the women's movement today, but I think that we should not discard biology. I think that we do need to look at some of the kinds of research that bear upon differential rates of depression. We know without a doubt that there's a genetic factor operating in depression . . . but that factor is the same for men and for women. We know that there is some limited evidence that estrogen therapy relieves some forms of depression. We should not throw out that piece of information; it is important. There are many psychosocial theories: sociologists, psychologists, and feminists in particular have offered a great number of explanations. The disadvantaged social status of women, all the legal and economic discriminations that we heard talked about this morning, are just plain depressing for women. One women in four, in contrast to one man in eighteen, lives on an income of less than $4000 a year. That's pretty depressing, given what lunch cost me today. Another psychosocial explanation is that women experience larger number of stressful life experiences than men. And certainly in recent years that stress has been compounded by the dual roles that many women fill in the home and in the labor market. Yet another explanation, one that is controversial is the learned helplessness model that was discussed in another session here at this conference.

The most convincing evidence that social role plays a part in the vulnerability of women for depression is that marriage has a protective effect for men and a detrimental effect for women. Current thinking in depression is that multiple factors interact to produce depression, and it may be that we need multiple kinds of intervention. What do we see when we look at the treatment system, and what do women encounter in the treatment system? The first thing is that when Myrna Wiseman studied depression in the community, she found that 43 percent of women received no treatment for this depression. That means nine million women lie in their beds and cry and receive no treatment from anyone. Of those who go for treatment, 54 percent go to their private practitioner. And the likelihood is very great that they receive some medication and a pat on the back and are sent home. Only 15 percent of those men and women, as a matter of fact, enter in the psychiatric treatment system. So when we are talking about changing the service delivery system for women, we should not only be talking about changing the mental health system, it should be the entire medical system because that is where the bulk of patients go.

When the 15 percent of women get into the psychiatric treatment system, what do they find? Two-thirds of the patients are women, but 90 percent of the psychiatrists and 60 percent of the psychologists are men. We know therapists, regardless of gender or field of training, prefer women as patients. The women who are most apt to be accepted for therapy are better educated, white, middle class, and only mildly disturbed. They are also more likely to be covered by insurance. There are a variety of women's self-help groups that have grown up in recent years; to the best of my knowledge, there have only been descriptive studies of these treatments and interventions. There have been no evaluations of them. One reason for that is that the evaluations of treatment and of therapy is an extraordinarily difficult research issue. It's difficult to do research on this because questions of outcome are not just a question of fact. They inevitably are a matter of value. If one wants to know whether therapy has been helpful, who does one ask? The patient? The physician? The therapist? They have invested so much time and money in the activity, they are most apt to say, yes, of course, it's been effective. Do you ask the spouse of the patient? The patient's spouse may feel that the therapy was a disaster because the patient has been more independent, more assertive, and more demanding. Furthermore, our evaluation instruments are problematic. At least one scale designed to measure change in psychotherapy considers a man improved when he can return to work, and a woman improved when she willingly returns to housework. By this criteria, a number of us are in very bad shape.

Some research evaluating treatment outcomes show that about two-thirds of nonpsychotic patients show significant improvements after treatment, regardless of the type of psychotherapy. One recent study has reported that running seems to be as about as effective a treatment for depression as any form of psychotherapy. If two-thirds of those treated have shown some change, however, what about the one-third who have not been impacted by the treatment? We need to know more about those people.

Let us now look just a moment at the current service system. Services, as I mentioned before, are primarily available through physicians. Next of course are private practitioners, at $50 for a 50-minute hour. Then there are the sliding scale services at the more than 700 community mental health centers in this country. For inpatients there are the state hospital systems as well as the alternative services developed for women. I mentioned before that it was important to evaluate these services. It is especially important that we have some evidence that these services are effective at least for some women, especially if we have any hope that they are to be covered by national health insurance when such legislation eventually passes. We must lay the groundwork for the funding of such services.

I really want to leave you today with some very specific kinds of actions to take; I could go on recounting the ills that have befallen women and there are many, but let me see if I can raise some issues on which some action is appropriate now.

First of all, the key service program of the National Institute of Mental Health for the last 20 years has been the Community Mental Health Centers. They operate in some 726 communities. Legislation to change this program was introduced on Tuesday, the day before yesterday, by President and Mrs. Carter to Congress. It is entitled *The Mental Health Systems Act.* It is important that this act be reviewed for its impact on women before it passes Congress. It is important that those of you who are actively working in the health and mental health delivery systems for women review this act. Get a copy of it from your Congressional representative; you have the opportunity now, before the act is passed to have input into it and to testify before . . . hearings on the act. This is an opportunity that will not come again for a number of years. We should change the act if necessary before it passes rather than criticize it after it passes. The act provides, among other things, for a greater integration of mental health services with general health services offered through health maintenance organizations and other comprehensive health services. It also provides for the development of something called "Initiation Grants." Put that in quotes and write it down. This portion of the act will provide for the development of single services in contrast to the comprehensive services now required under the Community Mental Health Systems Act. That is, individual communities can come in and request only one kind of specialized service. It is entirely possible that some of the special services developed by women and for women could be funded under this revised legislation, if and when it passes. Under these "Initiation Grants" special counseling for women in crisis, shelters for battered women, or other specialized services could be funded. Inquiry about the details of this program should be made from the Director of Special Mental Health Services.

If we hope to change the types of services that are delivered in this country, we must impact on the training of those people who provide the services, and it's primarily the psychiatrists, psychologists, social workers, psychiatric nurses, and community aides in programs. Most of those people are trained under grants from the National Institute of Mental Health. As yet, these grants in the program have never been reviewed for sexism in the curricula. It would be possible, if someone were to submit a research and evaluation proposal to look at these training programs to see what the curricula are like. It would also be appropriate to submit proposals to provide training for the trainers in these programs on the psychology of women. Such a proposal has never been received from the National Institute of Mental Health.

One of the major new initiatives that has come out of the President's Commission on Mental Health, at the instigation of Mrs. Carter is a prevention program. It's likely that there will be between five and six million new dollars for this program next year. Among the initiatives that are in that program is depression in women. It would be appropriate to design a proposal to attempt some innovative ways to reduce the incidence of depression among the high-risk groups that I described in the very beginning of this talk, the women between the ages of 25 and 44 who have children in the home.

I think, in closing, I'd like to say that we've spent 10 years defining the problem and dispelling myths about women's mental health and mental illness; it's time now for us to reshape the mental health delivery system, and one of the opportunities that we have is in the new Mental Health Systems Act, and I seriously hope that you will contact your Congressional representative and make input into that act. Thank you.

Chapter 15

INNOVATIVE ALCOHOLISM PROGRAMS FOR WOMEN

Norma Finkelstein

The Women's Alcoholism Program of CASPAR was started with a treatment grant from the National Institute on Alcohol Abuse and Alcoholism in 1975. When I wrote this grant, I had been working with alcoholics for four years as a social worker at the Cambridge and Somerville Alcoholism Program. I was appalled and outraged at the lack of attention given to the problems of alcoholic women. They were either treated as "intruders" or as nonexistent. The occasional woman who "wandered in" for alcoholism treatment baffled programs and threw treatment staff into chaos. The realities of women's lives, and their differences from mens' lives, issues such as children, economic dependency, sexuality, were ignored and never dealt with.

At that time (1974), there were three halfway houses for alcoholic men in Cambridge and none for women. When asked why no houses for women were being planned, the answer was always that there would not be enough alcoholic women to fill one. Today, our halfway house, Womanplace, is consistently full and has an average waiting list of 50 women.

Our initial grant from the Institute was primarily to finance a halfway house and outreach services. Since then we have grown quite a bit. National Institute on Alcohol Abuse and Alcoholism money is now less than 50 percent of our operating budget. We provide specialized, separate services within the framework of a parent organization, CASPAR, Inc. CASPAR stands for the Cambridge and Somerville Program for Alcoholism Rehabilitation and includes two detoxification centers, an emergency walk-in service, a dry drop-in center, three male halfway houses, an outpatient service and an alcohol education component. There have been advantages and disadvantages to this structure. Our overall goal has always been two pronged: 1) to bring more and different kinds of women into treatment; 2) to provide women and their families with a full range of services along the recovery continuum, from emergency counseling through detoxification, residential care, and out-patient services.

The Women's Alcoholism Program believes that a woman's problems must be dealt with in the context of a woman's total experience in society. To treat the "whole woman," we must deal with every aspect of her reality, including needs for child care, medical care, education, jobs, parenting skills, assertiveness training, and sexuality counseling. Women are also not a homogenous group. The needs of a woman during treatment and recovery may be different depending on her ethnic and racial background, age, social class, and sexual preference. We try to recognize these differences in treatment and provide all women with a range of treatment options.

The women who come to us often have very low self-esteem, no job skills, and poor interpersonal relationships. We attempt to assist them in recovering from alcoholism and in restructuring their lives so they will not need to return to self-destructive drinking patterns. This assistance comes in many forms: counseling, advocacy work, legal assistance, arranging for educational and job training programs, and so on. Most of all, we want women to begin to like themselves and other women, to develop confidence in themselves, and to build supportive caring relationships with others. Our experience has shown us that in order to do this women need some separate space from men, particularly in the early stages of their recovery. It is only in all-women's discussion groups that alcoholic women begin talking about issues that they had not dared to speak about in co-ed treatment groups, issues that are central to themselves and their alcohol abuse. Our unique position as a Women's Program within a large co-educational alcoholism treatment organization has enabled us to offer women a variety of treatment choices. For example, all women have access to co-educational treatment groups. Very few women, approximately 25 percent, choose to attend co-educational groups exclusively. On the other hand, over 50 percent of the women we see do chose to only attend women's groups.

I would now like to briefly describe the major components of the Women's Alcoholism Program. I will be glad to go into more detail regarding any of these during the question period.

WOMEN'S ALCOHOLISM PROGRAM COMPONENTS

Outreach/Consultation

The Women's Program felt from the beginning that we could not sit back and wait for the alcoholic woman to walk in the door and that we must go out and find her and bring her into treatment —the earlier the better. Besides extensive public relations efforts, the Women's Program has two full-time outreach workers who are essentially involved in a two-pronged approach.

The first approach involves alcohol education and alcoholism training and consultation to a variety of human service providers and health care organizations. Because the alcoholic woman is more likely to pursue treatment from a psychiatrist, medical doctor, or social agency, we view this work as intervention at the first point that a woman seeks treatment so that chances for early and accurate diagnosis and referral are greatly improved. Our Alcohol and Alcoholism Education Program is structured to explore attitudes, increase factual knowledge, teach diagnostic tools, acquaint individuals with resources, and examine the particular needs of the female alcoholic.

It has been our experience that unless given repeated exposure most providers lose confidence in their ability to work with the alcoholic woman. For this reason, we work to maintain ongoing consultation relationships with the agencies we have trained. This is usually done either on a on-call case consultation basis or by regular group consultation meetings with treatment providers. For example, we are beginning a monthly consultation group for 15 to 20 feminist therapists from our area. During this time, they will be able to discuss cases they have questions about and problems with as well as receive further training and assistance in appropriate diagnosis, treatment, and referral resources.

The growing numbers of women using our treatment services is a primary example of the success of our outreach. Within a year, we were able to triple the number of women using CASPAR's outpatient services. The Women's Program currently sees between 350 and 400 women per year and many of them are referred directly from the staffs of the agencies we have trained. In addition, more women coming to our services are in the early stages of alcoholism, or perhaps just beginning to question their drinking. We feel this is a direct result of our outreach efforts. As the number of women increase and we continue to reach women in early alcoholism or alcohol abuse, the general characteristics of women using our services have broadened. We are seeing women from ages 16 to 75 and from many different communities.

Our second approach involves training on women's treatment issues for alcoholism providers. As we began bringing more women into treatment, we felt the need to do consciousness raising around attitudes towards women within the CASPAR staff. We began by conducting a six-week training series on the alcoholic woman. Since then we have conducted this series several times with CASPAR staff as well as with other state and local alcoholism agencies. We have recently developed this material into a course entitled "A Course on Women Problem Drinkers, Anonymous Alcoholics."

We continue to conduct special workshops for CASPAR staff on issues particular to women. All new staff at CASPAR participate in workshops conducted by the Women's Program to sensitize them to the special needs of alcoholic women.

Inpatient Services

All women in both of CASPAR's detoxification centers are seen by a counselor from the Women's Program and our family social worker also works with their families and friends. The Women's Program provides training and consultation to the staff of both of these units.

Outpatient Services

We provide women with both individual and group counseling on an outpatient basis. At the present time, there are five different women's groups conducted, which consist of two day-time and one evening alcoholism discussion groups, a group for lesbians, and a mother's group. Child care is provided for some of these groups depending on their location. As mentioned before, women may also attend the co-educational groups run by the outpatient department. We also see women on an emergency walk-in basis at CASPAR's walk-in service at Cambridge City Hospital and have helped to stimulate other community resources for women such as "Women For Sobriety," a feminist AA group called "The Sisterhood Group," an alcoholism discussion group at a local women's center, and a group called "Amethyst Women," which sponsors drug free social events for alcoholic lesbians and their friends.

Services for Families and Significant Others

Our counseling component for families and significant others is based on our belief that a woman cannot be treated for her alcoholism in a vacuum, that alcoholism affects not only the individual with the illness but those people close to her as well, and that these people, in turn, have an effect on the alcoholic woman's recovery.

All significant others of women in our program are seen by our family social worker or student interns under her supervision. This includes families of women in detox, at our halfway house, and our day treatment center.

We also run four outpatient groups for significant others:

1. A weekly open discussion group for families and friends.
2. A group for children (ages 6 to 10) of alcoholic women. By next year we hope to add a second children's group.
3. A parallel group for the mothers of these children conducted at the same time.
4. A group for lesbians whose lives have been affected by another's alcoholism.

Residential Treatment Program

Womanplace, a recovery home for 15 women, has been in operation for two years. Womanplace provides its residents with a structured rehabilitation program including group and individual counseling, alcoholism education, exercise and dance classes, AA meetings, assertiveness training, discussions on women's issues and issues for mothers, health issues, and a vocational educational guidance goup. Women at Womanplace also may attend both women's outpatient groups as well as co-educational ones. Residents share chores and cooking and have daily house meetings to iron out grievances, problems, etc.

Women stay at Womanplace on the average of four to five months, but many stay up to one year. The staff is constantly involved in issues relating to child custody and vocational training. We have no residential component for children but we have had children visit their mothers for weekends at the house or stay several weeks at a time.

Besides children, issues of economic independence and fear of "making it" in the outside world, particularly going to work, are primary. We have found that while concretely working on building up a woman's skills, we must also provide her with a place to explore her fears regarding work and receive support from others to begin to take steps towards economic independence.

Day Treatment Program for Women and Children

This is our newest program and recently opened with six women and three preschool children. The program is located in a three-story single family house in Cambridge and will eventually serve 10 to 15 alcoholic women and 10 preschool children at one time. The Day Treatment Program, like Womanplace, is highly structured and limited to four months (by the funding agency, the Massachusetts Division of Alcoholism). The program is very much like the one at Womanplace with an added emphasis on parenting skills and parent-child interactions. The children's component includes alcohol and alcoholism education, diagnosis and evaluation regarding special needs, and a variety of preschool learning and play activities supervised by a trained child care teacher. After school groups are being arranged for the older children, so all children will be involved in the overall rehabilitation process.

We are hoping by this program to reach women still in earlier stages of alcoholism before they have lost their children and offer these women support and skill building to both recover from alcoholism and have healthy parenting relationships with their children. We also see the provision of comprehensive children's services as the first line in the prevention of alcoholism in these children.

In summary, we believe we have been successful in breaking down the stigma regarding alcoholic women in our community, drawing many different kinds of women into treatment and creating a comprehensive treatment program for alcoholic women and their significant others. Our experience verifies for us that alcoholic women do indeed exist in great numbers and that they will respond and seek treatment when alcoholism programs are designed that are relevant to them and their families. Thank you.

Chapter 16

MOTIVATION AND THE ALCOHOLIC WOMAN

Sheila B. Blume

MOTIVATION

There is perhaps no subject as important to the treatment of alcoholism as that of motivation. It is not only the first step, but also the continuing force in the alcoholic person's search for health. Yet, it is important that we understand from the beginning that there is not a single "motivation," but a variety of motivating factors, all of which have important roles to play. The classification I find most convenient in thinking about this subject is "initial" and "ideal" motivation.

Initial motivation refers to anything that will induce the alcoholic person to begin treatment, often originating as an "either/or" situation, precipitated from outside. Such motivations include concern over health, job, family, or fears of the future, or even spite. Ideal motivation is an internal state toward which the patient and therapist work in treatment.

Let me present a description of these motivations from an autobiography by a lovely lady; *"I'm Black and I'm Sober,"* by Chaney Allen. On page 219, Ms. Allen says:

I want to share a very important mistake that I made. When I first called for help, I was sick and I needed and wanted help, but I did not enter the Program to get sober for myself. I wanted to get Grant back. And when he said I was not going to stop drinking, I stayed sober to show him that I could. The result was, when we separated and I no longer had to show him, I got drunk. That was not a good enough reason to attempt sobriety.

So I learned, as I listened, that I must stay sober for myself only, not husband, wife, children, parents or boss. No one but Chaney. Stay sober for the first person who is hurt by the first drink. . . .

Thus, she describes her initial motivation, which in her case did not develop appropriately, and her later experience of ideal motivation.

INITIAL MOTIVATION

In America today, we have three successful organized intervention models to establish initial motivation for treatment in alcoholism: drinking driver programs, occupational alcoholism programs, and public intoxicant programs. One outstanding factor that these three programs have in common is that they have been successful mostly in reaching males. Studies on alcoholic patients in treatment have shown that while men most often enter treatment because of problems on the job or with the law, women most often cite health and family problems as precipitating factors. Thus, if we want to reach alcoholic women, we must do a better job at sensitizing our physicians and other health professionals, and our lawyers and social agencies to identify and refer these patients. In addition, we must improve our exisiting intervention models to reach more women, for example, by establishing more occupational programs in industries where many females work.

The main obstacles to the initial motivation of the alcoholic woman are denial, fear and shame. Denial is an unconscious defense mechanism, best overcome indirectly rather than attacked head-on. The therapist must distinguish denial from its conscious analog, lying, and react appropriately. Whereas most of us react to a lie with anger, reacting this way to a denial will effectively cut off helpful communication. Denial should stimulate the therapist to ask herself, *What is the purpose of the denial? Against what is the patient defending?* The answer will vary and, therefore, the approach will vary with the patient.

Fear is to be expected in any alcoholic person who has not yet accepted the disease. Although the alcoholic state is painful, the pain is at least familiar, while treatment represents a journey into the unknown. Any unfamiliar journey is less fearful with a guide (counselor or therapist, in this case), or when made as part of a group (therapy group, AA, or Women for Sobriety group). The best antidote to fear is helpful company.

Shame is perhaps the hardest obstacle to overcome in the alcoholic woman. From the society around her, she accepts the current myths and misconceptions about alcoholism and thereby carries a triple load of shame. First, having a problem with alcohol in our culture is in itself considered a shameful sign of personal weakness. Second, in women excessive drinking is considered even more shameful because women are expected to embody the so-called higher values of society. Third, alcoholism in women is wrongly supposed to be linked with sexual promiscuity, adding a burden of shame at being considered a potential or actual "loose woman." To counteract this shame, our most powerful weapon is the disease concept of alcoholism. This idea should be presented very early in treatment and stressed through readings, contacts with other recovering alcoholic men and women, and family counseling sessions. If family members are introduced to Al-Anon and Alateen, their improved attitudes will help to lift this crushing triple burden of shame. Even in the absence of sufficient initial motivation to bring the alcoholic woman herself into treatment, influencing the home atmosphere through family counseling often creates enough change to establish such motivation for the first time. The family will learn when and how to approach the sick alcoholic with a sympathetic but realistic offer of help, and how to create a constructive either-or situation.

IDEAL MOTIVATION

Once the woman enters treatment, however, one must immediately begin working toward the ideal motivation. To reach this state, the alcoholic woman confronts basic questions about her life, such as "Who am I?" and, "Do I deserve to recover to be happy?" She must care enough about herself to do what is right for her. Often ideas and ideals of femininity and woman's role in society are reexamined and revised. In our society, it is common for a woman to be defined primarily through her relationships to others: as some-one's wife, someone's mother, someone's widow. The alcoholic woman redefines herself, not merely through others, but as an indi-vidual. She often learns for the first time to express her wants directly and balance her concerns against those of others. The family will find her changing in many ways beyond simply not drinking, and may require help in readjusting to her new role and the "constructive selfishness" Chaney Allen describes.

As an aid in achieving this ideal motivation, establishing the positive identity of recovering alcoholic is essential. Contact with other recovering alcoholic women who serve as role models is help-ful. Also crucial to recovery is the attitude of the caregivers—we the professionals who are there to offer our help. Do we feel genuine concern for the alcoholic woman? respect? love? or do we collude to keep them in babyhood?

I would like to close by sharing with you 12 steps for the professional. This paper was written for the first Summer School of the Caribbean Institute on Alcoholism in St. Thomas by one of our students, an alcoholism counselor from Trinidad. Those of you who are familiar with AA will recognize the format. I think all of us will appreciate its value.

I write at the conclusion of the course and I feel bound to offer twelve suggestions (steps) of my own to help the social worker and therapist:

1. We admitted we were victims of prejudice and erroneous concepts about alcoholism and alcoholics.
2. We came to believe that this was a serious impediment to the work of helping to restore the alcoholic to sobriety and sanity.
3. We made a serious and diligent study of the subject.
4. We made a searching and honest appraisal of our attitudes and disposition towards the alcoholic.
5. We gradually discarded our prejudices and acquired new knowl-edge and insights into the baffling disease of alcoholism and subtle complications of alcoholic behavior.
6. We sought to understand the alcoholic and were not afraid to achieve this by visiting with him in his home and environs.
7. We attended AA meetings whenever possible.
8. We visited, counseled, and consoled the spouse and relatives of the alcoholic.
9. We constantly kept abreast with the latest developments on the subject.
10. We sought through mediation and study, not only to increase our knowledge of the subject but our capacity to love and understand.

11. We were willing to make sacrifices to become apostles of love and understanding to the still suffering alcoholic.
12. Having shed our prejudices and armed with new insights, we humbly sought, both by precept and example, to influence our fellow workers to undertake a similar exercise.

Christmah Sammy
June 26, 1975

Chapter 17

BREAKING CYCLES
OF VICTIMIZATION

The Shelter as an
Affirmative Institution

Peggy Ann McGarry
Dennis McGrath

The issue of wife abuse has been continually gaining public attention in recent years. Beginning with Del Martin's *Battered Wives* (1976), the first book published in the United States dealing explicitly with battered women, there has been a clear increase in newspaper accounts, magazine articles, as well as scholarly publications.

The transition from public recognition to effective public policy, though, is slow and difficult. Those working to reduce domestic violence against women are in serious danger of having the all too brief public attention span pass on to other issues before they are able to build the political coalitions needed to secure adequate public funding. Agencies such as Health, Education, and Welfare, Housing and Urban Development, and Law Enforcement Assistance Administration funds have changed their regulations in some areas to make existing funds available to domestic violence services. There has been no real increase in the *amount* of funding, however, and so domestic violence competes with other, more established, interests. Attempts to create new funding streams for services to victims have so far been defeated in the Congress.

At this point the most significant and comprehensive services for abused women and their children are being provided by private shelters throughout the country. If a woman needs a place to stay after 5:00 P.M. or on the weekend, if she has exhausted her money residing at the "Y," or if relatives are unable to take her in yet again, the private shelter is often the only place she can go. As of the middle of 1976 there were only 11 such facilities in the entire country, but since then many more have opened, usually growing out of the women's movement and largely run by volunteers or poorly paid staff members motivated by a commitment to the problem.

Because of this situation there are two critical policy issues that need to be addressed. The first is the question of how domestic violence against women can be placed on the national agenda at a time when new claims on government budgets are being actively resisted by legislatures, and well-financed campaigns are being mounted to roll back recent gains of the women's movement. The second issue, addressed in this paper, is the direction that private shelters, the only substantial resource now available to battered women and their children, should take. Our concern, then, is to clarify the focus of shelter policy and programs so they can provide the most appropriate services and so they can be a model for the larger-scale programs to be developed if the political battles are won.

The central goal of a Shelter for abused women, which should be reflected in all policies and programs, is to break the cycle of victimization and to help women so they can independently act to improve their lives and permanently free themselves from the threat of further violence.

The theoretical literature and publications in social service journals have largely emphasized the goal of breaking the "cycle of violence," the intergenerationally transmitted behavior patterns that encourage and normatively condone intrafamily violence (Galdston, 1975; Steinmetz, 1977). This, of course, is critical, but must be complimented by recognizing a second goal of breaking the "cycle of control," the interlocking effects of institutional functioning and traditional sex-role ideology that define the limits of women's place, designate women as appropriate victims of violence, and lock them into abusive relationships. Taken together these two goals can be conceptualized as efforts to intervene in the "cycle of victimization," by counteracting the effects of prior socialization in the family of origin and by advocating the rights of abused women in encounters with police, courts, prosecutors, hospitals and social service agencies.

The Cycle of Violence

Much current work in criminology has emphasized the role of the victim in shaping crime patterns, rather than maintaining an exclusive focus on the offender (Schafer, 1968, Wolfgang, 1958). Since crime is an interactional event the behavior of both the victim and offender, as well as their prior learning, motivation, and sense of options will influence the outcome of the offense. Within the work on domestic violence, this orientation has been pursued through the concept of a "cycle of violence."

There is fairly broad agreement among researchers that exposure to violence in the family of origin will tend to influence later adult behavior. Owen and Strauss (1975), basing their conclusions on a secondary analysis of a national sample, assert that the more an individual is exposed to violence during childhood, *either as an observer or victim,* the more likely the individual is to be violent as an adult. Gayford (1975), in studying the backgrounds of 100 battered wives discovered that 51 percent of the assaultive husbands had been exposed, as children, to models of intrafamily violence. Gelles (1976), in his study of family violence, reported that 66 percent of the women who had observed violence between their parents were themselves ultimately the victims of violence when they married. Pizzey (1974), in describing her work in England, recounts the impact of abuse on the woman's children. She notes that boys frequently act out in aggressive and destructive ways, while girls tend to be passive and withdrawn. Steinmetz (1977), in summarizing much of the work on child abuse comments that "such studies suggest that the abusive or rejecting parent was often abused or rejected himself as a child and thus is using child-rearing techniques that resemble those with which he was raised (p. 99).

Two critical points, though, must be made with regard to this extensive literature. The first is that exposure to violence in the family of origin influences the likelihood of being both victim and offender, i.e., the probable commitment to both violence and victimization. The role models available in the family prepare girls for later abuse as much as they help pattern future male aggressiveness. The legacy of female socialization has been very fruitfully studied, especially through the notions of "learning helplessness" and "altruistic madness."

Therapist Lenore Walker (1978) employs the social learning theory of learned helplessness to understand how a battered woman's perception of the degree of control she has over events contributes to her ability to act or to a virtual paralysis of will. In reviewing her clinical experience, Walker notes that "once the women are operating from a belief of helplessness, the perception becomes reality and they become passive, submissive, helpless" (p. 47). She relates this outcome of victimization, the psychological foreclosure of options by the victim, to prior female socialization. Walker emphasizes that women are continually and systematically taught that their personal worth and autonomy depend on their relationship to men, rather than on the quality of their personal response to life situations. Such cultural indoctrination throughout childhood ill prepares women for adult autonomy and causes them to enter marriage at a psychological disadvantage. Richardson (1977) reinforces this line of analysis by arguing that traditional sex-role socialization leads women to be more other-invested than self-invested. Those exhibiting a high degree of commitment to traditional standards of feminity tend toward what he terms "altruistic madness," the embodiment of the expectation of the expectation that a woman is to "govern her behavior with respect to the significant others in her life in such a manner that she is preoccupied with these others; prepossessed with their welfare" (p. 9).

The second point is less often recognized by researchers and concerns the reasons why the early exposure to violence has such efficacy in influencing later behavior. The related issue is why there are such strong gender-related patterns in response to exposure, such as those described by Pizzey. Pagelow has very effectively shown that the ultimate reaction to childhood exposure to domestic violence is conditioned by the degree of acceptance of what she terms "traditional ideology" (Pagelow, 1977, 1978). This refers to the complex of ideas and norms defining and legitimating sex-role stereotypic behavior and male hierarchic dominance.

Pagelow's point is that exposure to domestic violence in childhood heightens the woman's potential for victim status when such learning is combined with the inculcation of a traditional patriarchial ideology that circumscribes women's place and encourages self-investment in even unsatisfactory marital relationships. As a consequence, any resocialization of victims of wife-abuse must be coupled with attempts to neutralize this sex-role ideology and transmit a less restricted view of women's place.

The Cycle of Control

The concept of a traditional patriarchial ideology that encourages male violence and female acceptance of battering helps provide a conceptual bridge between the roots of domestic violence in prior socialization and its source in institutional functioning. The notion of a traditional ideology suggests that sex-role stereotypes enhancing violence are transmitted, represented, and "made real" to women through their encounters, not only with parents, but with representatives of major societal institutions. We must, therefore, better understand, and learn to intervene in, not only the cycle of violence that transmits violent behavior patterns intergenerationally, but also the cycle of control that continues to define women as socially appropriate victims and locks them into abusive relationships.

Even if we accept a family learning model we are still left with the larger structural and political question of why women and children are confined to a subordinate status within the family and why legal, medical, and social service institutions inhibit them from leaving the violent situation and from choosing alternative family forms. We are still left with the task of understanding why domestic abuse has been condoned or ignored by the general public and the reasons for the nonenforcement of laws whose application would provide women some protection.

We must, therefore, link our understanding of the consequences of family learning patterns with the structural constraints that assign women to a subordinate status in marriage, child care, and work, and which deny women equal grounds for ending marriage or adequate support to live alone or in nontraditional arrangements (Chester & Streather 1972; Marsden 1978; Feinstein 1979).

Just as there is a cycle of violence produced by the intergenerational transmission of violent behavior patterns within the family, there is a cycle of control produced by the intergenerational reproduction of women's place, restricting free choice, and denying protection from domestic violence.

In terms of legal tradition and practice, Blackstone traces the persistence of the common law right of husbands to physically discipline their wives until the middle of the 17th century. The Supreme Court of Mississippi in a 1824 case held that a husband should be permitted to moderately chastise his wife. The court found such behavior acceptable in cases of great emergency "without subjecting himself to vexatious prosecutions for assault and battery, resulting in the discredit and shame of all parties concerned" (Eisenberg & Micklow, 1977, pp. 138–139).

Although the chastisement right was formally repudiated by the end of the 19th century, the abused woman's lack of legal protection has been well-documented (Fields, 1977; Fromson, 1977; Parnas, 1973). In Pennsylvania, for example, the police, who are usually the first to receive the victim's call for assistance, are unprepared to handle the situation or provide even minimum protection.

Pennsylvania does have a "Protection from Abuse" Act that enables a battered spouse to file a petition in Family Court on behalf of herself and/or her children asking for a restraining order and the abusive spouse's eviction from the family home (Schickling, 1977). While the law requires a hearing on the petition within 10 days, the petition must be filed by an attorney. For a woman with no financial means of her own, this involves waiting as long as two weeks for an appointment with a Community Legal Services (CLS) attorney, thus further restricting legal protection for the victim. CLS estimates that its attorneys have brought 80 percent of all such petitions currently filed with Family Court.

With legal protection so hard to obtain, the victimized family members are rarely in a position to successfully gain assistance with their other problems. For example, in order to obtain Public Assistance, food stamps, or medical assistance for herself and her children, a battered woman must already be living apart from the abusive spouse. Such problems in obtaining services from social service agencies are quite widespread and have been discussed in depth by others (Nicholas, 1976; Schechter, 1978).

There has been much attention paid in recent years to the tremendous postwar increase in female labor force participation. Many analysts have argued that the growth in numbers of working women, including those with preschool children, has served to alter women's place and gives them more freedom, both in society and in the family. Women have traditionally had far fewer opportunities to earn a living on an equal basis with men, so marriage has been essential to their economic well-being. Several economic analyses of traditional family life emphasize that marriage has had a strong utilitarian dimension because a woman's social and economic standing has depended far more on her choice of mate, than on her ability, degree of education or any other personal characteristic (Sawhill, 1977). The assertion is often made, therefore, that increased attachment to the labor force and rising income of women will tend to equalize power relations between the spouses, producing more "symmetrical families," and improving women's standing in public institutions (Young & Willmott, 1973).

A careful analysis of the trends, though, does not support this interpretation. Greater participation in the paid labor force has not provided most women with economic independence or significantly expanded marital freedom. In 1976, for instance, almost two out of three of the 15 million persons over 16 defined by the government as poor were women, as were over 70 percent of the aged poor (Bureau of the Census 1977). When these patterns are combined with the continually higher female unemployment rates, it becomes clear that women continue to experience substantial economic insecurity.

Among working women a substantial wage gap, noted for over a century, has also continued to exist, undercutting the potential for economic independence and sustaining the priority and necessity of marriage, even when the relationship is abusive or otherwise unsatisfactory (Abbott, 1910). Fully employed women still earn only $6 for every $10 earned by men (Sexton, 1977). Furthermore, even when age, education, race, regions, hours and weeks worked, and time spent in the labor force are controlled, there still exists a 43 percent differential between male and female income (Suter & Miller, 1973).

The reasons for a continuing income gap and the lack of economic independence help clarify the structural barriers preventing an expansion of women's place and reinforcing the cycle of victimization by foreclosing alternatives to marriage.

Although women, including married women, have increasingly entered the labor market, the growth of female workers has occurred principally in low wage industries and occupations with short mobility ladders. This has been largely explained by Oppenheimer (1970) in terms of demographic shifts, accompanied by changes in supply and demand for labor in the American economy. She discovered that the demand for women workers had increased at the same time that a smaller than usual pool of eligible women was available for market work. The shift in the economy from industrial to service jobs after World War II, along with the baby boom created a great demand for teachers, clerical, and sales workers, and many other low-level white collar positions. Such jobs were sex-labeled as "women's work," so females were not likely to be crowded out by male competitors. On the supply side, though, there was a shortage of single or older women with the appropriate training, so the marital barrier to employment softened, as did restrictions on women with young children.

Thus, although the composition of the labor force has changed, it is still sex segregated, and much of the income gap can be accounted for by the different jobs held by men and women. Today 60 percent of all women workers are in 10 occupations, and 14 of 17 occupations that were predominantly female in 1900 are still so today (Feinstein, 1979). Fuchs notes that of the 100 occupations employing over 100,000 workers, only 46 employ as many as 35,000 of each sex (Fuchs, 1971). Other researchers note that most industries paying average weekly wages of less than $100 are primarily staffed by women (Waldman & McEaddy, 1974). In addition to intensive sex segregation of employment, women are less likely to have union protection and more likely to suffer job discrimination (Chapman, 1976).

The other major reason for the income gap and lack of economic independence for women is the difference in work experience, largely due to their continued primary responsibility for child rearing. The earnings of men and women begin at roughly the same point, but men's continue to rise while women's income peak much earlier. Women's work experience is much more likely to be interrupted, while men's tends to be continuous. As two economists note:

> The periods of time women spend at home rather than in the work force —particularly when associated with marriage or the birth of the first child—result in a net depreciation of their human capital and their earning power. The earnings depreciation for married women amounts to, on the average, 1.5 percent per year (Mincer & Polachek, 1974).

THE SHELTER AS AN AFFIRMATIVE INSTITUTION

In light of the previous discussion of the dual roots of domestic assault, Shelters should be viewed, and structured, as affirmative institutions. Their ultimate goal should be to counter prior socialization by presenting positive models of female behavior and to counter institutional restrictions of women's lives by being women-controlled institutions advocating victim's rights in dealing with police, courts, prosecutors, social service agencies, and medical institutions.

A shelter, in our view, should be operated as a haven, not a hospital, as a refuge rather than a treatment center. It is important that a medical model and clinical categories not be employed, that the source of the woman's distress be located in social conditions rather than in their psyches. Rather than being treated as patients, residents should be assisted in meeting their pressing needs and helped toward the achievement of full autonomy.

This distinction in program philosophy is not always clearly recognized, but must be highlighted since the model underlying the provision of services has profound implications for the way residents are dealt with.

In the Philadelphia Shelter operated by Women Against Abuse many more women seek refuge than can be housed in the facility, with an average of 25 to 35 being turned away each week for lack of space. As a result of the need produced by the high incidence of abuse, admission procedures give priority to women in the greatest need, for example, those without money or family to take them in, and those who have suffered serious injury and/or those whose lives are threatened.

Because of this a large proportion of the residents enter the facility exhibiting a variety of trauma symptoms. Many have been physically and emotionally battered for long periods, have lived in fear for their lives, as well as for their children, and often have untreated injuries and physical illnesses. They are forced to leave their customary and familiar surroundings, bringing with them few belongings and still fearful that their partners will pursue them.

Such circumstances, therefore, predispose staff members to assume a therapeutic stance and, unintentionally, to maintain a continuity of dependence. But if a shelter is to be a truly affirmative institution the violence that women have suffered must be recognized, but they must not be institutionally confirmed as a victim. One way that this issue is addressed is the terminology used by staff in referring to the women served by the shelter. At Women Against Abuse they are called residents, or collectively "the women." Another Shelter in Pennsylvania uses the term *guest* rather than that of "client" with its traditional connotations.

Shelter programs and procedures must emphasize that staff and volunteers are there as a resource, to counsel, provide information and outline available resources, not to "treat" or to make decisions for the resident. The loss of autonomy that the woman has suffered along with her abuse must be restored as quickly as possible and not institutionally perpetuated.

This aspect of program philosophy must also be understood in terms of actual shelter patterns. The average stay of women and their children in private facilities throughout the country is under three weeks, which is roughly the time needed for staff to outline options and services; assist in securing housing, employment, or public benefits; institute legal action; or aid in reconciliation and return. A shelter, by its very nature, is a transitional facility and its appropriate and achievable goals must be clearly recognized.

Staff members and volunteers, though, can and should take advantage of the shelter as an alternative living arrangement. In many cases it is the first time in their lives that women have lived apart from parents and husbands. One implication of emphasizing the rights and autonomy of the women is that residents must assume responsibility for the cooperative running of the household during their stay. In the Philadelphia shelter, as with most others, this involves very concrete activities, such as taking turns in preparing meals, cleaning, and care of children (when they are not supervised by child care workers).

In many cases, the women have experienced tremendous control by their abusive partners, who restricted their movements, sparingly doled out household money, made them account for every free minute and, in general, forced them into the role of dependent child. Because of this, the experience of cooperatively maintaining a household is an important step in overcoming prior socialization and the effects of their recent victimization.

The shelter is also in many cases, the first experience the woman (and her children) have had of a nonviolent living arrangement. Staff and volunteers can serve an important function in acting as role models in the nonviolent resolution of conflict and childrearing. The Philadelphia shelter, like a number of other facilities, also offers formal parenting classes for interested residents as a further attempt to break the cycle of violence by teaching alternatives to force in parent-child interaction.

Shelters must also actively seek structural ways to integrate residents into the formulation of policy. One way this can be done is to assign a minimum of places on the Board of Directors for former residents.

Finally, if shelters are to be affirmative institutions acting to break the cycle of victimization we must recognize that until the political battle for adequate funding is won, the tremendous demand for a haven from abuse that exists cannot be fully met. Besides providing refuge and telephone counseling, shelters must continually confront public agencies, pointing out ways they can better serve the needs of battered women.

REFERENCES

Abbott, E. *Women in industry.* New York: Appleton, 1910.

Bureau of the Census. *A statistical portrait of women in the U.S.* Current Population Reports, Special Study Series P-23, No. 58, 1977.

Chapman, J. R., & Gates, M. (Ed). *The victimization of women.* Beverly Hills: Sage, 1978.

Chester R., & Streather, J. Cruelty in english divorce. *Journal of Marriage and the Family,* 1972.

Eisenberg, S. E., & Micklow, P. L. *The assaulted wife: 'catch 22' revisited. Women's Rights Law Reporter,* 1977, *3* 138–161.

Feinstein, K. W. (Ed). *Working women and families.* Beverly Hills: Sage, 1979.

Fields, M. Representing battered wives, or what to do until the police arrive. *Family Law Reporter,* 1977, *3.*

Fromson, T. The case for legal remedies for abused women. *New York University Review of Law and Social Change,* 1977, *6,* 135–174.

Fuchs, V. Differences in hourly earnings between men and women. *Monthly Labor Review,* 1971, 10–14.

Galdston, R. Preventing the abuse of little children. *American Journal of Orthopsychiatry,* 1975, *45,* 372–381.

Gayford, J. J. Wife battering: A preliminary survey of 100 cases. *British Medical Journal,* 1975, *1* 194–197.

Gelles, R. J. *The violent home.* Beverly Hills: Sage, 1974.

Gelles, R. J. Abused wives: Why do they stay. *Journal of Marriage and the Family,* 1976.

Marsden, D. Sociological perspectives on family violence. In Martin J. P. (Ed.). *Violence and the family.* New York: John Wiley, 1978.

Mincer, J., & Polachek, S. Family investment in human capital: Earnings of women. *Journal of Political Economy,* 1974, 76–108.

Oppenheimer, V. *The female labor force in the United States.* Berkeley, Ca.: University of California, Population Monograph Series no. 5. 1970.

Owen, D. J., & Strauss, M. A. Childhood violence and adult approval of violence. *Aggressive Behavior,* 1975, *1* 193–211.

Pagelow, M. D. "Secondary Battering: Breaking the Cycle of Domestic Violence." Paper presented at the annual meeting of the Sociologists for Women in Society Section of the American Sociological Association, September 5–9, 1977.

Pagelow, M. D. Social learning theory and sex roles: Violence begins in the home. Paper presented at the annual meeting of the Society for the Study of Social Problems, September, 1978.

Parnas, R. I. Prosecutorial and judicial handling of family violence. *Criminal Law Bulletin,* 1973, *9,* 733–768.

Pizzey, E. *Scream quietly or the neighbours will hear.* Middlesex: Penguin, 1974.

Richardson, L. A. Women and altruistic madness: A study of sex-based vulnerability. Pater presented at the annual meeting of the American Sociological Association, Chicago, 1977.

Sawhill, I. V. Economic perspectives on the family. *Daedalus,* 1977, *106,* 115–125.

Schechter, S. Psychic battering: The institutional response to battered women. Paper presented at the Midwest Conference on Abuse of Women, St. Louis University Medical Center, May, 1978.

Schafer, S. *Theories in criminology.* New York: Random House, 1969.

Schickling, B. H. Relief for victims of intra-family assaults—The Pennsylvania Protection from Abuse Act. *Dickinson Law Review,* 1977, *81,* 815–822.

Sexton, P. C. *Women and work.* Washington, D.C., U.S. Department of Labor, Monograph 46, 1977.

Steinmetz, S. K. *The cycle of violence.* New York: Praeger, 1977.

Suter, L. E., & Miller, H. P. Income differences between men and career women. *American Journal of Sociology,* 1973, *78,* 962–974.

Waldman, E., McEaddy, B. J. Where women work—An analysis by industry and occupation. *Monthly Labor Review,* 1974

Walker, L. E. *The battered woman.* New York: Harper and Row, 1978.

Wolfgang, M. E. *Patterns of criminal homicide.* Philadelphia: University of Pennsylvania Press, 1958.

Young, M., & Willmott, P. *The symmetrical family.* New York: Pantheon, 1973.

Chapter 18

THE MYTHOLOGY OF RAPE

Susan Halpern

Before other panel members discuss the impact of public attention on the victim, the rapist and on legislation, I would like to present an overview of a variety of myths that affect all these issues. I hope that this will provide a framework within which these aspects of rape can be viewed.

Keep in mind that we are all affected by these myths and that they color not only how we view the victim but how the victim views herself.

RESISTANCE PREVENTS RAPE

One extension of this is that if you resist you will not be raped. Therefore, a "good" woman cannot be raped.

In a courtroom, this need for a show of resistance necessitates the victim have overt trauma (evidence). Without this evidence, the victim is believed to have consented to the rape.

In fact, there are numerous reasons for a victim *submitting* to the rape. *Submission does not imply consent.* Reasons for submission include:

1. more than one assailant
2. presence of weapons
3. assailant stronger
4. fear of death (in which case rape seems the only choice)
5. difficulty in responding aggressively (femininity is equated with passivity and passivity is a learned behavior pattern for most women, which is difficult to overcome under stress)

You Get What You Deserve

"She dressed suggestively or acted provocatively, so she got what she deserved." This shifts the blame away from the assailant. The assailant initiated the act, which is ignored.

Double message implied. Society approves suggestive dress. Media promote this. Where is the line to be drawn?

Provocative actions also a difficult area. Why is a woman hitching a ride "asking for it?" Why is a woman alone in a bar "fair game?"

Problem lies in the unwritten message that is implicit in our sexual code: women need male protection, whether or not it is asked for. Women who act independently threaten this code and are therefore seen as fair game.

Women Fantasize Rape

Most fantasies revolve around consensual sexual activity with a desirable partner. The act is pleasurable even though submission is involved. Rape is forced sexual intercourse and is painful, therefore not pleasurable and is not with a desired partner. Rape is more a male fantasy than women's.

Frequent, False Accusations Will Increase

Common Fear

Rape is one of the most underreported crimes in the country. If the accusation so convenient and reliable, why is it underreported?

Only in rape cases is it assumed that the criminal justice system will not protect a defendant from a lying plaintiff.

RAPE ONLY OCCURS IN URBAN AREAS, AT NIGHT, TO A SINGLE WOMAN LIVING ALONE

This is not true. It occurs in rural and suburban areas, during daylight hours in apartments, houses, alleys, parking lots, to married as well as single women. In addition, it happens to children, adolescents, young women, and middle-aged and older women.

Chapter 19

IN THE PURSUIT OF JUSTICE
IN SENTENCING AND PRISON

David Fogel

This paper deals with effects of indeterminate sentencing on the prison population, prison life, and public credibility in the system. Although my interest may appear rather narrowly drawn for this discussion it is of crucial importance to those who live and work in the prison. *The topic is sentence reform and prison violence.*

A few caveats:

All reforms eventually fail.

The criminal justice system has very little to do with crime rates.

Prisons as penal sanctions represent an abomination. (They make inmates less safe as free citizens.)

Nothing I have to say is meant to convey my support for mandatory sentencing. I oppose the concept. I support determinate sentencing.

I do not believe that the current movement toward determinate sentencing represents a "pendulum swing."

The arguments I advance in favor of determinate sentencing are in the service of advancing the debate about the purpose of our system of justice and not intended as a panacea for its current woes.

My research, which led me to adopt the views you will hear about, stemmed from the urgency of continued mass violence in our prisons beginning in 1971 through 1973. I was commissioned by the Law Enforcement Assistance Administration's Mid-Western Region's (Illinois, Michigan, Ohio, Indiana, Wisconsin and Minnesota) State Directors of Corrections Departments (DOC) and the State Criminal Justice Planning Agency Directors (SPA) to undertake this work. My job was twofold: 1) to suggest reasons for the persistence of violence in prisons and 2) to operationalize the concept I had earlier written about named the "justice model."

A few peripheral issues that account for the violence and mindlessness of the prison experience are:

> Administrators as a group are notoriously ahistorical and are therefore not likely to benefit from their predecessor's tragic experiences.

> The field of corrections is insulated, isolated, and suffering from a fatal mix: high discretion and low visibility.

> Role confusion within the walls (prison staff) and in the field (parole officers) is rampant. Guards remain professional fossils: bitter, radicalized, and both undertrained and underpaid. While parole officers go on their daily appointed rounds with Freud in one hand and a .38 in their other, guards still work at salaries generally lower than zookeepers and garbagemen.

> The field has bounced aimlessly through two centuries from panacea to panacea always biting off indigestable chunks as its mission and overpromising.

> My last peripheral issue, which I believe contributes to prison violence, is the physical environment, the fortress prison itself. The 19th century legacy of cellular confinement undermines all ameliorative efforts to humanize the prison experience. Inexorably the fortress prison degrades both the keeper and the kept.

These have been peripheral issues. I find the central issues related to prison violence to be how you get in and how you get out of prison, both however resting on some sort of theory of the purpose of the criminal law. My reading of the purpose of the criminal law is that it is intended to punish. When the punishment becomes a prison sentence then all that is intended is that the prisoner be deprived of liberty for a specified period of time.

SENTENCING OR HOW YOU GET IN

As a result of sentencing disparities inherent in the vast amount of discretion available, particularly in indeterminate sentencing jurisdictions, prisoners begin to develop a gnawing *sense of injustice*. Convicts simply speak to each other and draw invidious comparisons. Further sentencing, in unreformed states, is lawless in the sense of being procedureless (see Marvin Frankel, "Criminal Sentences"). In the United States, sentences are Draconian in length. Other Western nations get by at 25 percent of our rate of incarceration. Sentences in indeterminate jurisdictions are largely unreviewable. With plea bargaining at the front end of the criminal justice system and parole boards actually determining when a prisoner is to be released, we find that traditional judicial power in sentencing has badly eroded. Where judicial discretion abounds as to minimum sentences, games are possible. For example, a liberal judge believing that he or she is dealing with a conservative parole board may give prisoner A a one-year minimum sentence with the thought in mind that A will be denied at his first parole board appearance and perhaps be paroled in two or three years. But you might also have a conservative judge believing he or she is dealing with a *liberal* parole board likely to parole A at his first appearance and therefore sets the minimum at two or three years.

Some states hand out 5,000 year sentences, or quaint numbers like 494 years, or a 1,000 minimum to a 3,000 maximum, multiple life sentences, or even life plus a day.

PAROLE OR HOW DO YOU GET OUT?

The rehabilitation model of corrections relies on the indeterminate sentence and the parole board as a release mechanism. In theory, the judge plays a minor role establishing the minimum and maximum sentence. In some states, the judge simply sentenced "to the term prescribed by law," which might be 1 to 20 or zero to life. The prison authorities then diagnose the convict, prescribe a treatment course of action, and make periodic assessment of the convict's progress for the parole board. The board evaluates the reports to assess the convict's "clinical progress" and/or "parole readiness." This sounds fine but in practice it lends itself to enormous injustices and distortion, which include:

Parole boards are political appointees heavily loaded toward law enforcement or former prison officials.

They can't predict.

Parole release authority has become a tool for increasing terms of imprisonment and enforcing prison discipline.

Blacks and women* pay a special surcharge in the way of additional prison time.

Until quite recently parole boards were largely invisible and until the early 1970s were not (in one large state) required to even let a prisoner know why parole was being denied.

*As cited in *Fair and Certain Punishment* (New York: McGraw Hill, 1976, p. 142) by Alan M. Dershowitz:

Tappan. op.cit., pp. 532, 535. Presumably higher sentences in a high-crime jurisdiction reflect an effort to deter crime in response to the high rate. Another factor cited is that 13 of the 18 definite-sentence jurisdictions are southern states; this region traditionally has employed a policy of low sentences except in special cases.

These factors, however, cannot explain intrastate sentence-duration disparities, such as existed in Connecticut until 1968. A statute there permitted the possibility of certain women offenders on indeterminate terms being subject to maximum sentences longer than those that could be given to men serving relatively determinate terms for the identical offenses. Two 1968 cases invalidated the scheme. *United States ex rel Robinson v. York,* 281 F. Supp 8 (D. Conn. 1968); *Liberti v. York,* 28 Conn Supp. 9, 246 A.2d 106 (Sup. Ct. 1968).

Laws in Pennsylvania and New Jersey until recently required many women to receive indeterminate sentences with the maximum set at the maximum allowed for the crime, while men could receive shorter minimum-maximum terms at the discretion of the judge. The laws were invalidated on equal-protection grounds. *Commonwealth v. Daniel,* 430 Pa. 642, 243 A.2d 400 (1968); *State V. Chambers,* 63 N.J. 287, 307 A.2d 78 (1973). The sentencing schemes did not necessarily mean that women served longer sentences than men, although a study has indicated that mandatory indeterminate terms usually do result in female offenders serving more time than their male counterparts; see Comment, "Sex and Sentencing," *Southwestern Law Journal,* 26 (1972):890. At the very least the Pennsylvania and New Jersey statutes made women subject for reincarceration for parole violations for a longer period than most men; see 430 Pa. at 647 n.*, 243 A.2d at 402–403 n.6. The Supreme Court of New Jersey characterized the rationale of the statutes as follows: ". . . that females are better subjects for rehabilitation, thereby justifying a potentially longer period of detention for that purpose. . . ." 63 N.J. at 296, 307, A.2d at 82.

Parole boards have to assess something in order to justify a release decision. Some prisons have fuller programs than others. For example, one might have a semblance of clinical services (group therapy, AA, drug counseling, religious programs). Here you will typically find convicts flocking to whatever they believe the parole board wants of them in attendance. Another correctional facility might have only a farm and a piggery or a shoe or a glove factory. Obviously the parole aspirant must show diligence in whatever is available.

A late colleague of mine, Hans W. Mattick, said that the rehabilitative model generally but parole release in particular transformed American prisons into great drama centers with the convicts as actors and parole boards serving as drama critics handing out "Oscars," "Emmys," and paroles. The McKay report investigating the Attica rebellion found religious class attendance was a reliable ticket out of that prison. In Nevada it was a Sunday religious service attendance. In Minnesota for a time AA was your way out whether you drank or not. In Patuxent, it was through group therapy.

Of course there are other ways out. In California under Ronald Reagan the prison population was driven *down,* largely through accelerated parole release, by 7,000 in the 1966 to 1972 period for reasons of "economy" and *up* by 4500 in the 1972 to 1974 period as a "get tough" step in preparation for Reagan's presidential bid. Properly understood parole statistics may be better understood as a function of parole board members' behavior rather than individual convicts' parolability.

Of course, there are more exotic ways of release, witness the creativity of Tennessee's Governor Ray Blanton's parole and pardon process. Yet DOC's rhetoric will still speak to the rehabilitation of its convicts.

SENTENCE REFORM

Simply put we need to reduce the rhetoric, narrow the purposes of the criminal law, and structure the abounding discretion. Initially, we need to abandon the fruitless search for a *unified theory of crime or the criminal.* The criminal law should be as it was intended to be the community's collective outrage against certain kinds of unacceptable and/or unlawful behavior. The law as Stephen Shaffer has suggested is at any time the "command of the sovereign." A criminal sanction is simply punishment. When the punishment becomes a prison sentence it is meant to be a deprivation of liberty not to be executed retributively. It needs to be executed reasonably, fairly, humanely, and constitutionally. Elements of sentencing fairness include reduced disparity for similar criminal acts, procedural regularity, and reviewability through an appellate process.

We need therefore to create much greater *degrees of certainty.* The prison experience needs to be put on the continuum of justice. Uncertainty about release has been found (by a California Legislative Commission and the Attica Commission) to be a festering sore that leads to hostility and potential violence in the prison.

Volition has to be carried all the way. Our laws demand it as necessary as a basis for incarceration in a prison. The criminal act and intent must be in union. One without the other will not equal a prison sentence. In other words, not only did you do what was charged but you meant to do it, or, *you are responsible, you are volitional.* Only then can a judge sentence you to prison. Once there, the volitional and responsible nature of the defendant—now convict —leave him.

A way of returning to *responsibility-under-the-law* is to unhook treatment (clinical progress) from the release date. This is called determinate sentencing. A fixed sentence is imposed rather than a minimum and maximum. The judge is still permitted discretion within a narrow range, but is expected under what is called the *presumptive* sentence to give three and five, respectively. He or she may reduce in the lower range to two years if mitigating circumstances were found present or increase to four years if aggravating circumstances were found present. In either case, the aggravating and mitigating factors are stated in the statute and put on the public record when a judge uses either one.

When the prisoner leaves the courtroom he or she knows exactly how much time has to be done. The imposed sentence is said to be *flat time.* In Illinois, we allow the sentence imposed to be mitigated only by the prisoner who we assume to be volitional as the court itself found. This is done through a mechanism called vested day-for-day good time. The sentence is reduced one day for each lawful day the prisoner spends in prison. No clinician assesses the "good day." It is given as under a presumption of lawful behavior in the absence of on-the-record evidence to the contrary. When good time is in jeopardy then the procedure for taking it away is due process protected. With flat time sentencing prisoners "max out" of prison, thus the parole board can be abolished except for the residual prison population.

The movement to reform sentencing structures needs to clearly state its intention. New laws should unambiguously state the intention of the criminal law and just as unambiguously state the principle that sentencing authorities should have to affirmatively exhaust all nonincarcerative outcomes before a prison sentence may be imposed. This means making larger investments at the front end of the criminal justice system in probation, fines, work release, restitution, community service orders, and a host of other creative sentencing alternatives to incarceration.

Most of what I have stated has to do with justice in sentencing but the justice rather than rehabilitative model is also intended to deliver justice-as-fairness inside the prison as well. This includes some of the following prison programs:

Ombudsman

Access to the courts through well-established law libraries and civil legal assistance prison programs

A semblance of inmate self-governance to keep the thread of personal responsibility intact

Conjugal visiting

The right to refuse treatment and conversely the right to choose (here to be read as) programs of self-improvement. If offenders are truly volitional then programs for their own self-improvement can with some assistance be freely chosen by them.

This is not an abandonment of rehabilitation but a transformation of its coercive and seductive elements through the promise of earlier release, to a voluntary course of action by the inmate. Where clinical coercion ends individual responsibility on the part of the convict may begin. After all, what greater calling can prison work have than to teach non-law-abiders to be law abiding through treating them lawfully and as aspiring volitional actors.

This sentence reform movement has developed odd political coalitions. Normally warring factions have coalesced under the banner of greater certainty, straight talk, reduced rhetoric and claims, justice-as-fairness and simple (but not Draconian) punishment.

Prisons will better serve a democratic society by operating under lawful constitutional standards of humaneness and prisoner involvement than by seeking their guidance from the latest psychological, medical, and/or religious fad. After all, much of the progress of the planet can be laid to the unregenerated convict whom we could not rehabilitate, such as Christ, Ghandi, Mrs. Pankhurst, Joan of Arc, and Malcolm X.

Chapter 20

THE ROLE OF THE FAMILY
IN TEENAGE PREGNANCY
Support or Sabotage

Violet Padayachi Cherry

Adolescence is generally viewed as a period of turmoil, conflict, and strife. An unwanted or unplanned pregnancy in early adolescence constitutes a major crisis for the girl who experiences it, the family which, most of the time has to take the financial burden of rearing or helping to rear the child, sometimes for the male involved, and most of all for the unwanted child. In a number of the known studies, however, there are little data on the consequences to the adolescent's family. Most researchers and professionals working with this population view the grandparents as sources of help for the pregnant girl, but few have asked what the pregnancy of the young daughter means to the parents.

The population of youngsters served in our program has been 94 percent black, 5 percent Hispanic, and 1 percent white. In spite of the known myths, minority families do not accept the pregnancy of an unmarried girl very readily and they are often angry, disappointed, and feel betrayed. They are concerned with social disgrace, and the financial burden that an additional child will present to an already overburdened family. Mothers have shared with us concerns for themselves. She may be a young woman herself, just beginning to see some freedom from responsibility towards her own children. She may be planning to continue her own education or hoping to work again and does not relish facing the responsibility of part-or full-time caring for a grandchild.

Furstenberg (1976) found that only 3 percent of the grandparents welcomed the pregnancy of their schoolage daughters. He comments: "Parents are all too aware of the likely consequences of early parenthood. They were angry at their daughters, themselves, or both."

Bryan-Logan and Dancy (1974) also find the pregnancy of a schoolage daughter to be a severe crisis for the girl's mother.

We found, like they did, that most daughters tried to conceal the pregnancy from their mothers as long as they could and, to some extent, the mothers act in collusion with them. When mothers suspect the pregnancy, they are unable to raise the question. This denial from both parties usually postpones the decisions about pregnancy until the fifth or sixth month when it is difficult, or too late, to consider ending the pregnancy. We have found, in some instances, that both the girl and mother will choose to ignore the situation, hoping that in some magical way the problem will go away. Another problem for the family is the question of continuing education for the adolescent mother. Many mothers become babysitters for their daughter's child and give up jobs and their own plans so that the young person may return to school. John A. Bruce (1978) refers to the adolescent childbearing as an offense against planning. He states: "When futurity is weak, the present is strong; the ability to prioritize behaviors, delay gratification, and make long-term investments of self, becomes meaningless."

Less than a decade ago, many unwed adolescents who carried their pregnancies to term released their children for adoption. The primary task for most professionals, therefore, was assisting pregnant teenagers toward the difficult process of giving up their newborn infant and to enable them to make the adjustment back to their former roles. Today, most young women who choose to go to full term with the pregnancy plan to keep and rear their children themselves. Of the 84 young people in our program who chose to have their babies, only 4 gave up their babies for adoption. A great many questions have been raised as to why young people keep their babies. At the present time, there is little disapproval in society and certainly very little punitiveness towards the young person who chooses to keep her infant. Helen Friedman (1975) explains the trend of keeping babies with three old cliches: "changing societal values, changing lifestyles and youth asserting itself." The young people have given us many reasons for choosing to keep their infant, but whatever their motivation towards pregnancy, bringing up the baby becomes a means of finding themselves and having someone who needs them and whom they can love in the most unqualified fashion. In other words, the means of proving their worth. To some of the girls we have worked with, the infant has meant a means of freedom and independence and the "emancipated minor" label can mean that she can set up an apartment of her own without interfering adults and the public assistance received is her own to manage. To many of our clients, the child has served as an excuse for her to drop out of school, to leave a job, or to give up the living arrangement that she cannot cope with. She expects the child also to provide a solution for her loneliness and her emptiness. She may keep the child as a means of reforming herself and hoping that being a parent will make her a better individual. The young person may also see the child as helping her to prove to her own mother that she is a better mother and she could provide better nurturing and mothering than she herself had received. The child may also be used to get attention from the family or the putative father. Bruce (1978), sees "adolescent sexuality in itself as a symbol rejecting the role of the child in the family, and is sometimes seen as a rejection of the parents."

In an attempt to better understand the dynamics of teenage pregnancy, we decided to take a historic view of the socialization process of such individuals. That is, to take a look at the developmental process of moral and normative behaviors of our teenage clients.

First, the preoedipal child learns new skills, behavior, and attitudes that underlie these phenomena in order to please the mother. Mothers, then, actively and inadvertently become an initial and critical factor in the socialization of a child. Research on attitudes reveals (and it is also rather apparent) that teenage pregnancy is not perceived as role appropriate or adult-approved behavior by minority mothers.

The second significant factor in the socialization process is the school. Instantaneously, a child is now subject to a reward system and discipline that is independent of the home. This sets up inherent conflict of dependence/independence issues in the child, frequently manifested by compulsive-independent behavior. Generally speaking, the more independent the child, the more she will identify with the socializing agent (namely, the school).

A third developmental phase of socialization is that of peer group influence. By this time, the individual is an adolescent who is experiencing more fluid boundaries than earlier stages. These "voluntary associations" with peers contrast strikingly with a child's ascribed membership in the family and school. In the absence of available and demonstratively loving parents, or in the presence of severely punitive parenting, the focus of the adolescent's behavior goes beyond independence from adults to adult-disapproved behavior.

Values at this point are typically antithetical to that of the parents and socializing agents. At the chronic acute level, this adult-disapproved behavior materializes into delinquency.

This brief, somewhat simplified look, at the socialization process, leaves us with some broad interpretations. First, medical, psychological, and social aspects of teenage pregnancy must be attended to. Second, values clarification, and a look toward resocialization must be a treatment component in dealing with teenage pregnancy, especially with regard to rates of recidivism. Finally, the attitudes and biases of the staff making the intervention must be measured around such a nonneutral issue, so that mixed or harmful messages are not transmitted to clients. I will say more about this later in the paper.

Let me at this point, backtrack a little and give you a historical perspective of our own program here in Englewood. Englewwod is a small town in northern New Jersey and is situated across the Hudson River, about five miles west of upper Manhattan. It is located in Bergen County which is one of the most affluent counties in the country. It has a varied population with income, skills, and living facilities, ranging from highest levels to the lowest.

The minority population in Englewood numbers approximately 40 percent black, 12 percent hispanic, and the remainder white, of various religious and ethnic backgrounds. Englewood has the second largest minority population in Bergen County. There is an estimated 1,600 individuals on public assistance and, at present, the unemployment level in the town is projected at 11 percent. The local health department is the governmental health agency for the city and serves the entire population of 25,000. All our services are free.

The Teenage Parent Program was designed to meet the individual needs of Englewood's adolescent mothers and their families and is now in its third and final year of funding from the Division of Maternal and Child Health of the New Jersey State Health Department. The goal of this program is twofold.

First, to provide comprehensive medical care, health education, social services, and mental health services to the adolescent mother and her child, the staff tries to assist and encourage the young mothers in the program to continue their own development in the areas of education, vocation, parenthood, and personal and social growth.

The second goal of the program is to reduce the number of unwanted, unplanned pregnancies among the city's adolescent population through preventative measure, education, and supportive services. Up to this point, approximately 200 young people have been served in our program, 84 of whom carried their pregnancy to full term. From January 1979 to September of 1979, our referrals included 23 new cases, over a nine-month period 29 prenatal cases, 2 postpartum, 2 opted for abortion.

Concrete services, outreach, individual and family counseling, education, career guidance, psychological evaluations and therapy, health education, medical care, infant care education, parenting education, and referral services are offered to the adolescent by a multidiciplinary team. This team is comprised of a program director, full-time social worker, public health nurse and pediatrician and the obstetrician and the nursing staff at the hospital. We have also used a bilingual social worker, since up to the end of 1978, we have served ten Hispanic girls. Psychological services are contracted through the local mental health organization.

The social worker is the coordinating person to whom all team members relay information and plans. Working together, the team assesses each client individually and plans accordingly. The frequency of contact, the location and the content of sessions, is determined by evaluating each client, her level of functioning, her knowledge, and her special needs. The client's family and the putative father of the baby are included in the diagnostic evaluation, teaching, and counseling, whenever possible.

Referrals to the program are received from numerous sources, such as a local hospital, schools, community agencies, family members, former clients, and by adolescents themselves. Once referral is received, contact is made by the social worker or the public health nurse. The client's needs are assessed and planning is initiated in this entry level session. The social worker explores with the client all possible options available to her. They include, keeping the child, having an abortion, placing the child in foster care or adoption, etc. It is important that the client is aware of all options, so that the decisions she makes are informed, well-thought-out, and best suited for her. If a client chooses to have an abortion, arrangements are made at Englewood Hospital, the local abortion center, or through a private physician, or the County Hospital. Both pre- and postabortion counseling are offered to the client, along with family planning education.

For the adolescent who decides to continue the pregnancy, prenatal care is arranged immediately. Approximately 80 percent of our clients receive antepartum care at the local hospital. The public health nurse and social worker follow the client's prenatal care very closely. If, occasionally, a client is so fearful of the clinic, the social worker or nurse may go out to her home and accompany her to the first clinic visit. Prior to this visit, there is an in-depth discussion of the clinic routine and procedures, in an attempt to make this experience as nonthreatening as possible.

Our public health nurse attends the Obstetric Clinic weekly; she serves an advocacy, educational, and supportive role for our clients, especially for those who lack the ability to effectively handle and negotiate services from an institution such as the hospital. She is available to them to answer questions and explain reasons for various tests and procedures. She is able to speak to the doctor on a weekly basis and share our concerns and information about clients and their progress. There are periodic meetings between the doctor, nurse, social worker, and hospital social service department to review and evalute and to cooperatively plan for the continued care of the client. The importance of good nutrition and prenatal care are continually stressed by all team members and extensive teaching is conducted in these two areas to demonstrate how it relates to fetal growth and development.

Following delivery, the nurse or social worker visits the client in the hospital. During this visit, the team members confer with the hospital staff about the client's labor and delivery, the health status of the mother and baby, and the maternal/child interaction as observed by the nurses. Discharge planning is initiated at this point.

Once the young mother is home, a newborn visit is made to assess the infant, the mother/child relationship, and the mother's knowledge of infant care. During the postpartum period, frequent home visits are made and, any difficulties she is experiencing either in relation to her own health or in caring for the baby, are addressed. Prior to her six weeks' postpartum checkup, all methods of contraceptives are explored with the young mother and she is assisted in choosing the one which is most appropriate for her. Approximately 75 percent of our mothers are presently using the pill or IUD method of birth control. Initially, our clients have a number of misconceptions and fears about birth control devices, which we seek to help them discuss and understand. We found that contraceptives were not used by the majority of adolescents prior to the pregnancy and, if they were used at all, their use was not consistent.

After the delivery of the infant, the Health Department provides maternal and child health supervision. There are two well-child conferences held twice weekly and the public health nurse, who has had continuity of contact with the young person, is always present with the social worker/coordinator available on call.

A complete feeding history is taken by the nurse, a developmental evaluation is done each time the child is seen and much health teaching takes place before the pediatrician sees the infant. The pediatrician reinforces what the nurses have been saying to the mother about nutrition, child development, safety, etc. The children are seen every two months during the first year and, if the pediatrician identifies a problem with the mother or infant, the public health nurse or social worker does a home visit to ensure that all recommendations have been followed. At the present time, 72 percent of our young people in the program use the well-child conference and the remainder use private pediatricians. Wherever possible, the extended family is encouraged and invited in and if we anticipate or identify problems that they are creating, the nurse and social worker follow up with a home visit and attempt to involve the family in the teaching related to meeting the needs of the child and young mother.

Up to this point, 54 percent of our teenage parents are working and they have a positive attitude about work, 40 percent of our clients receive aid to dependent families and children. An additional 16 percent of the women are supported by their families and/or husbands; 20 percent of our clients are married. Many others still have a good relationship with the father of the baby, but do not feel that they are ready to enter into marriage, 44 percent of our clients have completed high school, having either received a regular high school degree or a G.E.D. diploma. Twelve young women are presently continuing their education above high school; six of whom are enrolled in college and six others in job or vocational training; 29 percent of our clients are currently high school students and 16 percent are enrolled in G.E.D. programs; 11 percent have dropped out of school altogether.

A great deal of time is spent with clients focusing on education, educational needs, and career goals. We are constantly encouraging them to remain in school and to consider careers that will enable them to support themselves and their children, working them away from public assistance or dependency on families. Our local school system has provided little encouragement and support to these young people and we have often found it necessary to assume the role of guidance counselor, to explore educational and vocational options. The school is also lax in following the girl's attendance and thus we find ourselves monitoring it closely and offering the girls as many supports as possible to move her back into the mainstream of school. We are concerned about those young people on home instruction, because we feel that it reinforces their isolation, depression, and loneliness, and we also feel that they are losing out on certain academic areas and often fall behind their regular grade level. The G.E.D. program that is available is essentially geared to adults and attendance is not monitored. Some of our clients need to be highly motivated to complete this program.

The unique feature of our program is the continuity of care provided to the young people, almost from the time that they are first brought to our attention. They are exposed to the same team of professionals, who become familiar with their problems and enables them to establish a trusting relationship with the service. The program also stresses comprehensive care, with special focus on effective communication strategies between agency personnel within a framework of nonpunitive attitudes and strong advocacy.

Our program has not been in existence long enough for a definitive evaluation of accomplishments, however, there are strong indications that it is having some success. Although we continue to face the problem of a large number of missed appointments, the young people continue to reach out whenever there is a crisis. They have also brought in friends and siblings to educational sessions and we are beginning to see a greater responsiveness from parents. The frequency of prenatal complications, such as toxemia of pregnancy and low birth weight, seem to be minimal and the rate of premature deliveries has not been a common occurrence. The description of the program this far may convey an impression that we have had few problems or drawbacks. We are facing our final year of funding and, up to this point, we have no indication that the program costs for the service will be absorbed by the city. We will continue to look for other funding sources, as we believe that this is a high-risk group of clients and much of our work is preventive.

From the outset, we faced the problems of dealing with community attitudes to a program offering services to "unwed" mothers. We were accused of throwing valuable tax dollars away on an undeserving group of sexually promiscuous adolescents. The civic leaders felt that the program should have been initiated by and paid for by our very costly public school system. They questioned the possibility of duplication of services and "passing the buck."

The minority community's attitude to teenage pregnancies is exemplified by a comment by Staples (1971) who maintains that within the black community, no child is "illegitimate." Ladner (1971), states that "although one might regret getting pregnant, there is an absence of long term overt shame. Stigmatization of the mother and child is not a serious problem." Our own experience bears this out.

We were under pressure in the past three years to prove the cost-effectiveness of the program, to demonstrate that comprehensive services to this group meant that more young people returned to school and were planning for a career or employment. Were we able to decrease the number of adolescent pregnancies? Are the young mothers and infants in a better state of health? Have we stirred people to provide more services for this underserved population? Our impressions from a close exposure to the program is that many gains have been made, but we need to develop a concise and sophisticated instrument to measure change. Any continuing effort, therefore, must include program evaluation and analysis.

Appropriately trained staff, whose attitudes and biases have to be scrutinized and who have some ability to establish trusting relationships with adolescents, are difficult to recruit. Attitudes towards unplanned, unwanted, and out-of-wedlock pregnancies, especially in this young population still raises a lot of feelings and reactions, even from professionally trained staff. This dynamic, coupled with the use of paraprofessional staff, initially presented problems. Lesser trained staff were more comfortable addressing concrete crises rather than exploring feelings, attitudes, and values. Their own anxiety was heightened when they did not deliver a tangible service. We have questioned the large number of missed appointments by clients in the early phases of the program, who may have wanted more emotional support than "tangibles." The quality and content of social data taken in this early phase often lacked dynamic insights which may have been important indicators of other problems in the adolescent's life. We found that experience, professional competence, an understanding, accepting attitude to young people were crucial prerequisites in our staff. Limited funds for services often predicated who we could afford to hire. We have leaned more and more in the direction of carefully selecting and seeking the best trained individuals for critical positions in the project, even at the cost of higher salaries.

A noteworthy achievement in our program has been the success we have had in working with the local hospital whose obstetrical nursing and social service staff have made the difference in the quality of care the adolescent mothers receive during the antepartum, labor, and delivery phase. Our continued advocacy for clients with other social agencies, such as County Welfare, Community Action Program, Vocational Services, etc., has enabled these agencies to understand the far-reaching problem the adolescent faces during this critical period. We have succeeded in raising the consciousness of the community and parents in particular, as to the extent of the problem of teenage pregnancy, so that it can no longer be ignored any more. We perceive a more supportive and understanding attitude from erstwhile critics in the town, who are beginning to believe that prevention of problem is the most constructive approach for the future.

We have not, however, made any serious impact on the local school system, which still chooses to adopt the "ostrich" attitude. There are no facilities to ensure the continuing education of pregnant teenagers, not to mention their social, emotional, and health needs.

We have to persist in our efforts to make this system more responsive to the needs of this group of young people. They must assume the responsibility for teaching reproductive facts and parenting before children make decisions that affect their entire life patterns. They will only start this when they recognize that there are sexually active youngsters in the school population. Schools must also be more informed about the availability of family planning services for sexually active teens. Approximately 75 percent of the young people served in our program reported long-standing problems at school, with little or no intervention. There is often a history of poor achievement, with no remedial supports whatsoever. There must be more efforts directed at administrative, teaching, and pupil service personnel to sensitize them and move them towards offering more creative services to pregnant teenagers, teenager parents, and teenagers at risk.

Our intervention strategies have taken into account the importance of the young person's immediate family, focusing on the girl's

mother as having the most important influence in the decision making process. In our counseling efforts, we have had to defend the
adolescent's right to develop decision making skills, while acknowledging the mother's values and opinions.

In our program, families have not been enthusiastic about getting involved. Some of this may be due to the nature of the town,
which is small and understandably there is concern about confidentiality and protection from censure and gossip.

Our outreach to young people involved extensive home visits
and, at some time or other, at least 80 percent of the families have
been reached. Many mothers clearly indicate their unwillingness to
be involved in any program of counseling for their daughters. There
is concern for the health of the young mother and her infant and
continuing education and employment are key issues. However, any
attempt to look more closely at the mother/daughter relationship is
immediately discouraged.

At least 70 percent of the girls reported poor relationships with
their mothers, which included rejection and uncaring attitudes about
their well being. This was clearly evident in our own observations of
interactions between mothers and daughters.

Initially, we were somewhat intimidated by the parental rejection of overtures made by us. We are renewing our efforts to establish
rapport with them and reviewing our strategies to reach them.

We have offered special groups for grandmothers and have
addressed their special needs as well. Bell (1975) observes that "in
the youth-oriented culture, that characterizes the American middle
class, the problems of the adolescent are often stressed to the point
of ignoring the personal problems of the parents." We have taken
cognizance of this factor and feel that any hope to understand the
phenomena of teenage pregnancy may rest on us being able to interpret the interaction between parents and children. Eleanor Wright
Smith (1975), very eloquently states: "The genesis in mothering is in
childhood when the girl's experience of mothering sets the pattern
for the future." During pregnancy, she relives and redefines herself
in her relationship to significant others and to her unborn child. A
supportive relationship with the mother at this time can increase the
young woman's confidence in herself and her ability to become a
mother.

In our experience with pregnant teens, we found that many of
their mothers were openly hostile and often punitive towards the
girls.

With the Hispanic youngsters that we served, we found that the hostility and rage of the mother and their fear of the father's reaction to the pregnancy, often hurled them into flight from the family. Fifty percent of them left home to live with distant relatives, friends, putting distance between them and their families. Most of their families provided little or no financial support during pregnancy. The other 50 percent were stampeded into an early and often disastrous marriage to save the family from disgrace.

We found in approximately 10 percent of our clients, some very supportive families, who cooperated with the various agencies and obviously wanted the best for the girls. They have followed through on recommendations and participated fully in planning for prenatal, delivery, and postpartum care. All these girls made a very satisfactory adjustment to the birth of the baby, either married or went on to complete their education, obtain vocational training, or got jobs. In the more disruptive families, the girls were faced with continuous conflict with parents, got into horrendous power struggles over money or care of the infant, and were surrounded constantly by crises and upheavals which negatively affected them and their infant. We were often witness to a range of mixed messages young people received from parents, which added to their confusion and seriously hampered planning efforts. In our counseling contacts with the family, our staff were forced into mediating roles with the youngsters to dilute the rage and frustration between them.

Ongoing work with families will require careful examination of the means to reach one or both parents, or any significant family member of the young parent. We view the period, during pregnancy and the time thereafter, as critical for the family, as much as for the young person. It is a time of crisis for everyone.

Where family supports fail, however, we may need to explore other sources of help for the young person. A recent program, funded by the Ford Foundation in Brooklyn, New York, pair single mothers in their twenties and thirties with adolescent mothers. The women help one another to find housing, jobs, babysitting services, continuing education, and advocacy with city agencies. They counsel teenage mothers on birth control devices and relationships with men, how to deal with young children, cultural enrichment, etc. This program is called "The Sisterhood of Black Single Mothers" and exemplifies the model of the extended family without ties of blood relationships. The older women effectively use their own life experiences in a positive manner to educate and improve the coping strategies of the adolescent mother. A major goal, they say, is to help the young person "survive" this critical period in her life with a form of external family-type support.

Locating substitutes for the family may be as important and as crucial as mobilizing health care for the physical well-being of the young person during pregnancy or ensuring that an adoptive family is available for her and her child after delivery.

We might want to pause for a moment to reflect on the experiences of our colleagues in the mental health field who have learned over the years that treating an individual in isolation and sending them back into the complex and chaotic world of an emotionally unstable and destructive family is like putting someone out to sea in a boat without a compass or means of finding their way back to shore again. None of us should assume that families are benign to their respective members. Assessing the strengths and weaknesses of the family initially, might be crucial information in planning overall care for the young person and her infant.

We have found in our experiences that not all families stand by their youngsters when they find out about the pregnancy and do not reassure her they will see her through this dilemma. A significant number of families have thrown the girls out and let them fend for themselves. A fortunate few find substitute families, willing to see them through this critical period, others reconcile with families before the actual delivery of the child and are supported through that painful phase. Providing comprehensive care, therefore, for teenage parents may involve an assertive outreach to contact families and to mobilize for families to come to us; we must go to them.

It is a known fact that severely pathologic families have a devasting effect on individual family members and most psychiatric agencies offering treatment to the individuals rarely fail to take into consideration the impact of this system on the individual psyche. In considering comprehensive services for the adolescent mother, one might start by viewing her within the framework of her family and her community. All efforts to address the problem should take into consideration how both these systems can help or hurt the young person in redirecting her back to functioning as a total person. The following are some case studies to demonstrate how families have affected individuals we have worked with.

Case Study I

M. R. was referred to our program at the age of 15, when she was five months pregnant. She came from a single parent home and her mother had been diagnosed as a paranoid schizophrenic. Her father had left the family several years previously and there were known psychiatric problems with two of her four siblings. Throughout her pregnancy, M. R. appealed to us to get her out of the family as her mother was actively delusional and was often very threatening to M. R. There were many nuclear family conferences and, on occasion, members of the extended family were brought in to support the young person. Although all family members agreed that the mother was a destructive influence in M. R.'s life and, on occasion, concurred with the home evaluation of the psychiatrist from the local mental health agency that the mother should be hospitalized, no one individual was able to carry this through. M. R.'s brothers struggled with their own guilt about "putting their mother away." Although they recognized the problems that M. R. was having and the potential danger to her child when it was born, they were unable to make a decision to remove the mother or to consent to M. R. being placed in a foster home with her infant.

M. R. and her infant continued to live within the framework of the family, but she is supported by a concerned guidance counselor in the Alternate School and she recognizes her own need for assistance and seeks it from all the social agencies who stand by helplessly watching this family drama. Prognosis for the emotional and physical well-being of the infant and its mother in this very pathologic family is highly questionable. However, no one agency has been able to provide strong advocacy for this youngster to remove her from the family, although one could make a case for child neglect in terms of her emotional well-being. We found that even the Division of Youth and Family Service were unwilling to stick their neck out on this young person's behalf. M. R. has demonstrated very good mothering skills, but, in addition to a psychiatrically ill mother, she also constantly has to contend with an older sister, who wants to take over her baby. The family has afforded her physical protection, but very little emotional support.

Case Study II

D. G. is an eighth grader, referred to us at 14, when she was six months pregnant. Her mother had been ill with a brain tumor for most of her life and her father had been the chief support for the entire family. Her father was very involved with D. G. and provided her with support throughout her pregnancy and so did her older siblings. There had never been a great deal of supervision of D. G.'s activities and her father felt that she had drifted into this relationship with the young man and there had been too many opportunities for her to get into trouble. The family openly discussed the options of foster care and adoption, but supported D. G. in keeping her child when she made this decision. Her father encouraged her to keep all appointments with our agency and the hospital and, at the time of labor and delivery, the whole family were concerned and involved with the young person. D. G. responded very well to counseling and education given by the team and made a good adjustment as a mother in caring for her child. She has since returned to school and intends to complete high school. She keeps appointments with the well-child conference and uses all our services appropriately as well. She does not see the father of her child any longer, but has other involvements with young men; she has appropriately sought out family planning advice and is using a birth control device. In spite of the absence of her own mother's involvement, D. G. was able to work through the problem of an unwanted, unplanned pregnancy and emerge as a young person, who had some potential to be a good mother herself. She is concerned about the future of her child and has expressed that she wants to be more of a mother to him. There were good social service supports from our agency and from the director of a teen program at Community House. There was, therefore, some mother substitutes for this young person from outside the family.

Case Study III

S. R. is a 19-year-old Hispanic high school graduate who did not go to college because of her pregnancy. She lived with an intact family and three sisters. She reported, however, a poor relationship with her parents, especially her mother, whom she described as cold and having no affection for her and she felt that she was treated differently from her other siblings. She also felt that the family were judgmental and particularly rejecting of her because of the pregnancy. She was a good student and well motivated about continuing education possibilities. There was some family pressure for her to marry the father of her infant and he did eventually offer, but she refused this because he had questioned whether he was the father of the child. S. R. was eager to get out and away from the family, but was able to look at the problems this would present for her, since she had no money of her own, nor a job. She was willing to remain with the family for a year and said that she wanted thereafter to be independent and to be able to raise her own child. She was not close to anyone in her family, except her younger sister and felt that nobody understood her. This is a Colombian family and S. R. had come to this country when she was 11. She, more than anyone in her family, had had extreme difficulty in making transcultural adjustment from a rural community in Colombia to living in an urban setting in this country. She also had difficulty in making an adjustment to the school. However, she has some clear goals for herself and her child and one year later she has a job and plans to go back to college. Although she remains with the family, they have in no way accepted her or her child born out out of wedlock and this is a problem she struggles with until such time as she is able to fend for herself.

References

Bell, R. R. *Marriage and the family.* Homewood, Ill.: Dorsey Press, 1975.

Bryan-Logan B. N., Dancy B. L. Unwed pregnant adolescents. Their mothers dilemma. *Nursing Clinics of North America,* 1974, *9*(1), 57–68.

Friedman, H. L. The mother-daughter relationships: Its potential in treatment of young unwed mothers *Social Casework,* 1966, *47,* 502–506.

Furstenberg, F. F., Jr. *Unplanned parenthood: The social consequences of teenage childbearing.* New York: Free Press, 1976.

John, A. B. Adolescent-parents: A special case of the unplanned family. *The Family Coordinator,* 1978, *27.*

Ladner, J. *Tommorow's tomorrow.* New York: Anchor, 1971.

Smith, E. W. The role of the grandmother in adolescent pregnancy and parenting. *The Journal of School Health,* 1975, *45.*

Staples, R. The myth of the black matriarch. In R. Staples (Ed.). *The black family: Essay and studies.* Belmont, Ca.: Wadsworth, 1971.

Chapter 21

PREGNANCY AND DRINKING

Lucy Barry Robe

Despite all the medical reports about fetal alcohol syndrome and the scientific accounts of alcohol's toxicity to the unborn baby, most women still say, "That's fascinating, but I'm not an alcoholic. So how much drinking is safe for *me* during pregnancy?"

How Much Drinking is Safe During Pregnancy?

No one knows how much alcohol is acceptable for a pregnant woman yet. The research, which is in its infancy, is particularly tricky on a socially accepted drug like alcohol. But maybe we can help women of childbearing age to use their heads in the interim and make wise personal choices about drinking during pregnancy. An example follows.

Susie's pregnant; she learns that tetracycline stains both sets of an unborn baby's teeth (and that's the only *known* toxic effect of tetracycline during pregnancy). Does Susie still insist on taking this antibiotic? No. Why? Because Susie doesn't go to antibiotic parties, or have a couple of capsules of tetracycline before dinner with her husband to relax. Susie can select a different antibiotic if she gets flu and needs medication.

Does Susie fight the fact that she can't safely have a German measles vaccination? Of course not, for rubella vaccine, like tetracycline, is not a recreational drug. Furthermore, both Susie and her doctor know that rubella vaccine produces severe birth defects.

However, does Susie know that rubella vaccine affects only 3 percent of unborn babies, while nearly *half* of all unborn babies are affected in some way by their mothers' heavy drinking during pregnancy?

When the horrors of thalidomide were unveiled in the early 1960s, all women of childbearing age recoiled from this popular tranquilizer because about 8,000 babies worldwide were born with missing arms or legs. Yet up to 10,000 babies are born with full-blown fetal alcohol syndrome every year in the United States alone, and up to 25,000 per year have partial symptoms.

So how much drinking is safe during pregnancy?

If you knew that just a few thalidomide pills taken on a certain weekend would produce a baby with no arms, would you risk taking *half* a thalidomide that weekend? Would you figure that at worst your baby might "only" lack a couple of fingers as a result? Would those thalidomide pills *really* be that important to you during pregnancy?

MODERATE DRINKING

In the brief period since fetal alcohol syndrome was discovered six years ago, several studies have tested the effects of moderate drinking during pregnancy. Moderate drinking in the scientific sense usually means 2 to 4 drinks a day, including wine and beer.

Two drinks a day early in pregnancy decreases an unborn baby's birthweight by an average of one-fifth of a pound; two drinks a day in late pregnancy decreases birthweight by an average one-third of a pound. This may seem unimportant, but every ounce is critical if a baby is born prematurely. Also, decreased birthweight can be a warning signal of other things being wrong with a baby.

Another study showed three drinks a day resulting in lowered birthweight as well as lowered placental weight and increased risk of stillbirth, especially from abruptio placenta.

Newborns of moderate drinkers apparently feature four distinct behaviors: tremoring, positioning head to left (this indicates poor developmental progress), keeping eyes open more than normal, and touching hand to face more than normal. Dr. David W. Smith of the University of Washington, who discovered fetal alcohol syndrome with Dr. Kenneth Jones, says:

> A woman herself is a good barometer of how alcohol is affecting the fetus. If she's feeling how much she's had to drink, then the fetus is, too. It hits the baby at the same level. I'd like to see mothering start right from conception, not just from birth.

BINGE DRINKING

An average-sized woman takes about one hour to metabolize one bar shot of liquor, one glass of wine, or one can of beer. If she drinks faster than this, the excess remains in both her system and that of her unborn baby, diffusing in every cell of their bodies. An unborn baby's liver is not yet developed, thus alcohol behaves much like a chemical hammer.

During the first trimester, when the brain and all other organs are forming, alcohol stunts prenatal growth. If a pregnant woman attends a weekend festivity, such as a family wedding, house party, or school reunion, it is easy to see how cocktails and wine with every meal, plus a few drinks in between, would be more than she could normally metabolize. She could go on a so-called binge before she even knew she was pregnant.

Bearing in mind that two thalidomide pills a day taken in a specific 5-day period (days 26 to 30 of development) could result in a baby with no arms, we can say that until we know exactly when and how alcohol affects unborn babies any so-called binge drinking could be extremely risky during pregnancy.

HYPERACTIVITY AND OTHER RESULTS OF ALCOHOL

Several studies have shown a connection between maternal drinking during pregnancy and hyperactivity in the offspring of humans as well as animals.

Besides being mentally retarded, most children with full-blown fetal alcohol syndrome are hyperactive. They also have delayed gross motor development and poor fine motor control, learning and behavior problems in school, and are clinically uninhibited (i.e., no stranger anxiety; no intimidation).

In addition, children with fetal alcohol syndrome remain small in childhood. Their parents cannot "fatten them up"; their arms and legs are markedly skinny compared to those of their sisters and brothers.

Dr. Stanley Gitlow of New York's Mount Sinai School of Medicine feels from clinical observations that the most insidious effects of drinking alcohol during pregnancy are the subtle ones. "I see too many children of heavy drinkers with lowered intelligence and hyperactivity," says Dr. Gitlow. "These kids don't necessarily have the facial characteristics or organic problems that identify full-blown fetal alcohol syndrome."

The former president of the American Medical Society on Alcoholism, Gitlow, who coined the term *sedativism,* also says that if alcohol were discovered in a laboratory tomorrow, this drug would require a doctor's prescription, for alcohol has all the properties of an addictive, prescription drug. However, the Food and Drug Administration (FDA) might not give alcohol safety clearance for use by the public, since it is so obviously toxic to unborn babies. The FDA would certainly require clear warnings on alcohol to pregnant women.

Unfortunately, however, the FDA does not have jurisdiction over alcohol, which is controlled by the Bureau of Alcohol, Tobacco and Firearms (BATF). When the FDA recently suggested that warning labels be put on bottles to caution pregnant women that alcohol may be hazardous to their unborn babies, the BATF decided that a public education campaign should come first. The BATF wants more specific evidence that moderate drinking can harm an unborn baby, and that warning labels would be an effective deterrent to drinking during pregnancy. The BATF will conduct its campaign throughout 1979, and will then examine the possibility of a warning label again.

Fetal alcohol syndrome is the number one preventable cause of mental retardation today. Let us all help prevent it any way that we can.

Chapter 22

PROSTITUTION AND SEXUAL VIOLENCE

Jennifer James

This workshop examines two major categories of institutional response to the sexuality of women: women as criminals, primarily prostitution, and women as the victims of sexual crimes. A substantial number of women will encounter the institutional bias of the first; all women will at some point face the fear of or experience the second. Because of their utility as classic examples of societal responses to female sexuality in contrast to male, prostitution and juvenile promiscuity are discussed at length. Sexual crimes against women, such as rape, are also presented as classic victim situations where the double standard prevails, a standard that prescribes different sets of acceptable sexual behavior for men and women.

WOMEN AND CRIME

The involvement of women in criminal activity has been steadily growing since the 1950s. Their activities still include the stereotypic

Portions of this presentation have been published in Long Laws, J., & Schwartz, P. (eds.). *Sexual Scripts: The Social Construction of Female Sexuality.* Pepper Schwartz, Dryder Press 1977 "women's crimes" of prostitution, shoplifting, and larceny that can be committed in the context of "normal" female behavior and fit into the traditional perception of woman as a sexual object and a shopper. Larceny has been defined in some legal statutes as "the deceptive use of the feminine role" because charm may be used to steal.

Prostitution and juvenile promiscuity are uniquely labeled as female crimes because they cannot, according to many state laws, be committed by males. The threat to society inherent in these crimes is the threat of loss of control over female sexuality, not any actual damage to victims or property. The female body is a social resource because of her reproductive capacity and her position as a possession, first of father and then husband. As in the abortion arguments, the female is not considered by many to have the same personal ownership of her body as the male. Controlling her access to sexual intercourse, whether for commercial or pleasurable motivations, is considered appropriate by our society. Public law and enforcement agencies are the guardians of home, family, legitimacy, and the moral order. Prostitution and early trespass of sexual taboos by females are therefore condemned and controlled by them.

PROSTITUTION

The most common crime cited for adult women is prostitution. There are prostitutes in every American city of any size and the profession exists under a variety of guises and in numerous styles. The basis for the existence of prostitution is our social concept that male sexual energy requires an outlet beyond the inclinations of "good" women. The traditional view of the natural promiscuity of men still prevails and stimulates the traditional need for a pool of "loose" women to meet these sexual needs. The virginity cult of the Judeo-Christian tradition has always supported a spectrum of female sexual behavior with the whore at one end and the madonna at the other. Men are to avoid corrupting good women because of their importance to the social order as wives and mothers. A population of loose women is then necessary to protect good women because of their importance to the social order as wives and mothers. A population of loose women is then necessary to protect good women from the "normal" impulses of men.

Prostitutes work on the streets picking up passers-by and out of cars that circle various city blocks looking for customers. They work as dancers, body painters, maids, masseuses, and magazine sales-women. Prostitutes also work as models, strippers, stag-show danc-ers and waitresses, sense awareness counselors, and sexual therapists, any job that puts them in contact with potential customers, especially if the work provides easy opportunities for playing the sexual object and thus providing the lure. They work on call for hotels, through an answering or other referral service and follow conventions across the country. Some women work out of airport lounges, some migrant labor camps, and others on retainers to large corporations with clients to entertain. In a few rural areas in the United States, notably Nevada, houses of prostitution are legal or tolerated by local officials. The possibilities for commercialized sexual exchanges are almost endless and shift to meet the customer demand and avoid the law.

A complete social definition of prostitution would be *any sexual exchange where the reward is neither sexual nor affectional.* Women prostitute themselves when they exchange access to their body for material gain (clothes, apartment, promotion, entertainment) and in doing so use their bodies as a commodity. Women learn at an early age in our society the rewards of flirting. It may begin with learning to wink or sit on a man's lap, and extends through the push to be popular in high school. The idea conveyed is to be sexy but not cheap, an attractive package but not to be touched. Female attrac-tiveness becomes a key to success in high school with peers, as cheerleader, junior prom queen, as a promising date. Girls learn very quickly the short-term rewards of the games recommended by the proponents of "fascinating womenhood." The use of their sexual-ity to obtain favors and eventually to secure support is a part of the social interaction patterns females are taught. The ideal is to save enough of "it" for the right man or moment because other-wise the female devalues her most saleable commodity, that is, her sexuality.

A legal definition of prostitution is more narrow. It involves four main reflections of social concern: *cash, promiscuity, relationship to sexual partner, and subtlety.* The legal statutes refer to women who engage in sex for money or loiter with this intent. A woman is relatively safe making exchanges for commodities other than cash. Other exchanges such as an opportunity to become a model or an evening of entertainment cannot be so easily recognized. Gifts from sexual partners leave more room for the assumption of affection and love. Affection as the stimulator of sexual exchange is acceptable for women and is, in fact, one of the most common rationalizations for first sexual experiences. Cash represents a nonemotional commercial exchange that society cannot modify to fit the acceptable limitations on the permitting of sexual access by women.

Promiscuity is an important second aspect of the legal definition. A woman is safe, i.e., acceptable, if only a few men are involved or if she knows them well and they are therefore not strangers. She is not violating extensively the appropriate social construction of reality for women because the possibility of appropriate motivations, i.e., love, still exists. In addition, her self-identification can remain more of "party girl" than prostitute. The practical aspects of avoidance of the appearance of promiscuity or indiscriminate sexual exchange are also important. She will be less obvious to the public officials whose purpose is to control such behavior. A few men/customers will not be noticed and if they are known to her then they are not vice squad officers or agents.

A prostitute is safe violating the first three aspects of legal concern if she carefully accedes to the fourth: *subtlety*. The key to understanding prostitution is that the only women usually arrested are those who are overt in the management of their profession, that is, streetwalkers. Prostitutes who are subtle and conform to more traditional female behavior, that is, call girls, are rarely arrested. Streetwalkers work alone on the streets late at night. This is automatically a signal that they are behaving in an inappropriate manner for women. Good women do not go out unescorted at night or walk the streets alone. The other attributes of unsubtle prostitution provide the same comparison with good women: flashy clothes, make-up, aggressive approaches toward male passers-by, and frankly sexual verbal exchanges. The streetwalker is clearly offering herself as a commodity for sale and essentially forcing the hand of public agencies who claim they are required by the community to enforce appropriate moral standards. The concern of society reflected in the enforcement of the law is that sex for sale be invisible, or nearly so. The most noticeable as a social problem are therefore the most flagrant, that is, the streetwalkers.

All forms of prostitution in the United States are illegal with the exception of some rural counties in Nevada. F.B.I. arrest figures list 34,226 women arrested for prostitution in 1973 (Uniform Crime Reports, 1974). The vast majority of these arrests are for open solicitation: women who are obviously engaging in sexual services for money in a promiscuous and explicit manner. Attempts are occasionally made to arrest women who work in houses or massage and sauna parlors, but arrest figures of these women are less than 5 percent of the total. Their prostitution is at least partially hidden by the offering of other more legitimate services.

Violations of the prostitution statutes account for approximately 30 percent of most women's jail populations. Convicted prostitutes serve long jail sentences compared to other misdemeanants, such as shoplifters, or those involved in larceny or assault. The judicial attitude represented by these sentencing patterns has no justification with reference to the traditional crime concerns of danger to person or property loss. The apparent explanation is again the punishment of behavior in women that is outside traditional norms and therefore a threat to social order. The importance of controlling such behavior, because of the powerful nature of the sex drive, has always provided the justification for excessive punishment. Sexual immorality has traditionally been considered a greater threat to American social order than violence or theft.

The sentencing and imprisonment statistics support this concentration on female sexual morality. It has been reported that 70 percent of the women who are now inmates in American prisons were initially arrested for prostitution, indicating its possible importance as a labeling device and the jail experience as an introduction to other crimes. This adds up not only to a significant impact on the lives of individual women but a staggering outlay of time and money by police, court, and corrections officials.

The control of overt prostitution is achieved in the United States through two main types of laws: loitering with the intent to commit an act of prostitution, and offering and agreeing to an act of prostitution. The most common enforcement procedures involve the use of police officers as decoys. The officer behaves as he assumes a customer would behave, and when approached by a suspected prostitute elicits evidence of intent. The prostitute is arrested if she mentions money and sexual service in her verbal exchange with the officer. These arrest techniques frequently involve the officer in the possibility of entrapment and questionable sexual exchanges. Some jurisdictions use civilian agents who complete acts of sexual intercourse before the arrest is made. They view themselves as protecting society by committing immoral acts for moral reasons. The use of female agents to solicit and arrest customers is rare because it requires a violation of appropriate behavior for women and an unfair use of female sexuality to entrap men. In most states customers are rarely, if ever, arrested. A woman who has once been convicted of offering and agreeing, regardless of the circumstances, is subject to future arrests under loitering statutes as a "known prostitute." (A "known prostitute" is a woman who has been convicted of an act of prostitution within the past year.) If she is seen in an area "known to be inhabited by prostitutes" she may also be arrested for loitering. Loitering is a statute frequently used by enforcement agencies to control individuals labeled as deviants.

Prostitutes once arrested usually plead guilty because they cannot afford bail, usually have inadequate legal representation and are aware of the bias of the judge and are then subject to sentences ranging from 30 to 180 days in jail. Prostitutes who can afford good attorneys plead not guilty and are less likely to serve time because juries are reluctant to convict when questionable police tactics are revealed in court. There are variations in enforcement pressure from one locale to the next depending on the resources of a particular police department and the political pressure to "crack down on" or tolerate street solicitation.

Male homosexual prostitutes are arrested in many cities under the same procedures applied to females. The percentage of male arrests is, however, low. It has been increasing recently in some cities because of complaints and law suits by equal rights advocates. The arrest of males has been traditionally negligible because of societal tolerance to male sexual activity regardless of its overtness or commercial intent. In some states where the Equal Rights Amendment has not passed, only women can be found guilty of prostitution even when homosexual males are providing the same service. The author was in the booking area of a jail two years ago when a transvestite was brought in and charged with prostitution. The arresting officer had assumed the offender was a female. Later, when the jail matron pointed out that the offender was a male he was released.

Prostitution is defined as a problem by three basic groups: 1) law enforcement agencies, 2) public health agencies, and 3) social and moral traditionalists. Police departments define it as a problem because of the associated crime they say accompanies the street environment generated by the presence of prostitutes. Larceny, robbery, assault, and narcotics addiction are cited as crimes that are bred in the environment of prostitution. The causal relationship, however, has not been established and, in fact, associated crimes are not an issue where prostitution is legal. Local level public health officials, despite little evidence to support their views, suspect prostitution as the cause of rising venereal disease statistics. They desire either eradication or strict regulation with health inspections. The social and moral traditionalists are concerned about the prostitute as victim. The women, they state, are degraded, exploited, and abused by business and the men (i.e., pimps) behind it. The total elimination of prostitution is the only solution that will protect women from this life and society from this type of women. The moralists also take a religious tack defining promiscuity as a sin and therefore prostitution as a contributor to the moral decay of American society. Feminists are often caught between opposing views of the prostitute. Some maintain that prostitution represents the ultimate degradation of women because of its offering of her body as a commercial object. Others state unequivocally that the prostitute is the only "honest woman," a heroine who recognizes the sexual object reality of women in our society and makes sure she gets a fair and definite exchange for her labor.

Street solicitation is defined as a particular problem by the first three reform groups because of its obviousness and also by others who cannot be categorized as police, public health, or moralists. Some people object to being exposed to activities in the street although they would tolerate the activity if it were private. They find women lounging on street corners offensive, much as they do public drunks. The important issue seems to be their desire to avoid exposure to such obvious sexual activity unless they are seeking it themselves. Businessmen feel it chases away clientele, parents want to shield their children, and passers-by do not want to be subjected to sexual suggestion by glance or comment from a prostitute. This portion of the American public would tolerate prostitution as long as it was invisible.

The clinical and academic definitions of prostitution as a problem historically stem from the concept previously discussed of female "promiscuity" as deviant behavior. Sexual promiscuity in exchange for money is a deviant response to the ascribed role for women of chastity and sex as permissible only in the context of love and marriage. Commercialized sex is a threat to a social structure that links sexual activity to the stable relationship of marriage. Unmarried women supporting themselves as prostitutes violate not only the taboos of fornication and adultery, but the sexual double standard of sexual behavior. They present a threat to married women because they offer sexual service without responsibility and to the traditional control society has exercised over female sexuality.

The research available on prostitution does not discuss it in this context of male-female sex-role behavior. Instead, research into the causes of prostitution has concentrated on individual pathology rather than social institutions. The issue is why a particular woman chooses to prostitute instead of an examination of the reasons for the existence of the profession. Unfortunately many of the articles on prostitution draw conclusions from small, nonrandom samples. For example, Winick and Kinsie in their book *The Lively Commerce* (1971) allude to thousands of interviews with prostitutes that turn out to be interviews they conducted with police and probation officers who had, in turn, had the original contact with prostitutes.

A variety of characterizations of the prostitute are presented depending on the bias of the researcher and the circumstances of the population studied. Most of the research has been done by men whose view of female sexuality is frequently less objective than that of female researchers. Theodore Rubin (1961) found their early childhood experience deplorable because of significant material and emotional deprivation. He interviewed women in jail. Harold Greenwald's (1958) study of call girls reported a 75 percent incidence of broken homes but he only interviewed women who were his patients. Prostitutes are stereotyped by psychotherapists as lacking self-esteem, hostile toward males, unconsciously homosexual, narcissistic, rebelling against inadequate fathers, anxious, frigid, showing poor impulse control, morbidly dependent, and mentally defective (Caprio, 1963; Choisy, 1965; Deutsch, 1965; Glover, 1960; Kemp, 1936; Rubin, 1961; Segal, 1963). Yet prostitutes look no different from other women, they have no unusual physical characteristics, and they include the full range of intelligence (James, 1976). Other women who combine various aspects of the personality problems listed by therapists do not become prostitutes.

Surveys of prostitute populations involving larger, random samples under more carefully controlled circumstances provide less evidence of deviance from standard norms. The average age of the streetwalkers interviewed in a West Coast survey was 22.6. Of these women, 56.3 percent were black, 36.6 percent were white, and 7.0 percent were mixed between Indian, Asian, and Chicano (James, 1972). The high percentage of black women is an indication of their tendency to work on the streets more often than white women. This is a combination of street knowledge acquired while growing up in inner city ghettos, economic necessity, and the racism that blocks their access to other kinds of prostitution. The educational achievement level was 11.4, comparing favorably with basic census averages. Most prostitutes have held jobs in other areas. With the exception of addicts, they have access to other occupations but state they prefer the financial and working conditions on the street.

Reasons for Becoming a Prostitute

A summary of articles on prostitution indicates that the need for money or the desire for material wealth is the most common reward. Prostitution is viewed by many women as a lucrative profession. Little training or preparation is required, the equipment is their own, and customers are everywhere. The dream of success as a hooker is strong for women who see few other possibilities. Prostitutes at the top of the economic ladder can make between $50,000 and $75,000 a year. There are not many occupations easily open to women that can compare. Few prostitutes actually make it into the upper income brackets, but the possibility is a strong motivater.

The need for money is a more commonly cited factor than the desire for wealth. Welfare women prostitute to supplement their income; addicts to support their habits. Prostitution is the most obvious source of fast money for a woman who needs a hit of heroin or has bills to pay. Black women say it is one of the few nonmenial occupations open to them, a different kind of domestic labor. It is possible to make $100 a night working the street, which is good money compared to other available options as clerks, typists, or pressers in a dry-cleaning establishment. Women's salaries are very low compared to men's and prostitution is viewed by some women as a viable equalizer.

Working conditions are also a part of the economic factor. The negatives of the profession are publicized: jail, beatings, drugs, self-respect. The positives the women mention include choosing your own hours, no time clocks, wearing beautiful clothes, being desirable and saleable, choosing what to do and when, travel and easy work that is seldom boring. The attitude is often that their sexuality can provide them with money that in turn provides freedom. Streetwalkers say they would never work in a brothel because of the loss of independence; they could not choose their hours or their customers. Women who work Nevada houses like being able to lounge around looking beautiful. There are many working styles to choose from. The classic statement is "I'm getting paid for what I used to give away." The problem of separating emotional involvement from sexual activity is described as a separation of business and pleasure. Once characterized as a "loose" woman under noncommercial circumstance, the movement towards commercialized sex can be justified as the easiest means of support.

Some research sources identify certain occupations as leading women into prostitution. Cocktail waitresses, magazine saleswomen, go-go dancers, masseuse, and modeling are all occupations where women may be offered tips or sales if they will just give the customer a little more—the traditional use of feminine seductiveness. The cocktail waitress may be already selling her appearance in a "bunny" costume and the tip being offered may equal the money she makes in an eight-hour shift. Occupations that depend on female attractiveness may blend into female sexuality as the commodity. There may be a slow movement from tips received for flirting to direct payment for sexual services. Adventure is also cited as a lure. Prostitution can be exciting and adventurous as well as degrading and dangerous. Women who work the streets move into an environment usually reserved for men: they are unescorted, on the street after dark, and they can take care of themselves. There is adventure in the act of strolling the streets at night in order to attract men. Some women talk about the pleasure inherent in having a man desire them, willing to pay well for access to their bodies. The buyer-seller exchange, in many instances, places the women in a dominant position; the customer is vulnerable to her comments about his sexuality. The customer is revealing himself to a professional, an experienced woman who has seen and been with many men. Her look of disdain or murmurings of pleasure can make the difference between his feelings of safety as a man/lover or failure. The prostitute who supports a man also talks about the domination in her provision of his support. The prostitute may feel a sense of control as the wage earner.

Prostitutes also travel, which provide feelings of independence and adventure. Some move up and down the West or East Coast, others all over the United States. A prostitute who is intelligent and knows how to find customers and protect herself from the police can travel anywhere in the world and pay her way. Streetwalkers are not as likely to work outside the United States as call girls but many have been interviewed who have traveled to Alaska, Hawaii, the Bahamas, Puerto Rico, and Canada from their home base in Washington State (James, 1972).

Adventure also has a component that overlaps with the category of desire for social contacts and marriage. Some prostitutes believe they meet many more exciting, wealthy, higher status males than "straight" women have the opportunity to meet. They feel the option is always open for converting a customer into a boyfriend. The chance to marry well is not an infrequent fantasy of prostitutes, although it rarely happens. The belief is that men like to save (i.e., reform) women. The romantic literature suggests either that marrying a prostitute proves the man is strong enough to please her sexually or that prostitutes make good, faithful wives once rescued. A "bad" woman converted to a "good" woman has made an informed choice where a good woman has had no experience.

Research conducted by the author with streetwalkers supports these four areas of motivation but places strong emphasis on a fifth: early life experiences (James, 1972). Women who are raised in an environment where prostitution is a daily fact of life outside their front doors are more likely to see it as a possible occupation. Many prostitutes reported a relative (mother, sister, aunt) who was or had been part of the business. Their models of appropriate female sexual behavior include prostitution in contrast to the models set for most young women. Another key area of early life experience is institutionalization. Young girls who are sent to girls' homes or youth centers because they become dependents of the state, incorrigible, or run away from home are frequent recruits for prostitution. In an initial survey of 72 prostitutes, 18.2 percent had been institutionalized as juveniles (James, 1972). The connections between institutions and prostitution fall into two patterns: exposure to information about prostitution from experienced inmates and recruitment by inmates who work for a pimp. Knowledge of prostitution creates curiosity, admiration of the negative status of juvenile prostitutes, and a desire for the independence that can be gained if a girl can support herself. Juvenile prostitutes seem tough and worldly to other inmates and the ability to earn money is envied. Many juvenile runaways see prostitution as their only source of income and money as the only way to solve their problem of dependence until they are 18. They have already been labeled as "bad girls" by the institutionalization process and so feel they have little to lose if they shift further into the negative female image of the whore. Joining an existing group of prostitutes is seen as a way of preventing reinstitutionalization because of the protective solidarity of the "fast life." The pimp in charge will take care of them in exchange for their earnings as a prostitute. They accept the pimp as necessary to survive as a new prostitute and reconcile their dependence on him by the fact that they choose to be with him.

The persuasiveness of pimps is the last factor cited wiht any frequency in the literature. Pimps appeal to the traditional female dependence on strong male figures and the desire to be "somebody's woman." Some women begin working as prostitutes at the suggestion of their boyfriends, husbands, or a man they've only recently met. The persuasion is usually psychological, rarely, at least in recent decades, physical (James, 1974). Detailed descriptions of the interaction between pimp and prostitute produce a picture of a relationship that is little more than an exaggeration of the stereotyped male-female relationship in the larger society. Levels of love, brutality, and exploitation vary but the basic needs are similar. Any analysis of a prostitute's preference for working with a pimp is discussed later in this article. It can be understood by viewing it somewhat like marriages, whether abusive or not, as an individual woman's choice of companion.

There is no single answer to anyone's choice of profession, whether the activity is considered deviant or normal. The *primary* cause of women becoming prostitutes is the supply and demand equation that grows out of the sexual socialization process. Some men are socialized to view sex as a commodity that can be purchased. Quantity has traditionally had a higher value than quality of relationship in male reports of sexual encounters. Women who are socialized to view themselves as sexual objects may violate the ideal of the subtle sell for approved commodities and accept money.

The *secondary* causes of women becoming prostitutes are those that lead her to make the shift from subtle sexual sale to overt prostitution. These include abusive family circumstances, such as incest and divorce, which lessen the female's feeling that she can be a good girl and therefore undermines her sexual self-respect. Institutionalization that labels them as "deviant," and economic stress engendered by the need to support children and addiction, and a desire for a better standard of living are causes of prostitution. Early reinforcement for sexual appearance and pressures from male friends can also be significant. Girls who are popular in high school because they are well developed or easy may wander into more overt sexual exchange. These secondary causes facilitate the gradual or sudden development necessary for an individual's shift to overt prostitution.

The wider social factor of female sexuality as a commodity is based on two cultural aspects of sexuality: the first is the traditional view that men are promiscuous and the second is the consequent necessity of catering to their basic needs. Although we have no scientific research that supports these traditional attitudes about male sex drive, they are pervasive in the early literature of this century. Men patronize prostitutes because man is by nature polygamous, the "primitive sex instinct is one of the variety of promiscuity" (Robinson, 1929), or "Prostitution as we know it today is the result of Christian virtue, which would have man a perfect being, and of that animal instinct which drags him into the woman's arms (Mantagazza, 1932). These attitudes toward man's sexual nature, though more subtly expressed, are still current. Such values lead into the second traditional viewpoint—the importance of marriage as a social and economic matter. Men are to avoid other men's wives in order to guard against the disrupting nature of adultery. Prostitution is therefore a "societal evil," a threat to both family and female role traditions. The contradiction is in the accompanying view that a population of loose women is necessary to protect good women from the "normal" impulses of men.

The Customer

The male customer is the invisible partner in both professional and media articles on prostitution. He is virtually ignored because his actions are congruent with our expectations about male sexuality and he is therefore not given a criminal identify.

The Kinsey survey of sexuality in the human male provides the most comprehensive review of intercourse with prostitutes. That survey found that about 69 percent of the total white male sample in their population ultimately had some experience with prostitutes (Kinsey, 1948:597). Not more than 15 to 20 percent of these had regular intercourse with prostitutes. Young males were only infrequently represented in this group, with the majority of customers in the 37 to 40 age range. Later studies have shifted the age range upward into the forties (James, 1972; Stein, 1974). Kinsey further broke down his data on contact with prostitutes to an estimate of 3,190 contacts per week in a town of 100,000 inhabitants (Kinsey, 1948:603).

The only available full discussion of the customers of prostitutes is *Lovers, Friends and Slaves* by Martha Stein (1974). Her approach was primarily observation based on her training in social work, and her book is the first effort to describe the men who visit primarily upper class call girls. Stein outlines categories of customers to clarify her description of the male needs serviced by prostitutes. Those categories include: opportunists, fraternizers, promoters, adventurers, lovers, friends, slaves, guardians, and juveniles.

As this review indicates, articles on clients are limited. The main interest of most of the researchers has focused on the basic fact that men visit prostitutes and on the needs, accepted as falling within the normal range, that their visits fulfill. The customer as a social problem escapes examination.

The needs of customers, as presented in the literature, are surprisingly uniform throughout the literature. They are categorized in general, including Stein's types, as travelers, social, disabled, special, impotent, homosexual, therapist, quantity, variety, uninvolved, and lonely. The traveler is the classic salesman, conventioneer, or serviceman who finds himself away from home and desirous of sexual contact. The social customer desires to share his sexual experiences of his night out on the town with a group of friends. The disabled are handicapped individuals, such as paraplegics, who feel a professional is either more appropriate or their only opportunity. Men classified as "specials" go to prostitutes because their sexual needs might be classified as perverted by other women. The impotent male seeks sexual stimulation and/or therapy. The homosexual customer seeks male prostitutes. Customers whose needs come under therapy often just want someone to talk with about personal problems. The quantity need and the variety need are variations on the theme of potency achieved through numbers of sexual contacts and the desire for different types of women as partners. The uninvolved customer desires sex without the potential problems of pregnancy, personal emotion, or courting. The final category, loneliness, overlaps in some areas, as do others, but basically refers to individuals who find themselves in need of human contact.

The categories used by these authors to describe customers are clearly diverse yet some overlap when reviewing in depth the description of the customer and what he is seeking. Variety and ability to avoid involvement are the most frequently cited needs. It is expressed through the *quantity* ethic. The apparent object is the seduction of many women to provide points for potency. It begins in adolescent bull sessions reinforced by the commercialization in the media of many women chasing one man. Seduction can be a long, drawn-out affair. The professional woman provides a short cut. The exchange of cash on a direct basis eliminates the slower transaction of dinners, entertainment, and the development of rapport. One can have hundreds of women in the time it used to take for ten; and the actual cash outlay, deleting money as time, may be the same. The quantity is guaranteed; the score is easy to predict.

Quantity may also be a value in a second expressed need, the desire for *variety*. If variety is the stimulant sexually, the same factors of exchange involved in quantity apply. Some men have stereotypes of sexual attractiveness (large breasts, blond hair, satin pants) that the variety of prostitutes available can fulfill. Customers who prefer dark women as the sultry whore can hire black prostitutes to fill out needs not satisfiable in their social circle. The advertising media is saturated with images of the ideal sexual partner, yet few men have access to women who meet that fantasy. Cultural stereotypes often provide a "forbidden fruit" fantasy that only the prostitute can fulfill without the threat of repercussions. The cultural concept of the sensuous woman is exploited by the prostitutes who seek to dress, talk, walk, and perform like the fantasy that reinforces the whore-madonna split.

Other prostitutes may appeal to fantasies the customer may feel are perverse. A penchant for the very young or very old that is in conflict with the customer's place in social reality, a desire for obesity, a preference for long, flowing hair; these varieties of the female sex object are available on the street, in the studio, or through the phone business. Prostitutes learn very quickly to exchange customers to keep them from becoming bored and leaving on their own. On the street they will pass him to a friend or stable sister expecting a return exchange. (A stable sister is a prostitute who shares the same pimp with one or more other prostitutes.) In a phone system, the trades will be kept within a known circle of women until the customer's desire for variety takes him to another circle. Many women will try to vary their own art to keep a customer intrigued. Many nonprofessional women try the same attempts at variation with clothing and behavior to continue to attract their lifetime customer.

Variety is also an issue in the sexual service performed within the context of the exchange. Many men say they seek prostitutes because of sexual variation they cannot fulfill at home or elsewhere. The separation of women into good and bad in adolescence and by sexual reputation contributes heavily to the issue of sexual variety. There are taboos against discussing or engaging in certain sexual activities with good women, i.e., wives. Homemakers are de-sexualized by the sexual stereotypes and, again, the media images. Home becomes an inappropriate location for sexual variety and special activities. Variety may express itself in a desire for different positions, anal intercourse, cunnilingus, the use of oils, lotions, liquors, or tone of voice, body language, and direction of events. The professional woman provides an infinite variety of possibilities that can be granted on request or introduced through experience. The customer ends up with a full set of choices in contrast to the limitations of less experienced women.

The customer categories include men who want release of sexual tension without the problems of *involvement* in a relationship with a woman. He doesn't want the trouble of an affair that his wife might find out about or a single woman who will expect marriage or set him up by getting pregnant. He doesn't want to waste time entertaining a woman who may say no or the responsibility of providing her sexual gratification. A professional woman is discrete, does not expect to be entertained, always says yes, and will pretend gratification regardless of his commitment to pleasuring her. He has no responsibility for her sexual response. He pays for access to her body to achieve ejaculation and that's what he gets without games or problems.

Men who *travel* on business or are estranged from sexual partners through participating in the armed services, residence in work camps, or construction projects also provide business for the prostitute. The traveling salesman expresses his loneliness sexually as does the sailor, merchant marine, or migrant worker. Men have traditionally sought female companionship and sexual intercourse as a "home away from home" or "woman in every port" cure for loneliness. In contrast, women are socialized to resist similar solutions to loneliness. They face not only the reputation loss in a "pick-up" situation but potentially physical danger. For men, a shortage of available women in day-to-day contact, as in work camps, also sets up one side of an equation, the other of which is filled by a prostitute who provides sexual satisfaction for many men.

There are men who qualify as sexually disenfranchised because they are restricted or *disabled* and turn to professional women to fulfill their needs. American society, in contrast to many other simpler cultures, limits sexual access to many populations on the basis of age, race, culture, personality, intelligence, and handicap (Marshall & Suggs, 1971). Those who do not or feel they do not fall within the range of acceptable sexual partner find it is safer to pay for acceptance than risk continued or possible rejection or social condemnation.

Not all customers desire sexual contact. Some want a companion to take to dinner or a movie; others want someone to talk to for an hour. Women, especially experienced women, are seen as understanding, appropriate people to tell their troubles to. "Talkers" may have the prostitute ride out to the airport with them or sit in a hotel room while they tell the woman their troubles. The prostitute is the sympathetic ear in a situation where other women are too impatient or not to be trusted. The impotent man hopes that the prostitute will solve his problems. She will not let him see his lack of erection as a failure. He has paid to be protected. She can play whatever role is required—mother, sister, friend. She may dress up for him of just verbally fulfill his image needs. This is only one of the areas where the customer is, in a sense, seeking a therapist, someone to talk to. The women we interviewed often recognized their role as therapist with the joke that good whores and good "shrinks" always have more business than they know what to do with.

The last basic category is referred to by the prostitutes as *specials* or *freaks*, that is, men whose sexual trigger falls into the section of the sexual spectrum frequently labeled perverted. Depending on their individual experience, people have special fantasies that intensify sexual pleasure. In some cases, the fantasy is necessary to achieve erection and ejaculation. The range of triggers extends as far as imagination. Many are acceptable to some sexual partners such as transvestism or certain positions; most are acceptable to a prostitute who has worked more than six months. The requests that a professional gets eventually become commonplace and grist for discussion at the after-hours bar. A wife or girlfriend rarely has sufficient experience to find special requests acceptable. The man may feel ashamed of his need and conceal it from a possibly willing sexual partner in favor of the safety of reaction of the prostitute. With a professional he may not have to do more than hint at his desires for her to fill in the picture.

Some men use prostitutes as a *social-bonding* mechanism with their friends (Stein, 1974). Going "with the boys" to a "party" or massage parlor is viewed as entertainment, something men do together. The activity is kept from wives and other noninvolved associates. Stag parties for entertainment are still being held by the fathers of today's generation and some younger members of social and business clubs like the Elks, Eagles, Moose, etc. They often appear to be father-daughter affairs with most of the men in their forties joking with 21-year-old topless dancers that they say remind them of their daughters. Yet, they would be appalled at the thought of their own daughters' involvement. (Again, the double standard and the necessity of having two classes of women.)

The sexual needs of customers discussed above are loosely defined as normal, with the exception of the "freaks" or perverts. In fact, the customers of prostitutes, and their activities as such, have enjoyed a long tradition of "normality." Even during periods when intensive official attempts to end the business of prostitution were underway (e.g., descriptions by Anderson [1974] of Chicago, 1910–1915, and by Holmes [1972] of nationwide efforts at about the same time), customers' needs were accepted as "inevitable." At most, the men were chided for risking venereal disease and implored to practice self-control. The real villains, according to the reformers, were "those who made money by 'promoting' prostitution . . ., not (practitioners of) 'secret or clandestine vice' " (Anderson, 1974). Since men were considered to have a basic biologic need for these "secret" sexual outlets, it was seen as somehow immoral for women to demand money for relieving that need.

Today, men who purchase the services of prostitutes are still considered normal (nondeviant), even though their actions may be seen as unpalatable, or even immoral, according to the personal standards of the observer. Customers of prostitutes are, of course, acting outside the law, but where the law and the accepted male sex role come into conflict. The norms of sexual role playing overshadow the power of the law to label deviance. Men are expected to have a wide variety of sexual needs to actively seek fulfillment of those needs. As part of that search, men are allowed to illegally purchase the sexual services of women with relative impunity, as arrest statistics demonstrate.

The provision of sexual services to males by women, in contrast, is clearly labeled deviant. Males break few social rules in patronizing a prostitute; females break almost all the rules of their sex role in becoming prostitutes. Streetwalkers in particular place themselves at the wrong end of the whore-madonna spectrum: they accept money for sex; they are promiscuous; they are not in love with the customers; they are not subtle; and they engage in "abnormal" or deviant sex acts, which "respectable" women are not expected to do. The location of the streetwalker's place of business also labels her as deviant. Men may walk the streets freely wherever and whenever they wish; a woman downtown late at night without a male escort is ipso facto suspect.

Most importantly, however, the independent, promiscuous, overt sexuality of the prostitute challenges the traditional assumption that female sexuality is entirely dependent on and awakened only by male sexuality. As Davis (1937) states, "Women are either part of the family system, or they are prostitutes, members of a caste set apart." Unregulated sexuality is accepted from males; from females, whose sexual stability is the sine qua non of our family concept, however, ultrafamilial sex threatens the basic structures of society. So threatening is the idea of female sexual independence that we have laws defining juvenile women who engage in sexual intercourse without official permission as deviants "in danger of falling into habits of vice."

The Pimp

There are other men in the prostitute's life besides police and customers. Friends and acquaintances within the "fast life," as involvement in prostitution is called, are important to the life-style. Streetwalkers usually do not work alone. With exceptions, all streetwalkers have a man somewhere in the background. In other prostitution styles, such as the call girl system, a man is less important to business survival than on the street but he may still be viewed as an important part of a woman's life. He may be called a pimp, although prostitutes dislike the term. He is usually referred to by the woman as *my man*. The *man* may function as a pimp; he may be a boyfriend or husband, or a combination of pimp and boyfriend. In cases of lesbian prostitutes, this role of man is filled by a woman who treats her women in much the same fashion as the man would. The lesbian pimp usually works with very young girls, often runaways from home or juvenile institutions. They are afraid to work for a man and find a female is more supportive of their situation as new girls in the business.

A pimp is someone who acts as an agent for someone else and essentially recruits them for a percentage of their money. In past decades, the pimp took an active role in the finding of customers for prostitutes, but this is no longer the usual style. The pimp does not perform a direct service himself; he has others do it for him while he receives, manages, and controls the proceeds. Pimps are now referred to as *players, midnight executives,* and *fast-steppers.* An ethnosemantic analysis of the domain of pimp has been provided in an earlier paper (James, 1972b).

The ideal pimp fills many roles in his relationship with the prostitute; he is husband, boyfriend, father, lover, agent, and protector. As husband he may pay the bills, take care of the car, and father her children. His role as boyfriend includes taking her to parties and providing other entertainment. These two both overlap in his role of lover. As father, he may discipline her for inappropriate behavior and make all her decisions. The agent and protector provides bail money, retains the services of an attorney, and protects her from others on the street through his reputation as a strong man whose women are not to be "hassled." How well he fills any one of these roles depends on how "good a pimp" he is and his relationship with the woman. Although individual cases vary depending on particular circumstances, prostitutes give basic reasons for having a man: respect, business, and love.

Regardless of how people may wish to qualify the statement, women in our society feel they need a male companion if their position is to be respected. Women alone, if they are not elderly or widowed, are viewed as "needing a man." Unmarried daughters are harassed, women without men frequently feel their life is incomplete, and friends are forever trying to make a couple out of two singles. The same feelings of need for a male associate pervade the "fast life." In fact, sex-role behavior is conservative among prostitutes and a woman needs a man or she is regarded as an "outlaw," someone who is abnormal by the subculture's values. If her man is in prison or has recently been killed, she will have a period of grace, but few other excuses are acceptable.

A woman needs a man, not only because woman alone is incomplete, but for basic protection from harassment by other men. A prostitute without a pimp is considered fair game by other pimps who will attempt to "catch" her. She will be looked down by her colleagues and be more open to abuse from others on the street. Her pimp's name is significant as a "keep away" sign in the same way that a wedding ring traditionally has been. On the street, it becomes more important because of the threat of assault or robbery if a woman doesn't have a man "behind her." His reputation provides respect and therefore protection. He does not in fact appear on the street, but instead socializes with other pimps in bars or private homes. Protection from customers is left to the prostitute and her co-workers since the pimp is not around when she is working.

Respect has other dimensions besides a male associate and protection. A woman's status among her peers in "the life" is directly related to the status of her pimp. Just as the banker's wife is accorded more status than the truck driver's, a prostitute's reputation in large part depends on her pimp's. If he is well dressed, handsome, drives a prestige automobile, and handles himself well she will be highly respected; on the other hand, if he is less than stylish and unsuccessful in playing his role she will be looked down on. The woman is defined by the man for whom she works, and a really top pimp finds women asking and paying to be associated with him rather than waiting for him to recruit them.

A second major factor in the prostitute-pimp relationship is business. Many women feel that they need a man to take care of business details that women traditionally have not felt capable of handling. They need a man to tell them when to work, how to work, to keep them in line, to give them confidence, and to take care of them. The pimp ideally takes care of all accounts. He handles the money, pays the bills, makes the investments, and gives her an allowance. He provides a place to live, food, clothing, transportation, entertainment, medical care, and makes provisions for children. He is expected to take care of bail when she is arrested, provide a lawyer, and give her financial and moral support if she has to serve a sentence. The pimp takes care of her property and sees that her children are taken care of during the times she is working or serving a sentence. As one pimp put it, "I provide the mind and she provides the body. After all, that's the difference between a man and a woman." One of the older women interviewed put it this way:

> I gave him all of the money and, like I say, all my business was taken care of. I didn't have to worry about it. If I went to jail I'd be right out, if I needed an attorney he'd pay for it, and he sent money to my kids, and he was always buying me something. We had our little misunderstandings but nothing really serious. We did a lot of things together. We were in New York, he sent me to business school, and he went to a school of acting; we had a lot of fun. We traveled together, we even bought a house, but after the Feds were bothering me so much we had to give it up.

The third important consideration discussed by prostitutes is affection. As they point out, everyone needs someone to come home to, and for the prostitute, it has to be someone in "the life." The prostitute needs a man who understands the profession and accepts her. The pimp provides the prostitute with varying degrees of affection. He may be a wonderful lover or a controlling father. He supports her with talk of how special their relationship is and how they can make it together. To love and be loved was often stated as being the motivation to stay with a pimp.

The reasons offered by both pimps and prostitutes for this kind of relationship does not differ greatly from the reasons most men and women have for marrying. In reality, detailed description of the interaction between pimp and prostitute produces a picture of a relationship that is little more than an exaggeration of the male-female relationships in the larger society. Levels of love, respect and economic exchange vary but the needs are the same.

Misinformation surrounds the pimp-prostitute relationship. This situation is in part due to past behavior of pimps, sensationalist journalism, and a protectionist policy toward women. Some pimps have been brutal in the past and exploitive, but the interaction is changing. Prostitutes are demanding better treatment or are working alone; pimps are discovering that they can be more successful using psychological coercion. The women work harder if they are doing it for the maintenance of a positive relationship with their man and the police are less likely to become involved if there is no violence. However difficult it may be to accept, many women choose to prostitute and prefer to give their money to a pimp. In the context of male-female role behavior, this relationship represents more of an exaggeration of traditional interaction than a perversion. Understanding of the pimp-prostitute relationship should be based on the recognition of these dynamics.

The security of a particular pimp-prostitute relationship is, however, often bleak. The pressures inherent in the life-style, arrest, incarceration, and jealousy between women who share the same man all contribute to strained relationships. The ability to maintain the relationship between a single prostitute and her pimp is based on acceptance of the ethics of the life-style. Streetwalkers label themselves as outside the "straight" world and a part of the "fast life." In "the life" the rules are different. A man, as long as he meets his obligations to each woman, may have more than one woman as his partner. Each woman may believe she will eventually be the one he chooses to be with when they have "made it together" and no longer need to be involved in prostitution. Some of the women are only interested in a short-term relationship because of their desire for the protection derived from association with a pimp. They pose no threat to the long-term woman because they make no demands for a position as "main lady." The set-up of a pimp and his women is referred to as a stable. The duration of a stable is often only a few months as one or more of the women move to another man. A particular prostitute may stay with a pimp five, six even ten years, but she rarely settles down with him and lives out the dream of the promised secure life together as husband and wife. Most pimps, when they leave the profession, also leave their women. When they settle down it is with women who have not been prostitutes and often, in this situation, the pimp may become a conservative husband and father. The prostitutes seem to ignore the examples of the end result of most prostitute-pimp relationships. They state that for them it will be different. The dreams of the fast life are very potent. They can be likened to the dreams of marriage that are part of many teenage women's thoughts when they first fall in love. The problems are not seen as clearly as the cultural stereotype presented by bride's or housekeeping magazines.

Surprisingly enough, more prostitutes leave the profession successfully than do the pimps whom they support. Few pimps leave the life before they are destroyed by it through violence, imprisonment, or drug addiction (Milner & Milner, 1972). Prostitutes, if they have avoided alcoholism or drug addiction, drift out of the life as they get older. They take other jobs, go on welfare, and in some cases marry someone who has little knowledge of their past. Pimps, unless they are very successful in another status career, such as entertainment, rarely survive past forty. Most of them find it impossible to compromise and re-enter what they describe as the "square world." Only positions of fast-life status, such as writer, producer, bar owner, entertainer, or actor are viewed as viable alternatives. As they like to point out, "It's a hard life taking care of women and keeping them together with everyone on your back."

Attempts to End Prostitution

Attempts at ending prostitution have been total failures with the apparent exception of China. Russia and Cuba claim to have eliminated prostitution with similar Communist programs but there is evidence to the contrary. Journalists report the easy availability of prostitutes in both Moscow and Havana despite severe fines for customers and prison sentences for prostitutes. China's success seems to be based on the complete equality of the sexes in domestic, economic, and political spheres combined with the discipline and commitment required by "pure" Communist ideology. The supply of women has been eliminated by offering equal economic opportunities to them and the use of intensive five-year reorientation sentences. The demand has been eliminated through emphasis on discipline and heavy prison sentences.

Other countries have accepted the existence of prostitution and made various legal arrangements. Countries in the Middle East, the Far East, the Caribbean, and South America regulate it by requiring brothels to be licensed and by subjecting prostitutes to health inspections. France, Britain, Italy, Japan, Germany, and a total of 100 members of the United Nations have eliminated the crime of prostitution and have abandoned experiments at regulations (United Nations, 1951). The criminal laws in those countries seek instead to control public solicitation and to discourage the pimps and procurers who live off the earnings of prostitutes.

West Germany has become the most open of the countries in its treatment of prostitution. There, prostitution is considered a social necessity, and the government actively supports the building of pimp-free prostitution hostels where prostitutes can live and work in comfortable rooms with access to shopping centers, recreational facilities, and mandatory medical inspection. Sweden has a special employment stipulation whereby a woman can work as a prostitute only if she has another full-time job in a "legitimate" field. The emphasis is on making sure the woman has an alternative and a job to go to when she is too old to prostitute.

In the United States, a number of groups are working towards changes in the prostitution and other sex laws; these includes The National Organization for Women, American Civil Liberties Union, sections of the American Bar Association, and the National Council for Crime and Delinquency. The main thrust of their efforts is for decriminalization and acceptance of prostitution as a "victimless crime" or "crime without a complainant." These terms are used to refer to crimes where the "victim" does not file a complaint. Examples include vagrancy, gambling, pornography, homosexuality, public drunkenness, and prostitution. With prostitution, the only person who files a complaint is the police officer who, in passing as a customer, has been solicited by a prostitute. The victim is not the customer who actively seeks a service or the prostitute who willingly sells. Those who refer to the prostitute as a victim do so in a nonlegal sense. She is seen as a victim because of her life-syle, her immorality, and not as the victim of a crime.

The movement to change the prostitution statutes views decriminalization as the least abusive choice. It differs from legalization in that it removes prostitution from the criminal code entirely. An ideal approach would be to put all sexual behavior in private between consenting adults outside the purview of the law. Options for controls would depend upon the community's concern about the obviousness of the sexual activities, the possible disease problems, business and zoning regulations, and age of consent.

Taxation, health, and age requirements can be approached in a number of ways. The least abusive to the individual woman would be a small business license with a health card requirement. Prostitutes would obtain a license much as a masseuse does; her place of business would have to conform with zoning requirements; she would be required to report her income, be of age, and keep her health card current. Violations would mean the revocation of license and would be handled by a nonpolice administrative agency. Advertisements would be limited to discreet classified ads. Houses of prostitution would not be licensed.

Regulations such as the above would, of course, still limit personal freedom in a purely private area. The nonlicensed prostitute could still be prosecuted although her's would be a civil citation, not a criminal one. The idea of a "consenting adults" approach must be balanced by the reality of public expediency. Decriminalization, with some restrictions, is regarded as a provisional solution only while efforts are made to change the more fundamental causes of prostitution.

In summary, prostitution is a social and cultural phenomena that places women in a double-standard bind. The accepted range of male sexual behavior in our society is considerably wider than the accepted behavior convention of the middle class, and especially of middle class women. Lower class women, then, and particularly those who have been "set apart" by the label "deviant," must serve as substitutes for the middle class women so firmly restricted by their class proscriptions. Prostitution allows men an area freedom from sexual restraints and permission to move briefly into the deviant subculture.

The more highly restricted female sex role contains almost none of the sexual motivations and behaviors allowed to the male; nor does it allow a woman to serve as a professional accompanist for those men who would rent her participation in sexual activities. The prostitute is a deviant *woman* and her customer is a normal *man*.

The puritan aspect of middle class society means that the full acting out of the male sex role requires the existence of prostitution. As a result, the male need for purchased sexual service is, and long has been, accepted as "inevitable" and therefore not to be punished. The women, however, are in violation of their full role and dangerously at odds with the conventions of society. They are therefore jailed, stigmatized, and exiled from "decent" society.

Prostitution cannot be eliminated nor understood unless the demand for prostitution, as well as the supply, is recognized. Men must be able to view sex as something other than a commodity that can be purchased. Women must be able to see their value as much more than the attractiveness of their bodies. The sexual socialization process of males and females is the key to the existence of prostitution. The stigmatization of women as whores is the result of a promiscuity standard that does not exist for males.

JUVENILE PROMISCUITY

The sexual labeling of young females is based on the same set of sexual expectations that are applied to the prostitute. Specialists in the area of juvenile delinquency have traditionally described the female delinquent as a sexual delinquent (Vedder & Sommerville, 1970). Sexual acts by juvenile females violate behavioral expectations for young women but are rarely against the law for adults; yet they are treated by juvenile courts as criminal acts. The sexually uncontrolled adolescent girl is more threatening than her adult counterpart because of her youth and its equation with innocence and the responsibility of society, particularly males, to protect the chastity of virgins. In contrast, juvenile males are virtually never reported for inappropriate sexual activity unless it is also an adult offense such as rape or molestation. Males who are sexually active are viewed as exercising the male prerogative to be wild and uncontrolled while they are young and have no family responsibilities. They are encouraged to "sow wild oats" to be "one of the boys" and prove their manhood. Females must prove their feminity in the opposite direction, through passivity.

The difference in treatment is well-documented. Girls who are referred to juvenile authorities for any activity from shoplifting to runaway are almost automatically given gynecologic examinations to determine virginity, pregnancy, or infection with a venereal disease (Lind, 1973). These examinations may be used to prove the allegation of sexual promiscuity as well as to protect the health of the female. The court may use as evidence for institutionalization the intactness of the hymen. Boys are rarely, if ever, examined. Young women are placed "under the protection of the courts" and incarcerated in juvenile institutions for extended periods of time on the basis of their "moral state." Young men are rarely incarcerated unless a criminal act, that would also be an adult violation, has been committed. Discrepancies in treatment are justified by the importance of protecting females and controlling their sexual behavior. This double standard is also applied to age. Juvenile males obtain adult status and release at age 18. If designated as incorrigible, promiscuous, dependent, or simply a person in need of supervision, a female can be held until age 21. These practices are viewed as helping the female juvenile by providing support and protection until she is of marriageable age or able to be independent from her family and the state. In reality, examination of the workings of the juvenile court process provides evidence that in contrast to this suggestion of "gentleness" the court is in fact exceptionally harsh with juvenile females, especially in the areas concerned with sexual behavior.

A review of the delinquency labels applied to girls point out the sexual interpretations added to any unacceptable behavior. Incorrigible is a frequently used juvenile criminal category, the definition of which is dependent on parental concepts of acceptable female role behavior. Families, while desiring their daughters to be popular and attractive, are careful to encourage them to be sex objects with no accompanying sexuality. She is encouraged to attract boys but may be reported to the authorities if she stays out late, "runs around," or is suspected of being sexually involved. The fine line between good girl and bad girl, if stepped on, may result in a report of incorrigibility by rigid or nonsupportive parents. Teenage girls are to be admired but not touched. A designation by the courts of incorrigibility is frequently a result of behavior that indicates violations of sexual restrictions. Young women who smoke, violate liquor laws, skip school, or come home late place themselves in "danger of sexual infractions" and becoming "cheap girls," and are often reported by their mothers to juvenile authorities as impossible to handle. In contrast, juvenile males are reported most often by school authorities or police officers for clearly criminal activities such as burglary and auto theft. Many parents and the juvenile courts support a double standard that allots females a much narrower range of acceptable behavior.

Promiscuity is another classic label applied to juvenile females, but not to their male counterparts. Pregnant young women, especially if they desire an abortion, may be referred to the juvenile court and can be classified as delinquents. Families that suspect their daughters are involved in sexual activity can refer them to the court for examination or commit them to juvenile institutions for safe keeping. Strouse (1972), in an article on the labels applied to juvenile female delinquents, reports many such cases. One was a recent case in Connecticut where a 16-year-old girl was sent to the State Farm for Women because her parents and the court agreed that she was in "manifest danger of falling into habits of vice." The general supervision law under which she was committed was challenged and upheld on the assertion that her commitment was not a punishment but a "protective safeguard."

In jurisdictions where promiscuity is no longer an acceptable charge, incorrigibility or other labels are applied. Sarah Gold (1971) in an article on equal protection for juvenile girls notes that "An unstated fear or dislike of sexual promiscuity and illegitimate births by young women and girls is behind the unequal treatment implicit in the New York Family Court Act." This act created the PINS (Person in Need of Supervision) label for a juvenile in trouble but who has not committed a crime. An examination of a metropolitan juvenile court case list of 1500 by Reiss (1960) demonstrated that the judges involved refused to treat any form of sexual behavior on the part of boys, even the most bizarre forms, as warranting more than probationary status. The judges, however, regarded girls as the "cause" of sexual deviation of boys in all cases of sexual activity involving an adolescent couple and refused to hear the complaints of the girl and her family. Regardless of whether juvenile court officials are male or female, their decisions usually reflect the same double standard of sexual behavior that precipitates many young girl's arrest. These standards define the female as the seductive element in any sexual interaction.

Juvenile prostitution also has a wide definition in most juvenile courts. Parents or authorities may suspect the girl is involved in prostitution without direct proof or may prefer to avoid the label of prostitution when proof is available. When a clear charge of prostitution is made, the result is usually a long sentence in a juvenile institution because prostitution is viewed as an extremely deviant activity for young women. This is in contrast to acts of vandalism, burglary, and car theft among teenage boys who are occasionally viewed as "going through that stage" or actually demonstrating their masculinity through delinquent behavior.

Prostitution provides unique opportunities for juvenile women. As noted before, it enables them to support themselves at a much younger age than legal employment. They can learn enough to achieve independence from parents, travel enough to avoid pick-ups as runaways or probation violators, and feel they are adults because customers seek them out as women. The excitement, adventure, and income is "heady stuff" for an adolescent child-woman. If her parents are unresponsive, school boring, and juvenile authorities oppresive, the "fast life" offers an escape. Already labeled as "promiscuous," the juvenile feels there is little to lose and potential recognition as "cool" and "fast" to be gained. The money means independence, the most common factor these young women need, from the controls placed on them by their families, school, or the juvenile courts.

WOMEN AS VICTIMS

Crimes committed against women frequently involve the same institutional definitions of female sexuality that are significant in promiscuity and prostitution, a double standard that punishes women who cross the whore-madonna line, whether by choice or force. Rape and other sexual abuses of females, whether child or adult, appear to be increasing and public information on their circumstances is expanding. The police, hospitals, and courts deal with the victims of these crimes and their attitudes and practices are being questioned and investigated. Once an incident is reported these institutions process both the victim and the offender. The reputation of police departments in particular has been so fearsome for women that many never report their assault for fear the investigation will be more abusive than the crime of which they were a victim. She may accept the judgment of others that she asked to be raped, that she was somehow guilty of precipitating the assault. In the last five years, new research studies describing the handling of victims of sexual crimes have been published. One central message emerges from all of them: society's views of the crimes and of the victim amount to an indictment of female sexuality (Brownmiller, 1974; Burgess & Holstrom, 1975).

Susan Brownmiller's book *Against Our Will: Men, Women and Rape* provides an historical analysis of rape in our civilization and how much it reveals about current male-female relationships. She concludes that "the threat, use and cultural acceptance of sexual force is a pervasive process of intimidation that affects all women," whether they become actual victims of violence of not.

Rape

The rate of forcible rape in the United States supports the contention that sexual assault is a major problem for women. Crime statistics note that a forcible rape occurs every ten minutes. The volume of forcible rape offenders increased significantly from 1972 through 1977. This represented the greatest percentage increase for adult male offenders in 1977 among the crimes of violence (Uniform Crime Reports, 1978). The actual number of rapes that occur appears to be much greater than these data indicate because it is estimated that only one in four rapes are ever reported.

In a single city, Seattle, where intensive rape research and projects encouraging reporting are underway, the frequency of rape charges has increased 420 percent from 1966 (Seattle Police Department Statistics, 1978). The increased reporting of rapes may not be an accurate reflection of increased attacks; it may be a response to public consciousness raising that has resulted in increased willingness to report rape. Regardless, the number of women involved on a constant day-to-day basis makes rape one of the crimes women fear most.

The new awareness of the problem of rape has been generated in large part by organizations identified with the women's movement. Their analysis of the treatment of victims by police, medical personnel, and criminal justice systems have led to increased consciousness, rape relief programs, police training, and legislative changes in the legal requirements for prosecution. The programs that have grown out of women's movements' concern provide assistance in six main areas: 1) understanding the crime of forcible rape and eliminating the myths that impair the enforcement of the law; 2) education for women in self-protection, knowledge of rape practices, and survival if assaulted; 3) rape relief centers where women can report rape if they prefer not to go to the police and where they can receive aid and counseling; 4) police sensitivity training and the use of police women in responding to rape reports and conducting investigations; 5) the development of model legal codes and prosecution procedures to aid in conviction of offenders while protecting victims; and 6) research into the possible causative factors of rape built into our definitions of male and female sexuality.

The implementation of knowledge derived from these programs and a realistic understanding of rape is complicated by definitions of good and bad sexual conduct for women. One commonly expressed societal view is that women ask for rape because they dress seductively and act promiscuously. Hitchhiking, drinking in bars alone, or accepting dates from strangers are all viewed as "asking for it" by some jurors and many criminal justice personnel. Seductive clothing such as short skirts, halter tops or braless outfits are all seen as "come-ons" which leave the victimization in question.

> A victim's "moral character" may be admissible as a defense in some statutes. Again, the assumption is that an unchaste female, or a female with such a reputation, is more likely than not to consent to sexual intercourse in any given instance. (Amir, 1971:23)

Research on actual rape circumstances indicates that up to 70 percent of all rapes occur between complete strangers where knowledge of past sexual experience is unknown, and 38 percent occur within a woman's home or apartment where the offender has not previously observed the woman's clothing habits. A second commonly expressed view is that "a good woman cannot be raped," yet the background studies of rape victims indicate the full spectrum in terms of age, sexual experience, social class, religious beliefs, education, marital status, and personal habits. The theory that women can stop rape has also produced contradictions. Police officials advise women to be passive, to avoid resistance that might possibly increase injury. Juries, however, rarely convict the rapist without clear evidence of resistance. Statistics on the assaults and homicides accompanying rape put the victim in a very difficult position. If she fights, she may be seriously injured; if she does not resist she may not be accepted as a victim.

The myths and misunderstandings that surround the crime of rape are supported by the same double standards that were discussed in the context of prostitution and juvenile promiscuity. Women are expected to control sexual access to their bodies; men are not expected to control their sexual desires. A woman who mixes her sexual messages by violating traditional behavioral boundaries for women "gets what she deserves." These societal attitudes lead to abusive treatment by police, insensitivity on the part of medical personnel, abuse and defamation in court, and suspicion by husband, family, and friends. The classic question, "Tell me now, didn't you sort of enjoy it?" is still being asked.

While efforts to clarify these societal definitions and produce change in the handling of rape cases continue, emphasis is also being placed on the education of women in the avoidance of possible rape situations. Major studies of rape situations provide knowledge of the modus operandi of reported rape offenders. The most frequent victims of rape are single, younger women and the most common place of attack is within their own residences. The offender either breaks in or uses a ruse to get the woman to open her door. In Denver, Philadelphia, and New York, the majority of rape offenses occurred in the downtown city center area where there is the highest concentration of young, single women. In more than half the cases examined, the victim and the offender were total strangers: 67 percent in Denver, 63 percent in Seattle, 55 percent in Kansas City, and 52 percent in Philadelphia. These studies also report time of day, day of the week, and month of the year, pinpointing weekends between 8 P.M. and 2 A.M. as the most potentially dangerous time.

Knowledge of rape circumstances leads to standard advice to women that many women's groups feel is unfair and difficult to follow: Do not go out alone; don't open your door to strangers; never pick up or accept rides from strangers; and never put yourself in a position, even with an acquaintance, where you will be unable to defend yourself (Storaska, 1975). If you are assaulted, resist initially if there is any chance of someone coming to your assistance or of escape, then submit with minimal verbal comment, and call the police as soon as you are sure the attacker is gone. Given the reality of rape, this advice is good but its implications for the limiting of a woman's freedom are profound. Do not go out alone at night is advice few males would accept. How can a woman protect herself even with an acquaintance given the physical strength differences between men and women? Why are the restrictions directed more toward women than the men who are potentially the aggressors? Again, the double standard of control over male and female sexuality is apparent.

Investigations of rape provide additional examples of the effect of societal attitudes on rape convictions. The Denver study provides a breakdown of the usual police problems in attempting to clear rape cases. Of the 915 offenses reported during the two years of this study, only 16 percent were cleared by the arrest of the suspect. The reasons given for not being able to arrest or charge in the cases where the suspect was identified were as follows: 43.2 percent of the time the victim refused to prosecute or was unavailable; 24.9 percent was lack of evidence, either the victim did not resist enough or was labeled as "asking for it;" 10.6 percent of suspects were arrested previously by another jurisdiction, and in 17.5 percent the district attorney refused to file the case, usually because the victim's sexual reputation could be attacked. Of the total cases, 49 percent were inactive. The reasons were stated as lack of suspect identification, victim failed to cooperate, or lack of sufficient information. These statistics are similar to those available through other rape arrest analyses.

An analysis of the meaning behind these statistics clarifies the social role implications for the victim of rape. Victims refuse to report or prosecute because they want to avoid publicity that will identify them as a "violated" woman. Victims are afraid of the reactions of parents or spouse. They also fear retaliation from their attacker and an inability to protect themselves. Their socialization into nonaggressive behavior and their concern with sexual reputation often negates their ability to fight the assault, legally or socially. The main problems in the lack of evidence for prosecution are extent of injury and victim reputation. A victim who has not been seriously injured may be viewed as not having attempted to defend herself, in a sense cooperating in the assault. A victim who leads a sexually active life style may be considered as "unrapeable," that is, she has nothing to lose or her testimony is suspect.

The consensus in studies of police investigation of rape list these problems of insensitivity to the victim; inadequate response to the crime (i.e., disbelief in the occurrence of rape), insufficient staffing, and lack of knowledge or concern for the evidence required for prosecution. Some of these problems are being solved through public pressure to use policewomen and separate counseling agencies who act as advocates for the victim throughout the police investigation. Others are being met through improved training and knowledge of forensic procedures.

The attention rape has been getting as the result of women's movement criticism of the institutional responses to the victim have also led to renewed comments on the possible causes of rape. The direction of research has been toward the tensions built into our definitions of male and female sexuality. The aggressiveness expected of the male, the push to "score," the fearsome term *sissy* in combination with the female's desire to be attractive, desirable, popular, but not "easy" are conducive to the build-up of tension. Accusations of female seductiveness and male inability to resist recall similar arguments for prostitution. This tension creates many circumstances of pseudorape when no means yes and rape where no means no. The victim is caught by her forced involvement in traditional sexual gamesmanship. The rapists that have been studied are those who were caught and convicted. They fall into the lower end of the occupational- and social-class scales (Amir, 1971). Rapists fit almost equally into married and single categories and show few other distinguishing characteristics. They are young (21 to 24 years old) and usually have previous convictions for other crimes. Rape is often committed as an adjunct to another crime such as burglary or robbery. Rape is characterized by offenders as victim-precipitated because of "seductive" or "reckless" behavior on the part of the victim. In the latter sense, rape is viewed as an ever-present possibility if a woman is not careful. Explanations for rape are diverted away from the offender and back to the victim. Psychoanalytic explanations for rape are as confusing and diverse as those listed for prostitution. Rape is sometimes defined as a political act of vengeance and also as a neurotic revenge against a deprived childhood, a seductive mother, or a rejecting wife. In many cases, rape is not viewed as criminal behavior by the offender and no personality disturbances are identified. Rape in this sense is a traditional right if a woman violates her assigned role position.

Revision of criminal codes in many states is now taking place to redefine rape as a crime and provide more likely conviction as a deterrent to offenders. Statutes that require a corroborating witness (never required in robbery) are being reviewed and replaced because they demonstrate an antivictim bias. Bills are pending that disallow evidence of a rape victim's past sexual conduct "other than with the defendant." In California, such information is already prohibited. In New York, Connecticut, and Ohio requirements of corroboration by medical evidence of sperm or assault have been dropped. These amendments suggest the beginnings of a shift in institutional response that will make it more difficult in the future to write off the rape victim as in some way the provocateur or inventor of her own attack.

Sexual Abuse of Children

Rape is only one of the crimes involving female sexuality and, according to many researchers, is not as common as incest and molestation of children. Incest in the crime of sexual intercourse with a person within prohibited degrees of blood relationship usually including mother, father, aunt, uncle, brother, sister, and grandparents. Some state statutes also include step-parents and half-brothers and sisters. In practice, incest appears under many charges and is a more common activity than is publicly acknowledged. It is often filed as child molestation if sexual intercourse is denied but sexual activity with a child reported. Incest can also be charged under carnal knowledge, indecent liberties, statutory rape, child abuse, and child neglect. Female children are the victims of these offenses ten to one over male children and their cases are apparently given more attention because of the implications of their violation on their emotional stability and their future sexual reputation.

Incest is one of the few universal cultural taboos cited by anthropologists. There are no known societies, with the exception of the ancient royal lineage of the Egyptians, Incas, and Hawaiians, where it is permissible for father and daughter, mother and son, or brother and sister to have sexual intercourse or to marry. The reasons behind these restrictions are varied but an important element involving female sexuality is the reduction of mother-daughter competition, that is, Freud's Electra syndrome. The vast majority of reported incest involves father-daughter or stepfather-daughter relationships that represent, in fact, the competitive situation. Social restrictions against are also based on the importance of maintenance of the nuclear family, fear of genetic defect, and the abhorrence society has of adults who exploit the dependence and sexual immaturity of children.

The actual extent of incest is unknown because of the hidden nature of these crimes, but estimates indicate at least 4 percent of the population has been involved as a victim or offender (Kinsey, 1953; McDonald, 1971). Researchers report that most cases to unrecorded because of the desire of parents to protect their image, to protect the offender (who is usually the wage earner), a lack of sympathy for the child, or actual collusion by the mother in the sexual activities (Vincent, 1972). This situation may change as more knowledge about sexuality and the effects of incest are communicated and more awareness of children's and women's rights is developed.

Increased concern and awareness about incest is the result of basic changes in society's view of the rights of children and the effects of sexual abuse. One important factor affecting both the increased number of cases and awareness is the breakdown of many marriages and the resulting increase in strained family relationships. Because they do not live together, fathers and daughters in separated homes do not develop natural familiarity. The breakdown in marital, and consequently sexual, relationships between a father and mother may also place increased pressure on the daughter to become a wife surrogate. A direct result of the break-up of a marriage is also remarriage, which exposes the child to a step-father who may not feel as strong a compunction to observe incest taboos as a natural father. When the mother does not remarry there is still the problem of exposure of the children to her male friends or common-law arrangements.

Concern in other areas of physical abuse of children has also led to increased reporting of sexual abuse. Children's rights is an apparent outgrowth of the movement for women's rights. Some agencies of society are beginning to take a stand toward protection of children from sexual violence, just as the review of rape laws has begun to redefine women's victimization.

Research into adult and juvenile crime has also contributed to increased awareness of incest and other forms of sexual abuse. Female runaways, juvenile prostitutes, and young girls turned into youth centers as promiscuous or incorrigible are often found to be the victims of sexual abuse within their homes (James & Vitaliano, 1979). Corresponding research with adult female offenders, especially prostitutes and addicts, indicates the same significance of sexual abuse as a destructive influence on personal development (Vitaliano & James, 1979). The impairing of female child's sexual self-respect appears to have far reaching implications for her adjustment as a woman. In a society that labels women as whores or respectable and treats them accordingly, the violated child finds it difficult to avoid self-labeling. She is clearly no longer a "good girl" and, like the rape victim, she may be accused of seductive behavior. Regardless of her age, the female, who may be unable to, is supposed to resist the male. The implications are again that the prostitute or sexual crime victim is self-created; the male offender, however, is victim-precipitated.

The most common incest relationships reported are father-daughter followed by step-father-daughter, uncle-niece, grandfather-granddaughter, brother-sister, and infrequently, mother-son. The average age of the female child is 13; the age range in most studies is between 7 and 19, although infant cases have been reported. The age range of the offender is late thirties to early forties. It is important to note the two age concentrations: for the victim it is adolescence, just when she is beginning to develop sexually, and for the offender it falls at the time of the male "forties crisis," the period where doubts of sexual prowess may occur. The incest usually happens within the child's or the offender's home and continues over a period of years. Reporting of the offense is controlled by threats to the child or the passive submission of the child to the situation.

The discovery of such long-term sexual abuse is usually the result of a combination of factors. The mother discovers the activity and refuses to collude despite possible loss of the man and economic support. She may want to get even with the offender or protect the child. A more common pattern is the daughter's resistance to her father's jealous efforts to restrict her activities with boys her own age as she becomes older and more independent. She may run away, report him for beating her, or become difficult to manage. The incest activity may come out when the juvenile authorities become involved in her associated behaviors. In some cases, an older daughter seeks to protect a younger sister when she sees her father making advances, or she is jealous. The victim may also become pregnant and the offender is subsequently identified as responsible.

The problem of incest, aside from the nature of the taboo, lie in the institutional responses to the female child and the lack of assistance available to her. The male, when discovered, usually blames the seductive girl, and the mother frequently joins in. This view of the sexual interaction repeats the female as responsible for stopping sexual advances of an uncontrolled male theory. The attitude that women, even children, can control sexual access while men, even adults, have little or no control over their sexual needs. The child is left with the burden of guilt for her sexuality because she is often removed from the home and placed in a foster home or institution while the father remains with the family. She views herself as the offender because she is being punished and rejected by her family, ostensibly for her own protection. The problems of corroboration of the crime are similar to those of rape. The usual legal response because of the difficulties of prosecution is to refer the case to juvenile authorities. Charges are not pressed against the father, and the victim is institutionalized.

The molestation of children presents issues similar to those of incest without the report of intercourse. The incidence of various types of molestation is also estimated to be many times larger than reported. The reasons for nonreport are the same as for incest because in two-thirds of the known cases the offender is a family member or close friend. In contrast to the social myths, molestation is not a single event occurring most frequently between strangers in parks. It is an occurrence involving relatives or family friends in the victim's or offender's home. In almost half the cases, the offenses were repeated against the child more than once.

The response of the social institutions of the criminal justice system to reported molestation is often described as more abusive than the molestation itself. The child is rarely protected through lengthy police investigations, questionings, and court proceedings. The child may be accused of lying or attempting to attract attention if the incident involves a close family member. The child protective division of social and health institutions is unable, in many cases, to show understanding of the emotional impact of the crime and the problems it may create for the child. It is in fact easier to treat as a fantasy of the child than a reality. As in other sexual crimes, it is easier to depend on tradition and treat the female victim as an offender. When the male is accused and prosecuted he is also treated harshly but viewed as "sick," not seductive.

CONCLUSION

The existence of prostitution is based on the American cultural view of sex as a commodity that can be purchased. The media provides the affirmation of a sexually hyper society where many products are bought and sold with the promise of sexual satisfaction. The discussion of customers outlined the needs that create the demand; the discussion of prostitutes pointed out the possible reasons why women provide the supply. An end to prostitution is dependent not on legal reform but on the sexual socialization process that produces the supply and demand for the profession.

The causes of rape and sexual abuse of children are more difficult to ascertain. Putting aside the motivations of the offender we are left with the abusiveness of the institutionalized response to the victim. A case has been made that both rapist's motivations and institutional responses are products of the myths and tensions built into the double standard of sexual behavior. The current emphasis during male adolescence on "scoring," regardless of the intimacy of the relationship with the woman, depersonalizes sex, and offers quantity and not quality as the ego enhancer. Aggression and submission are not the relevant measures. The double standard sets a whore-madonna spectrum on which a woman's sexual reputation is measured and further personalizes sex by limiting it to "loose women." The argument becomes circular. Good girls and women do not get sexually assaulted; while girls and women who are sexually assaulted are no longer good. They are, in fact, precipitators of their assault by retrospective reputation. Throughout history, most societies have noted that a population of such loose women is necessary to meet male sexual appetites while protecting "good" women who were to become wives and mothers.

Prostitution also provides the population with an outlet to meet male desires for promiscuity. The male defines his masculinity through these paid encounters. The female defines her feminity as a "good woman" by refusing to be paid or gives it up by accepting the label "whore." The male customer buys an illusion of sexual success combined with physical release. Access to females is commensurate with success. To be a "ladies man" is a compliment whether he purchases the companion overtly or subtly through less obvious favors than cash, or forces himself on women. Behind the exchange is a socialized male-female need: the male need to feel he is an attractive, competent lover by whatever means; the female need to be desired as a sex object, preferably as a good woman, and receive some economic support as a result.

The sexual definition of male and female role behavior sets up the tension. Prostitution can be used to provide ideal situations for fulfilling these role expectations; it is the business of fantasy. As Martha Stein (1971) has pointed out in her book *Lovers, Friends and Slaves,*

> the ability to switch roles quickly is the core of the call girl's work. Men don't come to her hoping to find a relationship with a real woman, but with a three-dimensional responsive embodiment of a fantasy woman. They pay her for the opportunity to satisfy their desires with a partner, undiluted by intrusion of an unpaid partner's own desires and personality.

In a house, apartment, or regular phone business, the illusion may be built up over a number of visits. Marie, the working woman, calls John, the trick, tells him she misses him and asks him to come over. What she is really missing is the rent money because of a slow week. John turns up because a man should not refuse a woman's request to see him; Marie needs him, and Marie makes him feel good. He knows Marie thinks he's a wonderful lover with a good body because she has told him so. He knows he pleases Marie sexually because of the orgasm she has so quickly and easily with him. All is clearly articulated; there is no silent affirmation of pleasure, no room for doubt. In his mind the $30 he leaves her is not relevant to the exchange. The money may nag a little but basically he is just helping her out because she is a working woman. The commodity that John has purchased is the illusion of his desirability and his potency that, as for most women, becomes more important than the sexual release.

Some of the same illusions are present in rape. The rapist will force the victim to say he enjoys him and that he is a good lover. He will describe the rape as a conquest. The society supports the illusion that women enjoy being ravished and that men who "take what they want" are in some senses to be admired. In incest, the father will state his right to his daughter's body and his sensitivity as a sexual teacher. In the same family, the mother will point out the daughter's seductiveness and the fact that "she's always been that way." The society, the family, and the institutional structure created by them accept the double standard and respond accordingly.

The issues presented here of women's involvement with the criminal justice system as offenders and victims are now the subject of intensive review by those interested in civil rights and social change. Prostitution and sexual assault are central issues in the legal reform supported by the "women's movement." Further knowledge of the circumstances of these crimes and understanding of their causes is needed to protect both men and women from abuse. The importance of rational and sensitive response to women, whether as delinquents, prostitutes, or victims of sexual assault is now being discussed. The cost of continued judgments based on stereotypes rather than realities is clearly too high.

REFERENCES

Amir, M. *Forcible Rape*. Chicago: University of Chicago Press, 1971.

Anderson, E. Prostitution and social justice: Chicago 1910–1915. *Social Service Review*, 1974.

Brownmiller, S. *Against our will: Men, women and rape.* New York: Simon & Schuster, 1975.

Burgess, A. W. & L. L. Holstrom. *Rape trauma syndrome. American Journal of Psychiatry,* 1974, *131,* 981–986.

Caprio, F. *The sexually adequate female.* Secaucus, N. J.: The Citadel Press, 1963.

Chesney-Lind, M. Judicial enforcement of the female sex role: The family court and the female delinquent. *Issues In Criminology,* 1973, *2,* 51–69.

Choisy, M. *Psychoanalysis of the prostitute.* New York: Pyramid Books, 1965.

Davis, K. The sociology of prostitution. *American Sociological Review,* 1937, *2,* 744–755.

De Francis, V. Protecting the child victim of sex crimes committed by adults. *Federal Probation,* 1971, 15–20.

Deutsch, H. *Neuroses and character types.* New York, International Universities Press, 1965.

Glover, E. G. *Roots of crime.* Imago Publishing Company, 1960.

Gold, S. Equal protection for juvenile girls in need of supervision in New York state. *New York Law Review Forum,* 1971, *17,* (2).

Greenwald, H. *The call girl.* New York: Ballantine Books, 1958.

Holmes, K. A. Reflections by gaslight: Prostitution in another age. *Issues in Criminology,* 1972, 83.

James, J. A formal analysis of prostitution. Final report to the division of research. Part I—Basic statistical analysis; part II—Descriptive report: part III—Formal semantic analysis. Olympis, Wash.: Department of Social and Health Services, 1971.

James, J. Ongoing research. Funded by NIDA #DA 0091801, Female Criminal Involvement and Narcotics Addiction, 1977.

James, J. Two domains of the streetwalker argot. *Anthropological Linguistics,* 1972, *14,* (5), 172–181.

James, J. The prostitute-pimp relationship. *Medical Aspects of Human Sexuality,* 1973, *7,* 147–160.

James, J. & Meyerding, J. Early sexual experience and prostitution. *American Journal of Psychiatry,* 1977, *134,* 1381–1385.

James, J. & Vitaliano, P. Factors in the drift towards female sex role deviance (unpublished paper), 1979.

James, J. & Vitaliano, P. The transition from primary to secondary sexual deviance in females (unpublished paper).

Kemp, T. *Prostitution: An investigation of its causes, especially with regard to hereditary factors.* Levin and Munskgaard, 1936.

Kinsey, A. C., et al. *Sexual behavior in the human male.* Philadelphia: Saunders, 1948.

Kinsey, A. C., et al. *Sexual behavior in the human female.* Philadelphia: Saunders, 1953.

Mantegazza, P. *Anthropological studies of sexual relations of mankind.* Anthropological Press, 1932.

Marshall, D. S., & Suggs R. C. (Eds.): *Human sexual behavior.* Englewood Cliffs, N.J.: Prentice-Hall, 1971.

McDonald, J. M. *Rape offenders and their victims.* Springfield, Ill.: Charles C Thomas, 1971.

Milner, C. & Milner R. *Black players, the secret world of black pimps.* Boston: Little, Brown, 1972.

National Conference on Rape. *Rape.* Washington, D.C.: National League of Cities, 1974.

Reiss, A. J. Sex offenses: The marginal status of the adolescent. *Law and Contemporary Problems*, 1960, *25* (2): 309–333.

Robinson, W. J. *The oldest profession in the world.* New York: Eugenic, 1929.

Rubin, T. *In the life.* New York: MacMillan, 1961.

Seattle Police Department. *Annual report: 1973*, 1974.

Segal, M. Impulsive sexuality: Some clinical and theoretical observations. *International Journal of Psychoanalysis,* 1965, *44,* 407–417.

Stein, M. *Lovers, friends and slaves.* New York: Putnam, 1974.

Storaska, F. *How to say no to a rapist—and survive.* New York: Random House, 1975.

Strouse, J. To be minor or female: The legal rights of women under 21. *Ms. Magazine,* 1972, 70–75.

Uniform Crime Reports. *Crime in the United States.* Washington, D.C.: U.S. Government Printing Office, 1974.

United Nations. *International convention for the suppression of the white slave traffic.* New York, United Nations Publishing, 1951.

Vedder CB, & Sommerville, D. B. *The delinquent girl.* Springfield, Ill.: Charles C Thomas, 1975.

Vitaliano, P. & Jennifer J. Deviant female sexuality: some adolescent and adult correlates (unpublished paper), 1979.

Vitaliano, P. Boyer, D. & James, J. Perceptions of juvenile experience among females involved in prostitution versus property offenses. Unpublished paper, 1979.

Winick, C. & Kinsie, P. *The lively commerce: Prostitution in the United States.* New York: Quadrangle Books, 1971.

Chapter 23

YOUNG FEMALE OFFENDERS IN MASSACHUSETTS

Toward Leaving The Juvenile Justice System Successfully

Carol Peacock

I am pleased to see your recent memos supporting good family work for all DYS youth. As you begin to articulate our position further, I feel you should be familiar with our girls' specialized family work needs. In my previous five (5) years of direct involvement with DYS girls, I observed these girls' complex mother-daughter relationships. These mother-daughter ties tend to include at least some of the following characteristics, which can be addressed through skilled family counseling and outreach:

1. *The daughter has fixated at an infantile level, seeking still unfulfilled needs from her mother.* Because the mother has been unable to nurture her daughter adequately when small, the daughter has been unable to move beyond a dependency-nuturance level. Thus, these adolescent girls manifest signs of regression, behaviors inappropriate for their chronologic age.

I have observed, for instance, that many 17– 18-year-old girls sleep every night in the same beds with their mothers. These girls also often tend to obese, compulsively in need of all food their mothers

This chapter is a memorandum to John A. Calhoun, Commissioner, from Carol Peacock, Assistant Commissioner for Girls' Services, dated October 14, 1977, about Family Work for Department of Youth Services (DYS) Girls.

offer them. The chain smoking exhibited by these girls indicates habit, tension, and an adoption of street culture. I also suspect that there is a heavy oral component in this chain smoking.

2. *There is little boundary between a mother's ego and her daughter's.* Poverty is a factor in this instance. Often, growing daughters share bedrooms with mothers. Rarely does one find a private area for the mother and another private area for the daughter. Mothers and daughters keep their clothes in the same drawers, rummage through each other's pockets, and purses for cigarettes. They sometimes may steal money from each other. The mother often merges her own adult life with her daughter's; she will ask the daughter to accompany her on dates with men, for instance.

3. *The mother, having received inadequate nurturing as a child, often looks to her daughter to be her own mother.* Roles are frequently reversed, a daughter providing discipline and nurturance for her mother. Mothers often seek their daughter's permission to go out at night, and ask approval for the men they see. Often, these mothers are happiest, it seems, when they become ill and are being cared for by their daughters.

4. *Mother is an inconsistent limit-setter.* Since the birth of her children, the mother has set limits sporadically and unpredictably. Children are allowed to do as they please until the mother, unable to contain her unexpressed anger, blows up. By adolescence, the daughters often exhibit poor impulse control and resentment of authority. As the daughter begins to test and rebel against the mother, this inconsistency has serious consequences. The mother's anger is matched by the daughter's surprise and rage. Furious quarrels around misunderstood rules often cause a daughter to run away or to turn to the streets.

5. *The daughter sometimes expresses her independence through violence.* Mother-daughter quarrels often lead to an exchange of blows. I have found that some violence has occurred in approximately 75 percent of the mother-daughter relationships of court-involved girls. When a daughter is driven to hit her mother, her guilt is enormous. This guilt colors the relationship. In order to avoid future confrontations, the adolescent daughter sometimes supresses all feelings toward her mother during disagreements. The mother perceives the daughter as aloof and uncaring; the anger increases.

6. *Communication patterns between the mother and daughter are destructive ones.* By the time the daughter has reached adolescence, communication between mother and daughter is muddled, at

best. One mother-daughter couple I know expresses their need for each other through angry confrontation. (At least while they stand and shout at each other, there is a sense that each one has some feelings, albeit angry ones, for each other). Often, there are few channels for mother and daughter to express positive feelings toward each other. Their relationship is set in patterns of dependency, hostility, and vacillation.

7. *The mother is threatened by her daughter's success.* Because the mother has few friends or other interests, her daughter becomes one of her only sources of satisfaction. The mother may unconsciously try to keep her growing daughter in the home. Behind ever truant, for instance, there is usually a lonely mother who has encouraged her daughter to stay home. Thus, I am constantly aware of mothers who try to sabotage a daughter's success at a new school training, or job opportunity. A high school drop out returns to school; it is her mother who turns off the alarm and lets the daughter sleep. A girl is placed in an all-day job; the mother, jealous and lonely, goes on a drinking binge until the daughter, guilty and concerned, stays home to watch the mother. She is fired from her job.

8. *Mother resents daughter's emerging sexuality.* Often alone, and sexually unsatisfied herself, the mother often resents her daughter's sexual maturity and sexual experimentation. Many of these mothers have reached, or are approaching, menopause. A sense of becoming old, and unwanted, heightens the mother's depression and increases her ambivalence toward her own, growing daughter.

BIBLIOGRAPHY

American Bar Association, Female Offender Resource Center, unpublished document on juvenile offenders, February 18, 1977, p 2.

Boston Sunday Globe, New England Magazine, "New Hope for the Troubled Young," February 13, 1977, p 8.

Center for Criminal Justice, Harvard Law School. Quarterly Report of the DYS Project, July 1975, p. 14.

Department of Youth Services, Proposal *50–75 delinquent females.* June 13, 1974, p 3.

Katzeff, D. *Boston Magazine,* "Equal Crime," December 1977, p 209.

Mayor's Committee on Criminal Justice, "Facts about Female Juvenile Delinquency," 1975.

Spangenber, R. L. et al *History of the CHINS program,* Cambridge, Mass.: Abt Associates, 1977, p 4.

Chapter 24

THE UNIQUE EMPLOYMENT PROBLEMS OF FEMALE OFFENDERS RETURNING TO THE COMMUNITY AND LABOR MARKET

Barbara Taylor

In the past decade, the U.S. Department of Labor and the Law Enforcement Assistance Administration (LEAA) of the Department of Justice have funded numerous research efforts and demonstration projects to determine the realities of problems confronting offenders as they reenter the labor market and to test various mechanisms for improving access for offenders to primary employment opportunities. In general, these studies and "model" programs have included both males and females; therefore, lessons learned are generalized, and more importantly, have proven more applicable to former male inmates who outnumber females at a ratio of approximately 20 to 1. Efforts that have dealt exclusively with women have too often keyed in on the dearth of programs within female jails and prisons and have determined little about the actual "double bind" experienced by female exoffenders in securing and retaining jobs.

In the process of managing a number of in-prison and post-release employment and training programs for women offenders and conducting a major research study of the employment histories and aspirations of the census of the New York State Correctional Institution for Women at Bedford Hills, I have concluded the following:

As limited and fragmented are the preincarceration histories of men, the women's backgrounds are even worse.

In-jail and in-prison preemployment preparation for females is indeed more limited than for males. Further, the occupations for which females are trained are, for the most part, sex stereotyped despite pressure for change brought by the women's movement.

The vast majority of female offenders reflect the aspirations of the lower socioeconomic backgrounds from which they come. Most cannot envision themselves in occupations other than those traditionally relegated to women: clerical, sales, and nonprofessional service providers. Corrections planners, program administrators, and guidance personnel fail to provide alternative programming or sufficient one-to-one vocational advisement that could prepare women to secure more lucrative employment upon release.

Most female inmates (67 percent) are mothers; the majority renew familial units and return to the role of heads of households with dependent children. Transition services, particularly those that focus upon employment, fail to take the women's emotional need to be with their children after incarceration into adequate account; nor is access to day-care services ordinarily expedited.

Community based employment programs for offenders are typically staffed by job development and vocational counseling personnel who are "people" oriented, and lack sufficient knowledge of private sector employer expectations. These well-intentioned intermediaries may thereby compound the female offenders' problems in securing appropriate jobs by mismatching clients to employment situations.

For many female offenders (a high percentage of whom have never worked in any case), the economic reality is that welfare with its add-ons is financially better than employment at minimum wage. Often the punitive notion of meeting parole responsibilities is the only stimulus that propels then into the job market.

The stigma of a criminal background may be even more injurious to the female exoffender seeking employment than the male "excon", since public perception of women with records is that they must be particularly "tough" or they would have been diverted out of the system (as the majority of women are).

Most exoffender advocate agencies who provide employment and training services fail to follow-up with both male and female offenders once they have placed them in jobs. Given the fragility of the population and its inexperience in the "straight" employment world, this is reprehensible. The results are typically short-term job retention, and often rearrest.

Having depicted the somewhat depressing "state of the art," I should like to offer some alternative considerations for change; some of which might prove useful to program planners and operatives who genuinely seek to provide more effective preemployment and placement (with follow-through) services for female offenders.

Since current CETA regulations designate exoffenders as a primary population target, it is imperative that local advocates impel CETA prime sponsors to fund adequate numbers of programs that focus upon exoffender training and placement. Importantly, sufficient pressure must be brought to bear for the funding of exclusively female "slots" or totally female programs in the community.

Major city CETA prime sponsors must be encouraged to fund in-jail or in-prison preemployment and training programs for female inmates, even if the penal facility is outside the circumscribed boundaries of the prime sponsor area. *Note:* There is a precedent for this in the New York City Department of Employment's funding of a prerelease clerical program at the Bedford Hills Facility in Westchester County. It is clear that most inmates in any state will come from the urban areas, and will return to them.

Departments of Correction must bring a diversity of atypical employment training options into female institutions or, alternatively (and better), provide access for female inmates to manual skills training in male correctional facilities.

Optimal use must be made of work release so that women may be enabled to try out their recently acquired skills and/or on-the-job experience without the pressure of embarking upon new careers while attempting to regenerate families, and incurring rental and child care costs on very limited salaries.

Advocate agencies providing training and employment services must cease to exist in a vacuum. Active participation of employers must be sought as evaluators (including in-prison program visitation and feedback) and as components of on-going advisory boards whose advise is seriously considered. Personnel in job development and vocational counseling capacities must include individuals with private sector backgrounds.

So alien is the work environment to most female offenders that serious (and long-term) employment programs should necessarily consider transitional employment through "supported work" projects or adult work experience (available through CETA).

Vocational counseling must begin at the point of incarceration and continue through a minimum of one year in the labor market. While this process is staff-intensive, the retention results warrant its implementation. Advocate agencies should be penalized by funding sources for failure to maintain demonstrable contact with both client and employer for a minimum of 12 months.

Employment services for female offenders must necessarily include the totality of the individuals family construct. Programs must include a staffing configuration that maximizes the capability to assist the woman *and* her children.

Programs seriously intending to aid female exoffenders must avoid the tempting option of imposing middle class female aspirations upon clients. To many women involved in the criminal justice system, postrelease employment in clerical positions represents the fulfillment of personal dreams of upward social and economic mobility. In short, programs must listen to and understand the individualized experiences and aspirations of clients.

Chapter 25

VOCATIONAL REHABILITATION
Options for Women

Denise Cappelli

The purpose of this paper is to outline some of the problems that must be dealt with by vocational rehabilitation counselors working with female alcoholic clients, and to describe some of the techniques used to overcome these obstacles. These impediments have been experienced by counselors at the Nassau County Department of Drug and Alcohol Addiction, but their general applications are not specific to that geographic area.

The initial role of the vocational rehabilitation counselor is to focus on the career and vocational issues that relate to the client as she goes through the treatment process. The first noticeable obstacle facing the female client is the lack of career awareness on her part. In most cases, it seems that these clients, especially the older women, have not been programmed throughout their lives to think in terms of careers for themselves. Instead they have been considering duties as wives and mothers, and staying at home. This lack of career awareness manifests itself in several ways.

First, the female client knows little about occupations. Aside from an awareness of the stereotyped jobs as nurse, secretary, and teacher, they basically do not know about opportunities for women in other occupational areas.

Similarly, they do not know their own career potential. Not having thought about careers for themselves outside the home, they, therefore, have not concerned themselves with an evaluation of their own skills and potentials.

In most cases these clients have no training for careers outside the home, nor did the majority of our female clients possess valuable marketable skills. (It seems that while the boys were learning carpentry and mechanics in shop class, the girls were learning to cook and sew in home economics.)

Another handicap is the lack of employment experience or at least of recent employment. Once again, the older clients seem to more likely fit into this category. Women who marry and start families in early adulthood usually have short work histories, if any at all. For the most part, these are entry-level positions, because not enough time was accumulated for any significant job promotions. This lack of exposure to the world of work manifests itself in a basic unfamiliarity with general employment situation procedures and healthy work habits, low self-confidence regarding job seeking processes, and a fear of employment itself.

Once vocational rehabilitation counselors recognize the special needs of their female clients, they can attempt to address them effectively in counseling. Special programs and procedures must be added to the more traditional vocational counseling processes that relate to these specific needs.

In Nassau County, we have stablished a vocational evaluation center for our substance abuse clients. Participants attend the program five hours per day for a period of four to six weeks. Reading, spelling, and mathematics levels are obtained, and clerical, manual, and mechanical aptitudes are tested. In addition to the evaluation of basic skills and other vocational testing, the special needs of our clients are addressed.

Film strips and written materials on occupations are presented to the clients. Field trips are made to local training schools and job sites. Training requirements and working conditions are thus explained to clients.

Considering the limited work background of our clients, we have attempted to simulate the employment experience by having participants punch in and out on time cards and conduct themselves in a manner appropriate to being at work. In addition to the vocational testing mentioned previously, more subtle, yet equally critical issues such as attendance and punctuality; attitudes towards assignments, authority, and peers; and general work habits are assessed. This simulated work environment serves not only as an evaluative tool, but exposes clients to a "job" experience and helps to enhance their self-confidence in this area.

Addressing the need for an accurate picture of their own career potential, feedback on all levels of the evaluation is presented to the client upon the completion of the program, and at regular intervals during the process. Valid feedback is essential to help the client plan realistic vocational goals for herself. Subsequent to the completion of the evaluation, educational training, employment, and other appropriate referrals are made.

In addition to the previously mentioned vocational handicaps of the clients themselves, certain environmental factors also create obstacles. In most cases, these are more difficult to overcome.

First and foremost is the problem of finding adequate funding and financial resources for necessary skills training. According to the current regulations of the New York State Office of Vocational Rehabilitation, alcoholism is not considered a primary handicap. (We have been told that these regulations are about to be revised; however, changes have not occurred to date.) Therefore, the funding for occupational training that is available to drug abusers and persons with other emotional or physical handicaps is not accessible to the alcoholic. Although the NCDDAA treats spouses of alcoholics and other family members as primary clients, the state funding agencies in some cases do not. Because many of our female clients are spouses of alcoholics with no alcohol histories of their own, they are further disadvantaged by not being eligible for certain programs, such as the work evaluation center previously mentioned.

Another problem in this area is that state and federal educational funding programs such as BEOG, TAP, and CETA, when determining financial eligibility for their awards, use combined family income as their criteria. This works against women in the following ways: The woman whose husband is alcoholic and not providing adequate financial support to the household is still considered according to his gross income. The woman who is not living with her husband, yet is not legally separated from him, is also considered according to her husband's income. Because the financial guidelines for these awards are so extreme, the large majority of women who are not already receiving public assistance do not qualify to use these needed resources.

There are two other significant obstacles that our female clients in Nassau County must face when considering training and/or employment. The first is the lack of availability of public or moderately priced private day care centers for preschoolaged youngsters. Once again, with the exception of women on public assistance, most women in our area do not meet financial criteria for government sponsored day care centers and cannot afford private programs. The second problem is the lack of an adequate public transportation system. Because a considerable number of women do not have the unlimited use of a private motor vehicle, public transportation is vital for the daily attendance to school or at work.

As previously mentioned, environmental obstacles are even more difficult to overcome than the women's personal handicaps. This is because we do not have control over the powers that dictate policy, and our input is usually not encouraged. It therefore, becomes necessary for vocational rehabilitation counselors not only to be aware of all the resource agencies and their eligibility criteria; but their roles must also include actions of advocacy on behalf of their clients and, in many instances, training their clients themselves to be their own promoters.

Chapter 26

STEREOTYPES AND STIGMA

Barriers to Recovery

Jacquelyn H. Hall

The topic for today's session is particularly intriguing: What happens after treatment? When the crisis is over and the dust settles, how does a woman "keep her act together?" While I will focus my remarks on what happens after a woman experiences mental illness, the ideas also are pertinent to women whose personal crises have involved drugs, alcohol, or criminal justice.

I submit that there is a special double-edged sword cutting away at a woman's chances for full recovery when she is mentally ill. One edge keeps cutting because she is a woman, the other because she is or has been mentally ill. Together those two edges can slice big chunks out of any woman's potential for putting her life back together. These two "cutting edges" I speak of are *stereotyped sex roles and stigma.*

STEREOTYPED SEX ROLES

Ask most people in this society—in fact, ask yourself—to describe a mentally healthy person. I suspect that you may think of adjectives and ideas such as active, competent, independent, showing initiative, able to solve problems, and under control in times of crisis.

Now contrast those notions with some of the stereotypes about women. Far too often women are thought of as being passive, dependent, helpless, submissive, conforming, incompetent, and emotional.

Furthermore, this stereotype is compounded by society's assignment of, shall we say, a *contingent* role for women. A woman often has an identity that is contingent on someone else. For example: I am *their* mother, I am *his* wife, I am *his* secretary, I am *her* maid. In other words, I exist because I have a relationship to someone else who is real! A woman often has life plans that are contingent on someone else. A woman is trained to expect and relish a life in which her place of residence, lifestyle, educational aspirations, and work plans are designed to accommodate her husband's career decisions and her family's personal desires. There is evidence that if a woman is deviant—that is, if she becomes competent, competitive, independent, and powerful—the enjoyment of her success is well-tempered by rejection, isolation, suspicion, and skepticism from others.

Let us not forget that men also are victims of stereotyped sex roles. In this society, a man is expected to be independent, competitive, willing to assume leadership, able to solve problems, physically robust, emotionally stoic, and always able to control himself and others.

The male and the female stereotypes interact differently with the stigma of mental illness. But before I describe that complex interaction let us consider what *stigma* means.

STIGMA OF MENTAL ILLNESS

The word *stigma,* like the word *stereotype,* is difficult to define in simple language. But the experience of stigma, like the experience of stereotype, has a profound, palpable effect on its victims. Stigmatized individuals are people who deviate from what a person "ought" to be. Stigma, in general, is characterized by a situation in which one finds oneself disqualified from full social acceptance. Stigma, like stereotype, sometimes takes the form of flagrant discrimination, but (perhaps more often) also takes the form of sensitive nuances—little things—subtle actions and intuitive exchanges. In the case of mental illnesses, those nuances say, "You are quarantined from the rest of society because you have been mentally ill."

Our society stigmatizes several different types of people; one type includes people with some sort of character blemish. The character blemish means that a person is believed to be weak-willed or treacherous; and those characteristics are inferred from a known record of mental disorders, imprisonment, addiction, alcoholism, homosexuality, unemployment, suicidal attempts, or radical political behavior. Granted, the concept of mental illness as retribution for sin seems to be fading—at least from middle-class discussions—but there still are moral connotations associated with mental illness.

By definition, so-called normal people believe the person with a stigma—in this case mental illness—is not quite human. Operating on this assumption, the "normals" then exercise various discriminations that effectively, if unwittingly, undercut the stigmatized individual's chance of survival.

What is the stigmatized individual's view? Unfortunately, the crippling stereotypes about mental illness are so pervasive that they have often been internalized by ex-patients. Many who have been treated for mental illness maintain the belief that they themselves are weak, incapable, unpredictable, untrustworthy, "sick," "crazy," or whatever.

But if the stigmatized individual reacts defensively (especially if that person's stigma is because of mental illness) the "normals" view the defensiveness as one more expression of the illness. (And if the "normal" person happens to be a mental health professional they are even *more* likely to interpret defensiveness as pathology!) After all, that's how "normals" justify the way they treat a stigmatized individual.

While it is true that people are better informed about mental illness and better disposed toward mental patients than they have been in the past, still a major portion of the population continues to be frightened and repelled by the notion of mental illness. Just a year ago the President's Commission on Mental Health made the point clearly:

Mentally ill and mentally retarded persons discharged from hospitals face difficulties in being accepted by people in their home communities. Too often, they return to find ignorance, prejudice, and fear of mental illness, discrimination, and social ostracism . . . people who have mental health problems, or who have had them in the past, often are discriminated against when they seek housing or employment, when they are involved in divorce or custody proceedings, when they are asked to serve on juries, and even when they attempt to vote.

Physical illness tends to make people sympathetic, and generally there is a belief that when a person recovers from a physical illness he or she is whole again. This is not so with mental illness, which repels people, and ex-mental patients simply are *not* perceived with the same trust, good will, and restoration of the former "normal" status that is reassigned to ex-medical patients.

There is no doubt that generally when people encounter someone who has been labeled mentally ill, they are not pleased to meet that person. Encounters between "normals" and stigmatized persons tend to be overwhelmingly uncomfortable. On the one hand, the stigmatized individual may feel unsure how "normals" will identify and receive him or her. On the other hand, "normals" may feel that if they show direct sympathetic concern they may be overstepping personal boundaries; yet, if they act as if nothing is wrong, they may make impossible demands or unintentionally slight the other person. The net result is that the very anticipation of being in the presence of each other leads both people to avoid each other. And, naturally, that avoidance leads to isolation, suspicion, and misunderstandings.

STIGMA AND STEREOTYPES TOGETHER

Let us consider the stereotyped sex roles again, but this time let us think about what happens as they combine with the stigma of mental illness.

Research shows that males are more heavily stigmatized for deviant behavior, especially mental illness, than are females. After all, remember that men are expected to be emotionally stoic and "in control of themselves and others." Perhaps also where unpredictability, especially violence, is involved, men instill more fear in others because of their physical strength.

So a man who has a mental health crisis may suffer more self-imposed and more socially imposed shame and isolation. Yet his rearing, from the earliest ages, has trained him to stand strong, take charge, solve problems, and provide for himself and his family. Shame and stigma notwithstanding, typically he knows that those are his "duties" because he is a man. He is inundated with subtle or overt messages that encourage strength and self-sufficiency. When he continues to be weak and needs care, he is not easily forgiven.

There are advantages and disadvantages to this situation. It is an advantage for a man to be socially encouraged to get well and take care of himself. It is a disadvantage when he feels the stigma and stereotype so intensely that he will not seek out or use services and care that he genuinely needs. It also is a disadvantage when services and care are delivered grudgingly, further highlighting his failure to live up to chauvinistic expectations.

Females, more often than males, are thought of and treated as helpless and needing to be taken care of. Generally, women are not trained as well as men are to solve problems or to get what they want by their own actions. They are not necessarily expected to be "in control." They are (by popular opinion) emotional, dependent, and incompetent as mental patients are thought to be. So the role differential is not so great, that is, "mentally healthy" women are thought to be more like mental patients than mentally healthy men are. Therefore, when a woman becomes a patient, there is more tolerance for her. She bears some shame and stigma associated with mental illness, but not so much as her male counterpart does. She is forgiven when she needs care, after all, the care is only an extension of what a woman demands already. Women never were completely accountable for erratic behavior, emotionality, finances, or general life conditions, so this mentally ill woman certainly is not accountable.

Again, there are advantages and disadvantages. It is an advantage for a woman to be willing to ask for and use the care and services she needs, and it is an advantage when those services are rendered in a supportive manner. It is a disadvantage when she is perpetually unaccountable for her actions; when dependence, passivity, and submissiveness are condoned and even encouraged; when society maintains its suspicion and fear of her mental illness but does not encourage her to develop power over her own life. In short, it is a disadvantage when society does not even ask a woman to recover.

RECOVERY

There seems to be a pervasive, perhaps dangerous basic assumption underlying definitions even clinical measures of "recovery." That assumption has been that the "recovered" person willingly resumes the living conditions, responsibilities, and life-style that he or she had before mental health treatment was necessary. Indeed, the socially imposed burden on the ex-patient is to prove that the illness and the symptoms were peculiar "glitches" in an otherwise smooth running mechanical system that remains unchanged by the temporary detour through a psychiatric hospital or some other form of mental health treatment.

But mental illness is *not* a mere "glitch" in a mechanical system. It emerges from a complex web of life conditions, personality traits, and biologic factors; psychiatric or psychological treatment is a profound experience. Mental illness and its treatment touch a person's innermost being, and that person must be allowed to integrate the experience into his or her self-image and social identity. Granted, sometimes the changes that are wrought through insights gained in illness and in treatment may feel awkward at first. For example, a woman may refuse to be a long suffering servant to her family; a man may refuse to be a slave to the competitive marketplace. Either of them may want to talk about what it was like to be hospitalized. Either of them may be suspicious of society's so-called helping institutions, particularly mental health institutions.

Whatever the circumstances of a particular individual, let us not be guilty of perpetuating stigma and stereotypes, for they are *barriers to recovery.*

As long as we allow mentally ill people and the subject of mental illness to be closeted away with "shameful" family skeletons, we do not allow their reality to be integrated into our own lives; moreover, we do not allow the reality of illness and treatment to be constructively integrated into patients' lives. In short, we perpetuate the painful stigma associated with mental illness—and that is a *barrier to recovery.* And as long as we expect "successfully treated" patients to fall right into traditional womanly or manly roles, no matter what insights they may now have about the unhealthy constrictions of those roles, we perpetuate sex stereotyping, which is another *barrier to recovery.*

I ask you to extend your hands to mentally ill women and men. Help them be strong. Look carefully at services and check out post-intervention systems. For the sake of all of us, do not let the unnecessary barriers of *stigma* and *stereotypes* be imposed on people trying to recover.

Part III

MAKING CHANGE

It isn't that we haven't asked, it isn't that we haven't begged, it isn't that we haven't pleaded, it isn't that we haven't fought, it isn't that we haven't organized—we have done all of those things. We have asked and begged and pleaded for recognition in the power structures of this nation. We are now essentially in a situation in which under inflation, which all of us feel very painfully, we find our condition worse. You're discussing here the problems of women in crisis. They are not unrelated to the status of women in society, they're not unrelated to the stereotyping of women, they're not unrelated to the frustration and the despair, and the inability of society to really cope and deal with as total human beings in our midst. Why is it, if the polls show, as I just read to you, as they do for example about the Equal Rights Amendment, the majority of men and women support it, not only nationally but even in the states that have not ratified it —I mean the last six Presidents of this country have supported the Equal Rights Amendment, Democrats and Republicans, their wives support it, the AFL-CIO supports us, all kinds of organizations; the Girl Scouts support us. Everybody supports the Equal Rights Amendment. But yet we don't have it. Everyone believes that women should have equality, but yet we don't have it. And it's the third stage that I'm interested in, Doctor Mead, that is the stage we are in. We don't have it because those in power are unwilling to let us have it, because those in power actually, I believe, as we know traditionally, people with power and authority and wealth don't share it easily, people with fixed ideas or prejudice don't relinquish them painlessly, the status quo usually doesn't like the state of things to come. We know that. But I want to make this one point, the fundamental reason that we do not have equality, either in the Constitution or in the places of power or in the economy of our nation is because there is no question that fundamentally, the long-term implication of what women want is threatening to present power relationships, and that is why for the past few years, we've seen almost, as a matter of fact, a little countereffect offenses from well-organized ultra-right-wing movements that are encountering resistance to our equality, we see it from employers who know that if there's going to be equal pay for equal work, it's going to cost them more. But it's much deeper than that. See, women are never going to secure equality in a society that has no soul. We are not going to get child care, we are not going to get proper treatment of women and alcohol, we're not going to get

Remarks by the Honorable Bella S. Abzug, Civil Rights and Civil Liberties Attorney; Former US Representative; Founder of W.O.M.A.N.

the understanding of what we really require in terms of fighting the abuse that battered women have and so on in a society that decides that it's willing to spend a hundred and thirty-seven billion dollars on a military budget while they're only prepared to spend two billion dollars on programs that affect women and children. We are not . . . we are not going to get a national health insurance program, and women are the majority of the users, and they and their children need it desperately, in a society that's willing to cave in to those people who are the prime causes of inflation, those who have enormous economic controls and monopolies; we are now about, as consumers, to give them another eighteen billion dollars while we are unable to get programs to fight for the actual survival of not only women but children and men in our society. We are not going to be able to secure that equality in a society that doesn't recognize that unless there is a society in which people are well, in which people can have jobs, in which people—we have a famous activity in this moment in history. Our whole emphasis appears to be to look upon the people who are the least capable of taking care of themselves as being the ones who are causing our problems. Inflation obviously is caused by women and children on welfare. Inflation obviously is caused by consumers who go into the stores to buy things: food, clothing, housing, shelter. Well, in fact, we know that inflation is caused by those who have enormous control over the sources and areas of inflation: energy, housing, food processing, transportation, and so on. We don't see any effort to go after those people. We see the highest profits in the history of various corporations being reported at the same time we see the highest inflation in the last four years. So that in order for women to be able to become part and parcel of the economic resources of this nation, in order for women to have a voice in the political policy structures that perpetuate this unfairness and this inequality in society, it means that there's going to have to be a change, not only for women but in the priorities of this nation, for men and women. We are not going to have to fight men to secure our equality. What we really have to do is fight together with men in order to create a society in which we can share equally in the great resources of this nation.

On the other hand, as far as women are concerned, we will never turn back to a time when women were segregated in auxiliaries and prevented from using their skills and abilities and barred from places of power. Some significant progress has been made; some women have been able to make some steps up this so-called ladder of success.

But they are relatively few. They're relatively high visible people in very special areas of activity, professions, and so on and so forth.

I always wanted to be a lawyer, ever since I was a little kid of eleven, so I went to Hunter College. Those were the days when it was free, and I would never have been up here had I not been able to go to a free college, and I'm still for that. Anyhow, when I was at Hunter College, I decided I was going to go to law school, I had decided it when I was eleven years old, so I had heard that Harvard Law School was the best in the country, and, you know, there were very few women lawyers in those days, it's a long time ago, believe me. I was born the year we got to vote. 1920, right, I'm going to be 59. So, you know, it's an interesting coincidence, I was born that year, and therefore I'm a lawyer . . . quite a long time. Anyhow, this was in 1942—I might as well tell you everything . . . about this. And so I decided that I had to go to the best law school in the country, cause it was going to be tough for me. So I wrote a letter to Harvard, and Harvard wrote a letter back to me. And they said, Sorry, but we don't accept women. I was kind of outraged at that, as you can imagine, having a big reputation, bigger than I actually deserve for being outraged all the time, so I was pretty upset, and I turned to my mother . . . well, in those days we didn't have a woman's movement, so you turned to your mother . . . I turned to my mother and I said, don't you think this is outrageous, they don't want me there just because I'm a woman, and my mother said, Well, what do you want to go to Harvard for anyhow? She said, it's far away. See I lived in the Bronx. For you out-of-towners, the Bronx is one of the five boroughs, you're in a borough called Manhattan, we have Queens, we have Brooklyn, we have Staten Island, and we have the Bronx. Sort of. Anyhow, my mother said, it's far away and you don't have the carfare anyhow. If you go to Columbia, they'll probably give you a scholarship, after all, you're local, you know. It's right near the Bronx, it'll only cost five cents on the subway, and I did that. I went to Columbia, they gave me a scholarship, it cost five cents on the subway, and that's how I became an advocate of low-cost mass transportation. But I also became a lawyer. I became a lawyer and as some of you know, I practiced law for many many years. Well, anyhow this summer I had the great pleasure of seeing my younger daughter graduate from law school in a class where 30 percent were women.

So changes have been made, but they've essentially affecting a rather limited number of highly visible, qualified professional areas.

But I don't think we're going to have to turn back. I think women are moving forward. I think that we will no longer accept the condition in which only men rule the cities, the states, the nation, and the world, excluding half the human race from effective economic and political power. Not when the world is in such bad shape.

I get into lots of arguments about if we arrive at the stage where we do share power with men, whether we will create a better world. I believe we will. I believe when we have the opportunity, we can figure out ways to spend some of the four hundred billion dollars being spent on armaments each year for more rational and humane purposes, like feeding the hungry, and housing the homeless and creating jobs, preventing disease and ignorance and illiteracy. The problem is how do we get there? The problem is, can we be tough enough? The problem is, do we understand what our challenge really is? Do we understand that inherent in the struggle of women is really the potential for change for women and minorities and labor and elderly people in our society because we're a majority of every one of that group and have a responsibility in every one of those groups. And we have the need in every one of those groups because we are the most oppressed in every single way. And we therefore have the responsibility to lead, to create that change in this country. We have to be able to move forward in such a way that we are prepared to make our needs and our program a priority above all other programs, because it carries with it the need to create the changes that will create more equality for men and women. We have to emerge as a major independent political force. We have to emerge as a major economic force. We have to be able to register our numbers so that it can be clear that we could mobilize it, we have to be able to support women. Doctor Mead says we don't support women enough. I suppose that's true; I think we're learning; I think we're coming to understand that women have a great deal in common and there's a commonality of interest that requires us to band together. And that we would work together with men to create a better society, but we have to organize ourselves.

We have to be able to recognize that in 1979 and 1980, as we go into a presidential election, that we have to insist that the priorities that we have for the women you are discussing here today and the other women that I have mentioned, who are in conditions of great crisis, have to become a priority for all women, especially for women. If we run as delegates in conventions, we have to have a national platform, a platform for women which says, this is our program, we support nobody unless there is a commitment to this. We commit to nobody until there is a commitment to our needs; that goes for presidential nomination as well as a senatorial or a congressional or a state legislator in the states where the Equal Rights Amendment has not been ratified. It seems to me that our priority should be to visit electoral punishment on those state legislators who are standing in the way of the progress of the majority of the people in this country.

We have a particular responsibility because we are consumers and budgeteers. We have a responsibility to show that we can use our numbers to object to the kind of prices that are driving us to the point where we don't know whether we're going to be able to afford survival tomorrow. We ought to be able through consumer boycotts of all kinds to be able to express our views in our determination that we're not going to permit ourselves to be the victims of inflation, while corporate profits and a failure to do anything about the continuing inflation takes place, except to say that we should tighten our belts. Well, I tightened mine. You might notice, I've lost a lot of weight. But that is not how you fight inflation. The fifteen billion dollars that were cut were being proposed to be cut in the federal budget which affects the programs which we need here in this room, and that we need for women who need jobs and job training and who need health care and who need mental health care and who need to be able to be dealt with in the problems of alcoholism and drug abuse. That fifteen billion dollars, by the way, cut the programs for women so that we have fewer jobs and fewer job trainees. It cut the programs of maternal health and nutritional programs. It doesn't provide for a meaningful child care program, either for the people on welfare or for working people. It doesn't provide for health insurance, it even fails to provide the kind of money we need to fight the teenage pregnancy that is a virtual epidemic in this country. And as you know, there's a plan to cut from those people who can least afford to survive and those are the senior citizens of whom probably two-thirds are women. I say that the fifteen billion dollars and other economists who are representative of the whole full scale have said that that fifteen billion dollars that has been cut will have less than three-tenths of one percent impact on inflation. Now you are the professionals in the field of problems, in the field of crisis. But it's not enough to counsel, it's not enough to aid, it's not enough to help, you have to be the activists also, to lead toward the changes that have to be taking place. You have to participate in the activism in this society to create the change that will make this truly an egalitarian society.

My friend Millicent Fenwick, the Republican Congresswoman, tells this great story that when she was in the state legislature in New Jersey, she was fighting for the Equal Rights Amendment. One of her colleagues got up and said, "I don't know, Millicent, I don't agree with you, I don't think women should have equality, because I always believe that women should be kissable, cuddly, and smell good." Whereupon Millicent answered, "That's funny. Because that's how I always thought men should be." And then she added, "I hope you won't be disappointed as many times as I have been."

Well, really, the point of this story of mine is quite clear. We all want to be kissable, cuddly, and smell good. We all want to be loved; we all want to feel part of society. We all want to feel that our needs and our hopes and our problems and the problems of the women you discuss here today can be dealt with. I mean, after all, we were here from the beginning. Women fought at the frontiers of this nation. We have worked in its factories and its fields and its institutions and its homes. We say to America, we love you, God knows, we'd have to love to take the kind of stuff we've had to take all of these years. But we want you to love us, too. We want to feel that you listen to us and that you care about us. We want to feel that we're part of this country, that we have rights and we have the responsibilities that every other human being that is not a woman has. We want to work together with men, we want them to be kissable and cuddly too, we want to help them smell good. God knows, they're not smellin' so good right now. Because the crisis is not of our doing. We had no control, we've had no power. The actual reins of power have been in the hands of only one part of the population, and they need a lot of help and we want to help them, and we want to be able to help them so that we can look forward to another day, we can look forward to another day in which the generations that we helped to create can believe that there was a fight that took place, a fight not only for equality, but for a better world, a world which didn't allow oil to dictate policies at home and abroad, which didn't allow the reckless use of nuclear or a nuclear arms race to destroy us, but a world which dealt with building and a world which dealt with caring, a world in which it is understood that equality is at the core of this.

Chapter 27

POSTINTERVENTION AND SUPPORT SYSTEMS

Ruth W. Messinger

Good afternoon. Let me say, by way of introduction, and because of some of the critical things I intend to say, that I am a professional social worker as well as an elected official. I worked in both traditional and innovative programs before I ran for office. The criticisms I will offer of services that are available for women in crisis are criticisms of service with which I have been professionally involved.

Our topic today is "postintervention support systems." We cannot talk about what should happen after the fact if we don't first acknowledge what it is that has gone before. The term *postintervention* is dangerous because its connotation is favorable or at least neutral. It suggests somehow that the intervention we are following up on was voluntary, appropriate, nondiscriminatory, helpful, and therapeutic, and that therefore all we need to do is follow up on it better and provide the right kind of continued professional or lay assistance or support.

Unfortunately, I do not assume any of those premises. In fact, I think it is safer and fairer to assume the opposite, that the women-in-crisis, the women intervened with, were to some extent being blamed for the problems of our society, that they were and are the victim of discrimination on the basis probably of sex, race, age, and income, and that the intervention itself may have involved forced separation from family and community without any positive treatment.

Even the best interventions, those that offer a real opportunity for change and that have actual concrete results, do not deal adequately with the most fundamental aspects of the problems we are trying to solve. They do not because they cannot. Alone, they cannot change the nature of the society in which those women were functioning and to which they have to return. Also, they do not deal fully enough with the psychological impact of having been singled out, labeled, treated, perceived as a victim, or fear of being again out on one's own, after the intervention. And they rarely deal with the reaction of those in her immediate universe—her family, her community, her friends—and the problems that those persons have in adjusting to the intervention and then to the return.

What needs to happen is not only tackling some of those problems and make both the intervention and the postintervention experiences more positive but even more important, we have to help move toward a society in which we have to do a lot less intervention because there is a lot more support.

More specifically I'm talking about three major kinds of change. One is a very different professional response to the woman or the person in crisis. Two is a much more dramatic emphasis on new and different program services emphasizing prevention, support, and mutual self-help. Three is a rising tide of social concern, mutual on behalf of both the professionals and the population being served, with the fundamental problems in this society that make so many of these crises occur in the first place.

First, as professionals, we have been all too given to disappearing after the major intervention is made, leaving the person likely to go immediately back through the revolving door. We need to demand of ourselves and the rest of our professional colleagues a different understanding of what is involved for the woman-in-crisis, both psychologically and practically. We need to do whatever it is that allows us to understand what it is like to be her. I'm not really talking about anything much more complicated than a basic and fundamental act of empathy, but I think it is not easy, and therefore too often given lip service, but no reality.

I would urge all of us all the time to stay in touch with an experience of ourselves as prisoners, whether in the physical space, in a relationship, in a job, some experience that each of us has had in which we have felt irrationally or unfairly punished and confined.

That fundamental empathic experience is necessary to understanding the feelings of neglect, anger, and rage that the women we are talking about experience. Similiarly, I would urge us to get in touch with an experience of ourselves as a victim being "taken." Did I ask for this? Is this my fault? What is it that I have to change so that this won't happen again? As professionals, we need always to understand that it is easier to discuss food stamps regulations or arrange medical care, no matter how difficult those are, than it is to really be in touch with another person's pain, but that both of those abilities are necessary.

We need to expand our professional care-giving ability so that we begin to treat people as people, so that we have as one of our major goals in providing help or support the empowering of other people and the moving of those people beyond a professional relationship into an empowered life system. This involves increasing that person's ability to recognize and use their own strength, sharing our strength with them, and working constantly to put ourselves out of work. Also, it means acknowledging to those people we try to help that a lot that we ask them to do, a lot of aspects of the government system with which we ask them to be in contact are fundamentally oppressive and abusive and very often don't work the way they're supposed to.

I think I need to talk only briefly about providing support systems because most of you know what I mean and are trying to do it. I'm talking about systems in which the individuals who have been probably still are in crisis feel increasingly empowered to meet their own needs. Partly because they are finding themselves in a universe of people who have shared elements of their same experience and can help. For those of you who are in New York or know our programs, I would cite as examples the Fortune Society and Project Return; Greenhope, which is a half-way house and job training program for women ex-offenders; and a program called Pace that works with ex-hospitalized mothers by providing a day-care experience for their children and involving the mothers in that experience.

Finally, I wish to see a different emphasis on the part of all of us and the people with whom we work in moving toward comprehensive social change. It is, of course, the job of all of us to see that the programs that do make a difference get funding, that the money in this system begins to go where it is needed most. But I am talking about going beyond questions of program funding, beyond even the question of providing adequate employment opportunities for the women we are talking about. I am talking about working together to attack the fundamental sex, race, and class biases that have helped to create many women's problems and helped to exacerbate their readjustment difficulties.

It is our job to focus locally and nationally on the pervasive crises of race and of poverty, to become advocates for change on behalf of the people we serve, and to the greatest extent possible to involve them in those same actions. A huge effort is necessary in a time in which government is saying, "we can't provide, we can't afford, we can't meet service needs." We must help people—colleagues, clients, friends, the voting public—understand that we will have to pay over the long run for failing to attend to the fundamental problems in our country now. People must know how very little we provide for the poorest people in our society, and they must be asked to imagine what it would mean to return from a life crisis and continue to have to provide for yourself and your children on $2.08 per person per day. People must understand that the rate at which we are meeting the needs of the poorest people in our society is as if we were to say, "what we want to do is to fund hunger, disease, and illiteracy, to fund family break-up, and to fund street crime." People must realize that we provide so little money so badly and in such abusive systems that we create many of the problems we feel saddled with.

They are our responsibility. Only if we begin to tackle them directly will they be able to make the kind of system in which there are fewer crises. There is much more to do to help people get beyond those crises and return to full and productive lives. Let me leave you with one final thought, a quote that comes from ancient Greece and sums up what I've been saying, "There will be justice in Athens only when the uninjured parties are as indignant as the injured parties." Thank you.

Chapter 28

ESTABLISHING INTERDISCIPLINARY TREATMENT NETWORKS

Flora Koppel

Most service agencies, being comprised of humans, suffer from a somewhat parochial point of view. This tendency is frequently reinforced or even mandated by the bureaucratic procedures of funding agencies. It is obvious that in order to provide optimal service to clients combined with a prodigious utilization of all available resources, especially the resources proferred by other service providers, is of the essence. Thus, the issue we need to examine seems to be what does a coordinated interdisciplinary network look like and how can it best be achieved. It seems most expedient to begin this examination by looking at communication and coordination in an agency-to-agency level because any necessary changes at a higher governmental level will emerge from here.

The most likely starting point would seem to be a vigorous community education campaign to make known the parameters of one's service. In this case, the term *community* must be enlarged to include the larger as well as the surrounding community and even, optimally, to extend to relevant service providers in other states. To this end, a national information clearinghouse with a minimum of bureaucratic redtape would seem to be called for. Very often, the exact resource desperately required by a client may either be around the corner or far across the country. Too often, however, we may be equally unknowledgeable of the existence and the appropriate function of both services. A national information clearinghouse would help to minimize such information gaps and would help ensure a more interlocking, full-bodied treatment web with progressively fewer holes. Conferences such as this provide, of course, another means of information exchange.

None of the above, however, negates the responsibility for continuous ongoing educational efforts at the agency level, which may take varied forms. No matter what the form, however, such educative efforts ensure an enriched flow of appropriate referral sources bringing clients into the agency as well as a deeper, broader reservoir of resources to which a client can be referred out of the agency, as dictated by client need. Furthermore, hopefully, continuous educative efforts by all service providers would lead to more enlightened cooperation and coordination of endeavors.

In my agency, a regular two-week institute on alcoholism is offered for interested individuals as well as staff of agencies who would seem to benefit from a comprehensive understanding of the disease of alcoholism. Before the beginning of each institute cycle, contact is made with appropriate service providers who would potentially benefit from such training, both through mailing of literature and through personal contact by members of our Community Education Department. Agencies whose staff members attend the institute represent a wide range of disciplines, including Dept. of Social Services, Bureau of Child Welfare, drug programs, medical hospitals, alcoholism treatment facilities, parole, probation, mental health facilities, the clergy, the school system, etc. Thus, the foundation is laid for improved interagency and interdisciplinary understanding, the payoff of which is better interfacing of services. Ultimately, this must result in more consistent, comprehensive service for the client with fewer of those frustrating (often near fatal) treatment gaps that frequently seem to yawn before us and the client like bottomless pits.

Such interchange of information is particularly important in treatment for women. The available resource supply is so sparse that ingenious and creative interutilization of whatever services do exist is the only possibility for providing even a semblance of adequate treatment. Conscientious efforts by service providers to educate one another lays at least the cornerstone for such informed interutilization.

Furthermore, educative endeavors should not be conceptualized as the sole province of a small specialized department within each agency. Each counselor, therapist, etc., should conceive of him- or herself as an educator of sorts. At our agency, the counselor is encouraged to make immediate contact with the referral service as well as with all agencies (and individuals such as significant others) with whom the client may be integrally involved. Often the first task, especially in dealing with individuals from the disciplines, is to communicate as succinctly as possible the essence of the disease concept of alcoholism and some of the possible behavioral manifestations that may color all work with the alcoholic client. Certainly, the individual from the other agency should also be encouraged to communicate any information that may be helpful in understanding the agency's point of view, because this will certainly influence the cooperative interactions that must ensue in order to achieve optimal service for the client. Such an interchange initiates the efforts for the two or sometimes more than two agencies to work out a contract or set of cooperative guidelines for dealing with the particular client. In this, each should make clear the structures under which the agency operates; what the agency can and cannot provide; the methods, approaches, and techniques he or she is most likely to utilize; what he or she will need from the other agencies in terms of dealing with the client; and the role he or she envisions for each agency in the treatment process.

Such a contract, if thoughtfully and creatively set up, as well as cooperatively implemented, will ensure coordinated, comprehensive, and maximized service for the client. It will stimulate each agency and discipline to contribute that which it can most efficiently and effectively provide (which, of course, may differ from individual case to individual case) and the various discipline's contributions will interface in a way most beneficial, in the long run, for the client. In this way, two or more agencies may pull together, in the same direction, toward mutually agreed upon common goals. This will prevent the all-too-frequent occurrence where the client is put in an institutionally created double-bind situation often pulled in several directions at once by various agencies who are purportedly to be serving client needs, while in reality serving primarily agency needs and point-of-view, or, even worse, sometimes the prejudice and needs of the individual worker.

The kind of coordinated treatment best achieved through interdisciplinary cooperation is especially important when dealing with the women in crisis. She enters treatment with all the problems and needs of the man. She frequently has numerous additional problems and needs, however. She is generally more stigmatized by her alcoholism and, thus, is likely to have a more severely impaired self-image and sense of self-worth and a more highly developed sense of shame. She is more likely to be responsible for the care of children and, if she has had children removed from the home, she is likely to feel guilty and "less of a woman." The man in a similar situation is less likely to have this situation do serious damage to his sense of "being a man." The female often has fewer available resources for socializing, job training, and employment. The female alcoholic is less likely, according to many studies, to have an intact marriage. If she is still married, she is more likely to be married to an alcoholic spouse. The female may have unique health problems. It is possible that she may be pregnant, thus creating a necessity for adequate prenatal care (especially in view of recent concern regarding fetal alcohol syndrome). Additionally, pregnancy or prevention of pregnancy may be an ongoing issue. Many studies indicate that the female alcoholic is more likely to have a history of suicide attempts. They may be battered wives or girlfriends, in addition to their other problems. These are just some of the additional problems that a woman may bring to treatment. Ironically, however, not only is there a sparsity of literature and research regarding the female in crisis, in particular the female alcoholic, there is a sparsity of treatment facilities and resources that address her needs. For example, many halfway houses and long-term treatment facilities that treat alcoholism will not accept female alcoholics at all and those that do frequently have only a tiny percentage of available beds allotted for women. There are a handful, if that, of long-term treatment facilities that can treat a woman together with her children. Available child-care facilities are scarce and often require a great deal of time and bureaucratic maneuvering in order to get acceptance for the children of women who need child care to attend treatment. These are only examples of not gaps, but craters, that exist in treatment resources for women. Thus, it is obviously crucial that the few treatment resources that do exist be used both wisely and well. This makes interdisciplinary cooperation and coordination absolutely imperative in attempting to meet the needs of the women in crisis.

For example, our agency has attempted, in all of the ways described previously, to set up a working relationship with the Bureau of Child Welfare (BCW) and BCW workers. Presentations are made by our Community Education Department at BCW in-service training sessions. Frequently, BCW workers attend our alcoholism institute. When a client is either referred to our agency through BCW or has an ongoing BCW case, the counselor makes immediate contact with the appropriate BCW worker and tries to set up the type of working contract previously described. Thus, our agency and BCW may optimally be able to work together in many ways. Our agency, hopefully, can help the female alcoholic client stop drinking, resulting in an improved life for both herself and her children. Through various modalities, we can help her build up ego strengths, gain vocational skills, improve her interpersonal communication patterns, etc. All of this will better both her lot and that of her children.

If the alcoholic client does not stop drinking and participate in treatment, her children may be removed from the home or may not be returned. This may provide the "handle" often needed early in treatment before a client becomes self-motivated. On our part, we can help BCW gain a realistic assessment of the mother's readiness to handle her children. BCW may provide foster care facilities for children of an alcoholic mother who badly needs long-term treatment, but who is hampered from going into such treatment by child-care responsibilities. Of course, this separating of mother and child is not always optimally desireable (although sometimes, it may be) but such a temporary, voluntary separation is certainly preferable to a more permanent involuntary one that may result from her inability to participate in needed treatment. In other words, we do the best we can.

We have also, on many occasions, been able to negotiate written interagency agreements. One example of this is a recent agreement worked out with a neighboring hospital-connected alcoholism unit aimed at minimizing countertherapeutic manipulation by the client. Frequently, a client will leave one agency when he or she is unwilling to accept necessary treatment there and register in another agency, thereby still assuring his or her welfare grant or other fringe benefits of treatment. To preclude this type of situation, both agencies agreed on a strategy for validating the circumstances underlying the patient switching from one program to another.

I have only touched on the manifold functions that a well thought out, creatively implemented, interdisciplinary and interorganizational network could serve and have only briefly examined some of the mechanisms for achieving this. Hopefully, I have underlined the special importance such a network would assume for the alcoholic woman. Our task now is to think together and work together to achieve these ends on all systems levels, agency, community, and governmental. Such an achievement would benefit women in crisis that would, in turn, benefit society as a whole.

Chapter 29

SELF-POWER AND LEADERSHIP

Marlene Crosby Mainker

Nowhere in my script as a child or young person, or even up to age 33, did I think of myself as a leader or as someone who could have impact on other people. I'm now 39 and I only started talking to people in the last few years. Up until now, I was too quiet and shy; I lacked the confidence to make things happen for me; I lacked the confidence to project myself into leadership areas.

I am President of two corporations, one is for profit, called Clearinghouse, Inc., and the other is a nonprofit organization, called Womanpower Projects, Inc., both companies are located in Chatham, New Jersey. Both companies are devoted to many different kinds of projects to foster equality, to fight sexism, racism, ageism, and alcoholism.

One of the things our company does is career/life planning for both men and women. We help people enrich their self-images by getting them in touch with their skills. Our program includes one-on-one, small groups, and intensive two-day workshops focusing on skills and formulating career goals. I have women coming in who tell me that: "Oh, I'm just a housewife." After the workshops, they say: "Let me tell you what I can do!" It's a different change of attitude. The change occurred just by giving them tools to look at their life and assess it in a different light. Women on the whole, have had few role models. Even when I go to my office, I still look around and feel like I'm "playing office." It is not something that I was brought up to do. Women need mentors, they need other women and other men who will reach out and help them. We must learn how to develop people as mentors for us. One of the things that I have worked toward is getting a network going for women, so that they will have other resources to get in contact with each other. This conference is important, because it sets up a mechanism for women to talk to other women and men.

Because our company has fostered programs and has become an advocate for women, the State of New Jersey encouraged us to pursue a project to open a Career/Life Planning Center for Women Affected by Alcoholism. Right now, the proposal is awaiting Federal approval and we hope to open next Fall.

This particular project demonstrates how we can work towards doing innovative things to bring about a change in our society. I am very excited about this program. It's unique, it's unusual, it's going to fill a void that has not been filled before. Our program is a multifaceted approach to provide long-range rehabilitation through in-depth career/life planning. The goal focuses on the aftercare phase, enabling detoxified women to become emotionally and economically independent, giving them tools and support to change life patterns, practices, and goals. An integral part of this program will be child care for those attending the Center.

The women that are coming to my company now and the women that will attend the Alcoholism Center need the very same thing that I needed to effect changes in my life pattern. I believe that all of us, regardless of where we have been, are natural-born leaders, and are powerful as individuals. Our power remains intact, even if it has been hidden temporarily over the years. What we need are methods to uncover our hidden power and our ability to be leaders.

Before we begin to talk about a prescription for leadership and change, I would like to discuss why we even need to have a conversation like this. Why are women not natural born leaders? The answer has to do with the political power structure. I think Phyllis Chesler covers it very adequately in her book *Women, Money, and Power,* when she says that there are 13 powers in the world: Seven are controlled by men—physical, technological, scientific, military, religious, secular organized institutions, consumption. Each of the male powers can be bought with money; each is highly interchangeable or exhangeable with the other. These powers are exclusively male, although females are used to carry out their dictates. Two powers are controlled by men and women: social power and influence. The three powers that are exclusively female are physical beauty, sex, and motherhood. These last three powers are nonexchangeable, for the most part, short-lived, and nonvalued. The thirteenth power is money. Money is human energy trapped and counted in measures of gold, silver, and paper. Money is love, sex, life, time. Money power can buy and control the 12 powers. It is a power sacred to most men and foreign to women. Only the powerless live in a money culture and know nothing about money.

My point is that women have been an oppressed group, and if you look at oppression, you find that people that are oppressed feel powerless. They find themselves in powerless positions in many areas of our society. It's really only been since the women's movement of the last 10 years that there have been substantial changes coming forth in the laws (e.g., in equal credit).

What does it mean to have been brought up on a diet of sex-role stereotyping? Very often oppressed people who work their way through become oppressors. It's really a cyclic pattern. Women want to get in touch with their own feelings of power, which should not be power over other people, but power within ourselves, that is, positive power, good feelings about ourselves, a good self-image. How do we do that? How do we keep ourselves from becoming oppressors? How do we do something more positive? How do we foster other people getting in touch with their power?

What can we do about discrimination? What can we do about being oppressed? I want to recommend three things. *First, recognize it.* So many of the ways in which I was oppressed as a woman were things I was not aware of. I did not understand how society was set up and why certain things happened to me. I did not recognize oppression. I internalized the discrimination and came away feeling that everything that ever happened to me was all my fault. This is a typical powerless, oppressed method of responding to a world that is basically sexist and unequal. *The second thing,* after recognizing oppression and how we respond to it, is to *understand how it works,* and how the system is set up. *The third thing is to develop ways to combat it.* How do we break up the patterns of oppression? Not only for ourselves as women, but also for men, for minorities, for the handicapped, and for people recovering from alcoholism. In a study comparing women and men alcoholics, all of the women cited a major life crisis such as separation, divorce, death in the family, or children leaving home, as triggering the onset of heavy drinking. If a woman's identity is associated solely with her role as wife or mother, a change in her marriage or family situation will cause great stress—a "middle-age identity crisis." If a woman's worth is measured by her beauty, youth, or capability to bear children, then the loss of these qualities is a severely stressful life crisis, and may lead to alcoholism. The more we can transcend the images that society has laid at our feet, the less crippled we will be by its effects.

All of us, in a sense, are pioneers in this society, and it is we who are in transition, since we are not the people in power. Conflict for us, as women, is inevitable, no matter what path we choose. The way we can proceed and endure this struggle is to help other women see options, alternatives, and most important to be more tolerant of women who make choices that are different than the traditional woman.

In many ways, women today are caught in a no-win situation. Three life-styles for women exist. There is the traditional woman who spends 99 hours each week on home and family. This is a shrinking group of women. The "liberated" woman is a career person who goes after a career in a single-minded fashion, picking her own life-styles. She is punished for that choice because she is told she is imitating a man, or she's "not a woman." The traditional woman also gets punished because she sometimes feels that the majority of women are now working and her work is not valued, it is not counted in the gross national product, she does not have social security, and so on. Finally there is the woman who is in between—she has a career that is temporary or part-time, that career is second to her husband's work, she does not compete with men. Quite often, this woman holds two jobs ("superwoman"). She works every day, then she comes home and fulfills the work involved in being wife and mother and homemaker as well.

Personally, I hope that all women will have empathy for each other and learn not to compete with each other even though we were brought up to compete with each other over men. We have to begin to learn how to work synergistically with each other and to be supportive.

Power I am referring to does not mean dominance over someone else, but rather the power to realize your own abilities and work in a more equal society where no one is told what limits they have to put on themselves, their choice of life-styles or their career because of their role, their sex, their sexual preference, their color, or whatever; power to be able to choose for oneself what we as individuals want.

Once we achieve a position of feeling powerful and able to lead, we must impact on the society to foster change. I don't see women fitting into the society today as a goal, at least it is not a goal for me. I want society to change. I want day care; I want two people sharing one job; I want flexible working hours. In my office I have two people sharing one job. I want to be able to be a worker and to be able to live in a society that truly cares about children and family life. We are redefining family because we are no longer living in the world of nuclear families. But there must be a whole new range of services devised to fit the need of the kinds of life-styles that are emerging.

All we need to do to be leaders is to choose ourselves. Other people can choose to recognize us or not recognize us, but we don't need to be recognized as a leader to be a leader. All we need to do is choose to do it. People, particularly oppressed women, have difficulty taking initiative. Cultural patterns tell women that they are weak physically and mentally and when we begin to develop our inherent abilities and talents, we are often looked down upon as unfeminine, which is another penalty, another way of keeping us oppressed. Because if you are not a woman, then you must be a man, and nobody in this society is hated more, by both men and women, than a successful woman. That is part of recognizing it and understanding it, and overcoming it.

Political scientist, Hannah Arendt, defines freedom as "the ability to act and speak in the public sphere often with the consequence of making something happen, such as political action." Ending personal slavery, within ourselves, is the first step toward leadership, being able to speak out loud, and stand up for yourself is a big first step. Once an internal change is realized, external change can begin.

Chapter 30

FEDERAL SUPPORT

Understanding and Utilizing the Federal Dollar

Marilee Grygelko

Like it or not, dollar availability rather than programmatic need determine what community mental health care is given to anyone, whether they are female or male, black or white, rich or poor. In other words, money drives voluntary mental health care services in the community. Programs tend to spring up around accessible funding sources and not always around program need.

For example, funding often determines the type of care given and the location, duration, and cost of that care. Medicaid reimbursement formulas make it more lucrative and easier to admit a client to an inpatient psychiatric unit in a general hospital rather than to long-term outpatient care. Typically, inpatient care is staffed and provided on a medical model, and the two-week average length of stay in psychiatric units in general hospitals demonstrates clear progress toward crisis stabilization and recovery. Impatient psychiatric care in general hospitals is also revenue producing for a hospital because of lowering staffing costs and higher census than other hospital departments.

On the other hand, outpatient Medicaid reimbursement requires proof that a client's treatment is necessary, supervised by a physician, and shows demonstrable progress. In community ambulatory care programs, these factors are harder to document, and the high volume of outpatient care services and incidents often dissuades the meticulous record-keeping required to justify reimbursement. In addition, the types of programs needed as a result of examination of women's changing roles are often not fundable under traditional reimbursement formulas. Programs for battered spouses, child abuse, stress resulting from entry or re-entry into a professional world, and training for parenting have emerged in the past ten years, mostly as a result of feminism nudging people to look at themselves and each other in a different way. Such programs are not typically interventions needed for medical reasons, but they are interventions needed for social reasons. Traditional federal funding dollars such as Medicaid are not available for such programs. Title XX funding for social support programs is available and has been capped. As they currently exist, Federal entitlement and assistance programs offer little funding for the social and mental health programs now being developed as a result of a closer examination of women and their needs.

Other subtler factors tend to influence the lack of funding of the social and mental health programs now being developed. These factors are far-ranging and often ridiculous when viewed out of context, but they effect why such mental health programs have not been developed or, more importantly, have not been funded.

Women are the majority sex in the United States. Implicitly this society views any majority as able to take care of itself, and social programs are thus directed at "minorities." A crucial assumption of this implicit belief is that such a majority identifies itself, has power, and the cohesive ability to use it; by and large, women don't. Women have not been trained as managers and administrators. The power of the purse unfortunately still applies to women in the context of a department store rather than the management of an agency or institution.

Also, the overriding societal attitude is that women will survive, regardless of the kind of social and mental health programs available or not available to them. The assumption is that women are the backbone of the family and, in addition, have developed culturally in support groups based in both the family and in other women. Therefore, the investment of the social and mental health dollar is not as necessary here as elsewhere.

Strategies for Change

Given that dollars drive the community mental health system, how can they be accessed to develop needed mental health and social programs? With a future of ceilings on entitlement and categorical grant programs, the increase of block grants to states, and state and federally identified priorities for the shrinking dollar pool, what can the manager of a program of services do?

1. Identify your population, its current service needs and its service needs five years from the start of your program.
2. Develop a prioritized work plan for your agency based on those service needs, defining areas of funding expansion and retraction on several program fronts.
3. Key into a funding source with ongoing, multiple bases such as Medicaid or Title XX with state, local, and federal financial shares.
4. Develop shared service contracts and/or consortia with other providers or become affiliated with existing service providers, such as community mental health centers or health maintenance organizations.
5. Contract with a hospital or neighborhood health center to provide your agency's services to fill an explicit service need already identified. If such a service is not already identified, bring it to their attention.
6. Become board members of your area's health systems agency, which is the regional health and mental health planning agency that identifies the area's services needs.
7. Become a member of or develop contracts with the state level advisory councils for mental health, mental retardation, developmental disabilities, alcoholism, or substance abuse that are required by federal categorial grants to the states. Influence the state plans required of such advisory councils to include the service needs of women.
8. Know the federal agencies that provide assistance to mental health programs. The Department of Health, Education, and Welfare's (DHEW) regional offices have contact people for each of the federal assistance programs. Here in Region 2 the phone number to obtain a list of such people is (212) 264-4490.

9. Review the *Catalog of Federal Domestic Assistance* frequently. It lists all federal assistance programs by subject, by program, by current recipient, by granting federal agency, and by eligible agencies. It is available at DHEW regional offices, State A-95 clearinghouses, and most public libraries.

10. Contact your state's Department of State. In New York any local, municipal, or state official can contact the Department of State and access the FAPRS system (The Federal Aid Program Retrieval System) which is a listing of all federal assistance available to that state. It is updated semiannually, and in New York State you can have your local official call Gilbert Kelly (518) 474-5063 to get the listing for you.

11. Know who's on what Congressional committees and how and where to make contact to determine what federal assistance is available and how you can get it. The Congressional Record prints listings of who's on what committees and their office phone numbers and locations. Your local representative can also get you such listings. Know your representative and use him.

In essence, in order to access federal funding for mental health programs one should:

1. Determine a service needed by your area
2. Develop both short-range and long-range plans to meet that need
3. Examine and determine which possible long-term, multiple-aegis federal funding sources for primary support of your program
4. Where possible, develop shared service or subcontract arrangements with providers already expert in maximizing federal reimbursement. The skill of accessing federal reimbursement—whether it be time-limited grants or assistance programs—develops with experience using the bewildering maze of federal rules and regulations.

Although most federal assistance programs for mental health are medically oriented and those for social programs are soon to be capped, federal funding still offers the most consistent and broad based support around. Accessing those dollars in innovative ways is the strategy to develop.

POSTSCRIPT

Maj Fant

Being an executive woman from another country—Sweden—and one of the very few Europeans who participated in the first national conference of Women in Crisis, I'd like to share some of my feelings, my memories, and my thoughts.

I have delivered an official report on the concept of the conference to Sweden's National Board of Health and Welfare since they funded my trip. I also wrote some articles for Socionomforbundets Tidskrift, a magazine, published by Sweden's equivalent to NASW (National Association of Social Workers) where I am vice-president and a member of the editorial board.

It was a very powerful conference! Most valuable! I learned a lot and meeting all of these capable, competent women was beautiful. I often go to conferences, most of them male dominated. This one was the opposite and had a very special impact. I remember sitting in the big ballroom listening to the opening speeches, looking around at all of the women; what a colorful collection! Black and white, young and old, slim and obese, married and single; we all knew what it means to be a woman in a male society. I was suddenly aware of the "total sum of life experience" in the room. We differed a lot, but we had a lot in common as well. The love we had experienced in our lives; the sadness; the joys; the changes we had gone through; the crises.

Then Eleanor Holmes Norton spoke. I enjoyed her, I loved her poem.

I made the right choice to come here, I told myself. The following days I sat in at all integrated panels, all plenary sessions. I participated in workshops concerning drug addiction, which is my field, and in some dealing with being a career woman. The problems were familiar. The same games. The games *my* mother never taught *me*.

I really liked that many of the speakers told us where they came from. They told us their private and professional background in a way men rarely do, and never in conferences, that's for sure! I loved this personal approach. These women were incredible!

Some I will always remember. Some scenes, some words are forever such as:

> At the banquet when Bella S. Abzug said, "I take my hat off —it is too big and I can't think." Her wit, her courage. An outstanding women; if Sweden had a president I would vote for someone like Bella.

> In a workshop on fundraising and integrity I remember Anita Kurman Gulkin quoting a friend, "You must sit down next to the cow in order to milk it."

> On prostitution, Margo St. James characterizing her kiss-and-tell campaign as a weapon in the struggle for ERA. The ex-prostitute from Scapegoat saying "Oh boy, could I mention names."

> In the career workshop, Debbie Salem's three male boss stereotypes: the intellectual one, the father-type, the coming-on-to-you-type. We've all met them; the laughter was revealing. We knew all about male chauvinism.

Over a cup of tea one morning, I spoke with an executive from the Ford Foundation (Siobhan Oppenheimer Nicola) who had come to deliver a speech. She said, "My daughter came home from college this morning bursting with things she wanted to tell me. She just began 'Susan was raped, Kathy went on drugs, Barbara got cancer in her ankle and must stop her career as a ballet-dancer.' I, her mother, heard myself saying, 'Sorry, darling, can't talk to you right now, I have to go to the Women in Crisis conference.' "

I've been torn between family and career. I know the pain, the guilt feelings, and the constantly bad conscience that goes with it.

I would like to share some general observations with you.

Women's issues are political issues. We have to move from a personal level (consciousness-raising, support to other women, "sisterhood") to a political one. Women must get involved in political life. In Sweden the women's movement says "make the personal political."

The male role in society must be dealt with. No change in female roles can be made until the macho stereotype has undergone some profound change. Men must learn to take full responsibility not only in household chores but in accepting a full share of the responsibility for the care of the children.

I would like to see these two things dealt with in future conferences.

Finally, I would like to express my respect and admiration for the organizing of the Women in Crisis Conference. The structure, the balance between plenary sessions, panels and smaller group discussions were excellent. I am looking forward to the next conference and I hope to be in Washington with you. Happy 1980s!

APPENDIX

Women in Crisis Conference Addenda

ADDITIONAL SPEAKERS

Governor Hugh L. Carey
Thursday, May 17–9:30 A.M.   Plenary

Mayor Edward I. Koch
Saturday, May 19–2:00 P.M.   Plenary

Carol Bellamy
President, New York City Council
Saturday, May 19—2:00 P.M.   Plenary

Judge Lisa A. Richette
Judge, Pennsylvania Court of Common Pleas
Saturday, May 19–2:00 P.M.   Plenary

ROOM DESIGNATIONS

Conference Opening	Imperial Ballroom
Thursday—2:00 P.M. Plenary	Imperial Ballroom
Banquet	Imperial Ballroom

CONFERENCE STAFF

Jane Velez
Conference Administrator
Jean Keeler
Administrative Assistant
Charlotte Kuey
Conference Secretary

Judi Davis
Registration Coordinator
Arleen Costa
Conference Liaison
Arts, Letters, and Politics
Consultants

The Conference Administration wishes to thank all those people who have given so generously of their time and expertise that made this Conference possible. Special thank to Susan Shapiro, Violet Padayachi Cherry, Barbara Taylor, and Gwen Ingram and to the New York Urban Coalition for registration assistance. Our thanks, also, to the many photographers who lent their photos for exhibit and to Jan Engels and Sonia Moskowitz who edited and arranged their work.

First National Women in Crisis Conference

Women and Mental Health
Women and Alcohol
Women and Drug Abuse
Women and Justice

Sheraton Centre
New York City
May 17, 18, and 19, 1979

Sponsored by:
Project Return Foundation, Inc.

Cosponsored by:
The School of Social Welfare, SUNY at Stony Brook

This Conference was made possible in part by grants from: New York State Division of Substance Abuse Services; New York State Division of Alcoholism and Alcohol Abuse; New Jersey State Department of Health, Division of Alcohol, Narcotic and Drug Abuse; Project Return Foundation, Inc.; Exxon Corporation

NATIONAL ADVISORY BOARD

CARL AKINS, Executive Director, National Association of State Alcohol and Drug Abuse Directors

ANN BAXTER, Executive Director, California Women's Commission on Alcoholism. President, National Congress on State Task Forces Women and Alcoholism

MARLENE BECKMAN, Corrections Specialist, Law Enforcement Assistance Administration, Department of Justice

LYNN W. BUTTORFF

WILLIAM BUTYNSKI, Science Management Corporation, Washington, D.C.

JANE R. CHAPMAN, Co-Director, Center for Women's Policy Studies, Washington, D.C.

VIOLET PADAYACHI CHERRY, Director of Health Services, City of Englewood, New Jersey. Director of Alcohol Counseling and Treatment Center, Englewood, New Jersey

STEPHEN CHINLUND, Chairman, New York State Commission of Correction

NOREEN CONNELL, Chairperson, NOW, New York Chapter

ANTONIA D'ANGELO, Chairperson, Committee on Women and Alcoholism National Council on Alcoholism

JODY FORMAN-SHER, Special Assistant for Women's Affairs, National Institute of Drug Abuse

LINDA HARGNETT, Administrator, Planning and Program Development, State of Illinois Dangerous Drugs Commission

JONICA D. HOMILLER, President, Jonica D. Homiller Associates

GWEN INGRAM, Consultant

OLIVE JACOB, Deputy Director, New York State Division of Alcoholism and Alcohol Abuse

DR. SANFORD KRAVITZ, Dean, School of Social Welfare, SUNY at Stony Brook

DR. JEAN KIRKPATRICK, Executive Director, Women for Sobriety, Inc.

JULIO MARTINEZ, Director, New York State Division of Substance Abuse Services

DR. MARCELLA MAXWELL, Chairperson, New York City Commission on the Status of Women

DR. KATHLEEN MONAGHAN-LECKBAND, Sociologist, Marymount Manhattan College

DR. HELEN H. NOWLIS, Director of Alcohol, Drug Abuse, Education Programs Office of Education, Washington, D.C.

PAMELA O'SHEA, Chairperson, North American Women's Commission on Alcohol and Drugs, Minnesota

VIOLET J. PLANTZ, Executive Director, Women's Training and Support Program, Harrisburg, Pennsylvania

RICHARD J. RUSSO, Assistant Commissioner, New Jersey State Department of Health, Alcohol, Narcotic and Drug Abuse

RUTH SANCHEZ-DIRKS, Special Assistant to the Director, National Institute on Alcohol Abuse & Alcoholism

MARGUERITE SAUNDERS, Deputy Director, New York State Division of Substance Abuse Services

BARBARA TAYLOR, The American National Red Cross. Principal, Huggins-Taylor Associates

COOPERATING AGENCIES

Abused Women's Aid in Crisis (AWAIC)
Addiction Research and Treatment Corporation
Alcohol and Drug Problems Association of America
American Civil Liberties Union
American National Red Cross
Commission on Correction (State of New York)
Department of Correctional Services (State of New York)
Department of Health, Division of Alcohol, Narcotic and Drug Abuse (State of New Jersey)

Department of Mental Health, Mental Retardation and Alcoholism (City of New York)
Division of Alcoholism and Alcohol Abuse (State of New York)
Division of Substance Abuse Services (State of New York)
Fortune Society
Gaudenzia, Inc.
Girls Clubs of America, Inc.
Marymount Manhattan College
Mayor's Commission on the Status of Women (City of New York)
Mayor's Task Force on Rape (City of New York)
National Assembly of National Voluntary Health & Social Welfare Organizations
National Association on Drug Abuse Problems, Inc.
National Council on Alcoholism
National Council on Alcoholism (New York City Affiliate)
National Council on Crime and Delinquency
National Institute on Alcohol Abuse & Alcoholism (NIAAA)
National Institute of Drug Abuse (NIDA)
National Organization for Women (New York Chapter)
National Urban League, Inc.
National Women's Political Caucus
New York State Department of Correctional Services
New York Urban Coalition, Inc.
New York Women in Criminal Justice
Regional Coalition on the Special Needs of Women with Alcohol and Drug Abuse Problems
Salvation Army
South Forty Corporation
The Coalition of Voluntary Mental Health, Mental Retardation and Alcoholism Agencies, Inc.
Therapeutic Communities of America

Conference Planning Committee

Violet Padayachi Cherry, A.C.S.W., Director, Health Services, City of Englewood, New Jersey. Project Director, Teenage Parent Program, Englewood, N.J.
Lynne Hennecke, Doctoral Candidate, Teacher's College, Columbia University, New York, N.Y.
Mildred Kleiman, Coordinator of Vocational Services, NYS Division of Substance Abuse Services, New York, N.Y.
Rose Leone, C.S.W., C.R.C., Division Director of Youth Services, Project Return Foundation, Inc., New York, N.Y.
Sylvia Maples, Division Director of Voc/Ed Services, Project Return Foundation, Inc., New York, N.Y.
Dorothy Phelan, Senior Consultant, New York City Bureau of Alcoholism Services
Susan Shapiro, Special Assistant, Addiction Research and Treatment Corp., Brooklyn, N.Y.

Barbara Taylor, Consultant, The American Red Cross. Principal, Huggins-Taylor Associates, New York, N.Y.

Jane Velez, Conference Administrator, Project Return Foundation, Inc., New York, N.Y.

ALCOHOLISM TASK FORCE MEMBERS

Mary Bighorse, Social Services Program Coordinator, American Indian Community House, New York, N.Y.

Constance Boston, M.S.W., Coordinator, Alcoholism Services, Hartford Hospital, Hartford, Conn.

Frances Brisbane, Ph.D., Director, Alcohol Abuse and Alcoholism Specialization, School of Social Welfare, SUNY at Stony Brook

Officer Harry Cardona, Office of Community Affairs, New York City Police Department, New York, N.Y.

Violet Padayachi Cherry, A.C.S.W.,* Director, Health Services, City of Englewood, N.J., Project Director, Teenage Parent Program, Englewood, N.J.

Rozz Cole, M.S.W., Consultant to Alcohol Programs for Women, Minorities and the Aged, Somerset, N.J.

Penny Pearlman, M.S., Director, Family House, Eagleville Hospital and Rehabilitation Center, Norristown, Penn.

Karen Zuckerman, Community Based Services Specialist. Coordinator, New York State Division on Women, Alcoholism and Alcohol Abuse

Marion Spratt, Director, Women's Projects and Drinking Driver Education. New York City Affiliate, NCA. Special Advisor, Alcoholism Program, Marymount Manhattan College, New York, N.Y.

Clarice Staff, Staff Services, Coordinator, Regional Coalition on the Special Needs of Women with Alcohol and Drug Abuse Problems

B. Lorraine Stuart, R.N., M.P.S., Director, Bronx Citizen's Committee, Inc., Sobering Up Station, Bronx, N.Y.

Dorothy Phelan*, Senior Consultant, New York City Bureau of Alcoholism Services. Regional Coalition on the Special Needs of Women with Alcohol and Drug Abuse Problems

DRUG TASK FORCE MEMBERS

Delores Ali, A.S.W., Federal Trainer. Training Consultant, State of Connecticut. Connecticut Alcohol and Drug Abuse Council, Hartford, Conn.

Stephen J. Levy, Ph.D., Director, Alcoholism Treatment Program, Beth Israel Medical Center, New York, N.Y.

Anita Kurman-Gulkin, Executive Director, Greenwich House, N.Y.

Martha Ottenberg, Director, Outpatient Services, Interim House, Inc., Philadelphia, Penn.

*Co-Chairpersons

Donald J. Ottenberg, M.D., Executive Director, Eagleville Hospital and Rehabilitation Center. Clinical Associate Professor of Medicine, Temple University, School of Medicine, Penn.

Phyllis Halpern, Coordinator, Women's Programs, New Jersey State Department of Health, Division of Alcohol, Narcotic & Drug Abuse Control

Roz Cohen, Executive Assistant, Gaudenzia, Inc., Philadelphia, Penn.

Mildred Kleiman,* Coordinator of Vocational Services, New York State Division of Substance Abuse Services

Rose Leone, C.S.W., C.R.C.,* Division Director of Youth Services, Project Return Foundation, Inc., New York, N.Y.

Susan Shapiro,* Special Assistant, Addiction Research & Treatment Corp., Brooklyn, N.Y.

Clare L. Jones, Consultant in Human Services

JUSTICE TASK FORCE MEMBERS

Sharon Smolick, Assistant Director, ORA/NY

Martha Bernstein, Coordinator, Juvenile Justice Projects, Girls Clubs of America, New York, N.Y.

Helen Johnson, Second Assistant District Attorney, Bronx Supreme Court, Bronx, N.Y.

Gwen Ingram, Consultant, Juvenile Justice

Sister Mary Nerney, Director, Project Green Hope, Services for Women, New York, N.Y.

W. E. "Billie" Holiday, Commissioner, New York State Department of Parole

Renae Ogletree, Assistant Director of Training, Boys' Club of America

Robert Brown, Member, Board of Directors, Fortune Society, N.Y.

Carolyn Huggins, Principal, Huggins-Taylor Associates

Hildy Simmons, Office of the Deputy Mayor for Criminal Justice, New York, N.Y.

Roberta Ross, Director of Planning and Development, Girls Clubs of New York, New York, N.Y.

Barbara Taylor*, Consultant, The American Red Cross, Principal, Huggins-Taylor Associates

Helen Donner, Director, Immunization Programs, American Red Cross in Greater New York, New York, N.Y.

MENTAL HEALTH TASK FORCE MEMBERS

Violet Plantz, M.S.W., A.C.S.W., Executive Director, Women's Training and Support Programs, Harrisburg, Penn.

Olive Jacob, Deputy Director, NYS Division of Alcoholism and Alcohol Abuse, Albany, N.Y.

*Co-Chairpersons

Aphrodite Clamar, Ph.D., Feminist Psychotherapist in Private Practice, Consultant to Mental Health Agencies

Dr. Barbara Lewis, Feminist Psychotherapist, New York, N.Y.

Janet Steele-Holloway, M.S.W., Private Practice, New York City. Organizational Consultant in Applied Behavioral Sciences, New York, N.Y.

Joy Fields, M.H.A., Surveyor/Field Representative, Accreditation Council—Psychiatric Facilities. Joint Commission on Accreditation of Hospitals (J.C.A.H.), New York, N.Y.

CONFERENCE SCHEDULE

May 16, Wednesday	4:00 PM	Registration
May 17, Thursday	8:00–10:00 AM	Registration
	9:30 AM	Conference Opening
	10:45 AM–12:15 PM	Integrated Panels
		Modular Workshops
		Special Sessions
	2:00–3:30 PM	Plenary:
		Intervention/Service Delivery Systems
	3:45–5:15 PM	Integrated Panels
		Modular Workshops
		Special Sessions
	7:00 PM	Banquet
May 18, Friday	9:00–10:30 AM	Integrated Panels
		Modular Workshops
		Special Sessions
	10:45 AM–12:15 PM	Integrated Panels
		Modular Workshops
		Special Sessions
	2:00–3:30 PM	Plenary
		Postintervention/Support Systems
	3:45–5:15 PM	Integrated Panels
		Modular Workshops
		Special Sessions
May 19, Saturday	9:00–10:30 AM	Integrated Panels
		Modular Workshops
	10:45 AM–12:15 PM	Integrated Panels
		Modular Workshops
		Special Sessions
	2:00–3:30 PM	Plenary:
		Making Change

Special exhibit area in Albert Hall
Women in Crisis Photo Exhibit in Albert Hall

DAILY CONFERENCE SCHEDULE

Wed. 4:00 PM—Registration

Thurs. 8:00 AM—Registration

Thurs. 9:30 AM—Conference Opening

Jane Velez, Conference Administrator

Ed Menken, Senior Vice President, Project Return Foundation, Inc.

Dr. Sanford Kravitz, Dean, The School of Social Welfare, SUNY at Stony Brook

Julio A. Martinez, Director, New York State Division of Substance Abuse Services

Commissioner Eleanor Holmes Norton, United States Equal Employment Opportunity Commission

Thurs. 10:45 AM–12:15 PM—Integrated Panels

1   Breakdown in Familial and Social Systems   *(Buckingham A)*

Carol M. Anderson
Director, Western Psychiatric Institute
Pittsburgh, Penn.

Richard R. Clayton, Ph.D.
Professor of Sociology
University of Kentucky
Lexington, Ky.

Dr. Karen Morell
Director, Correctional Education and
   Research Programs
University of Washington
Seattle, Wash.

Armagene Perry, M.A.
Assistant Program Director
Social Service Delivery Training
   Program
Los Angeles, Calif.

2   Learned Helplessness: How Society creates the dependent woman.
     (Georgian B)

Edith S. Gomberg
University of Michigan
Center of Alcohol Studies
Rutgers University
New Brunswick, N.J.

Miriam Resnick, A.C.S.W.
(Private Practice)
Portland, Ore.

Helen M. Simon, R.N., Ph.D.
Research Consultant and Freelance
   Writer
New York, N. Y.

Dr. Penelope Russianoff
Clinical Psychologist
Faculty Member, New School
New York, N.Y.

3   Race and Class as Economic Factors   *(Buckingham B)*

Dr. Mary T. Howard
Dean, Urban Affairs
Director, James Kenney Campus
Mercer County Comm. College
Trenton, N.J.

Councilmember Miriam Friedlander
City Council
New York, N.Y.

Dolores Finger Wright
Director, Dept. Drug and Alcohol
   Concerns
Board of Church & Society
United Methodist Church
Washington, D. C.

4   Battering: The evolution and long-term impact of physical and emotional violence in the family setting.   *(Royal Ballroom B)*

Kathryn Conroy, C.S.W.
Director, Park Slope Programs
Sisters of the Good Shepherd Res.
Brooklyn, N.Y.

Beverly Learch, Director
Birch Hill Transitional
   Living Center for Women
Union Hill, N.Y.

P. J. Marschner
Director, Program Development
Center for Women's Policy Studies
Washington, D.C.

Peggy Ann McGarry
Women Against Abuse
Philadelphia, Penn.

Maria Roy—Moderator
Founder and President
Abused Women's Aid in Crisis, Inc.
New York, N.Y.

5   Update—Women and Substance Use/Abuse   *(Versailles Ballroom)*

Beth G. Reed—Moderator
Principal Investigator
Women's Drug Research Project
Assistant Professor
School of Social Work
University of Michigan

Margaret Wilmore
Program Administrator
NIAAA Division of
   Special Treatment and Rehab.
Rockville, Md.

Barbara Starrett, M.D.
Medical Director
Montefiore Hospital and
    Medical Center
Rikers Island Health Services
East Elmhurst, N.Y.

6   Women, Work and Worth   *(Loire 2/3)*

Jane Roberts Chapman
Co-Director
Center for Women's Policy Studies
Washington, D.C.

Louise Finney—Moderator
Ass't Industrial Commissioner
New York State Department of Labor
New York, N.Y.

Helen B. Stanton, C.A.C.
Washington Hospital Center
Washington, D.C.

Camille S. Tylden, A.C.S.W.
Mental Hygiene Clinic
Veterans Administration
    Medical Center
Lebanon, Penn.

7   Prevention: Recognizing and addressing problematic behavior in its
    developmental stages.   *(Malmaison 6)*

Mary Beth Collins
Commission on Alcohol &
    Substance Abuse
Prevention and Education
Albany, N.Y.

Patricia O'Gorman, Ph.D.—
    Moderator
Director, Department of Prevention
    and Education
National Council on Alcoholism
New York, N.Y.

Martha Bernstein
Coordinator
Juvenile Justice Projects
Girls Clubs of America
New York, N.Y.

Ellen Schertle Danfield
    Director Prevention Services
Dauphin County Mental Health
    and Mental Retardation Services
Harrisburg, Penn.

8   Women—Society's Victims   *(Chelsea A)*

Cindy Cohen
Member, Elizabeth Stone House
Jamaica Plain, Mass.

Josie Balaban Couture
President/Founder
The Other Victims of Alcoholism,
    Inc.
New York, N.Y.

Dr. Ruth Cowan—Moderator
Professor of Political Science
CUNY/NYCCC
Member, New York City Commission
    on the Status of Women
New York, N.Y.

Barbara Methvin
Executive Director
Eastern Women's Center
(Women's Medical Services)
New York, N.Y.

Modular Workshops

DRUG ABUSE:

D1   Biological Factors of Drug Addiction   *(Chambord 14)*

Mark Hochhauser, Ph.D.
Research Associate in
  Drug Education
University of Minnesota
Minneapolis, Minn.

Mary Jeanne Kreek, M.D.
Senior Research Associate
  and Physician
The Rockefeller University
New York, N.Y.

D2   Causes of Adolescent Drug Addiction   *(Loire 4/5)*

Jean Denes
Director—Moderator of Social
  Services
Chelsea School
Long Branch, N.J.

Dr. James J. Turanski
Program Director
The Door—Center for Alternatives
New York, N.Y.

ALCOHOL:

A1   Alcoholism and Women—the Disease Concept   *(Chelsea B)*

Dr. Eileen M. Corrigan
Professor, Rutgers University
Graduate School of Social Work
New Brunswick, N.J.

Lynne Hennecke
Doctoral Candidate
Teacher's College
Columbia University
New York, N.Y.

Dorothy Phelan—Moderator
Senior Consultant, New York City
  Bureau of Alcoholism Services
New York, N.Y.

A2   Sociocultural Factors in the Development of Alcoholism among Minority
      Women   *(Chambord 15)*

Susan Arellano
Director of Alcoholism Services
East Los Angeles Health Task Force
Los Angeles, Calif.

DeAnn Martin
Director, Alcoholism Project
New York, N.Y.

Rebecca Sanchez, M.S.W., C.S.W.—
  Moderator,
Director, Alcoholism Programs
Prospect Hospital
Bronx, N.Y.

A3   Sexuality and Alcoholism   *(Malmaison 7)*

Irene Gad-Luther, M.D., M.A.
Assistant Professor
Department of Psychology
College of St. Thomas
St. Paul, Minn.

Sandra Turner, A.C.S.W.—Moderator
Chief, Outreach Component
St. Vincent's Hospital—Alcohol
    Program
New York, N.Y.

Dr. Valerie Pinhas
Assistant Professor of Health
    Education
Nassau Community College
Garden City, N.Y.

Joy Witchel, C.A.C.
St. Vincent's Hospital
Adolescent Clinic
New York, N.Y.

MENTAL HEALTH:

MH1   Aging Women in America   *(Monte Carlo)*

Lawrence Faulkner—
    Attorney-Moderator
Executive Director
Legal Services for the Elderly
    Project of Erie County
    and Western New York, Inc.
Buffalo, N.Y.

Jane Porcino
Assistant Professor
Director Gerontology Project
School of Allied Health Professions
SUNY at Stony Brook
Co-Director, National Action
    Forum for Older Women

Special Session

S1   Special Problems of the Gay Woman   *(Biarritz)*

Sidney Abbott
Co-Author, *Sappho Was A Right-On
    Woman*
Co-Chair, New York Political
    Action Council (NYPAC)
New York, N.Y.

Ginny Vida
Editor, *Our Right To Love: A Lesbian
    Resource Book*
Media Director, National Gay
    Task Force
New York, N.Y.

Thurs. 2:00–3:30 PM—Plenary: Intervention/Service Delivery Systems

(Imperial A/B)

Severa Austin
Director, Bureau of Alternate Care
Dept. of Health and Social Services
Madison, Wisc.

Sheila B. Blume, M.D.
Director, New York State Division of
    Alcoholism and Alcohol Abuse
Albany, N.Y.

Joyce B. Lazar
Chief, Social Science Section and
Special Assistant to the
Division Director—
Research on Women
National Institute of Mental Health
Rockville, Md.

Dr. Sanford Kravitz—Moderator
Dean, School of Social Welfare
SUNY at Stony Brook

Jody Forman-Sher
Special Assistant for Women's Affairs,
   NIDA
Rockville, Md.

John DeLuca
Director, National Institute on
   Alcoholism
   and Alcohol Abuse
Rockville, Md.

Thurs. 3:45–5:15 PM—Integrated Panels

9   Pregnant Clients: service and support   *(Buckingham A)*

Dr. Richard Brotman
Associate Dean and
   Professor of Psychiatry
New York Medical College
New York, N.Y.

Violet Padayachi Cherry, A.C.S.W.
Director, Health Services
City of Englewood, N.J.
Project Director, Teenage
   Parent Program
Englewood, N.J.

M. Sharon Smolick
Assistant Project Director
OAR/NYC
New York, N.Y.

Sharyn M. Wright—Moderator
Harrisburg, Penn.

10   Sexism in Treatment: The stereotypic response to women   *(Albert Hall I)*

Stephen Levy, Ph.D.—Moderator
Director, Alcoholism Treatment
   Program
Beth Israel Medical Center
Assistant Professor of Psychiatry
Mount Sinai School of Medicine
New York, N.Y.

Barbara A. Lewis, Ph.D.
Feminist Psychotherapist in
   Private Practice
Psychotherapist Coordinator
   of Psychology, Committee of
National Organization for Women,
   New York City Chapter
New York, N.Y.

Dolores Niles, A.C.S.W.
Feminist Therapist
Mental Health Service
   for Women
Madison, Wisc.
Laurel L. Rans
Entropy Limited
Pittsburg, Penn.

12   Education and Training of Staff: Consciousness raising   *(Albert Hall II)*

Clare L. Jones
Consultant in Human Services

Maureen J. Carroll
Director, National Center for Alcohol
   Education
Arlington, Va.

Violent Plantz, M.S.W., A.C.S.W.—
   Moderator
Executive Director, Women's Training
   and Support Program
Harrisburg, Penn.

Jacqueline McMickens
Deputy Warden
NY Correctional Institution
   for Women

13   Realities of Prostitution   *(Loire 2/3)*

Jennifer James, Ph.D.—Moderator
Associate Professor
Department of Psychiatry and
   Behavioral Sciences
University of Washington Medical
   School

Margo St. James
Private Investigator
Publisher, *Coyote Howls*
Executive Director,
Victoria Woodhull Foundation
San Francisco, Calif.

14   Evaluation and Diagnosis of Clients' Problems   *(Loire 4/5)*

Herbert J. Freudenberger, Ph.D.
Independent Practice of
   Psychoanalysis
Staff Training/Educational Consultant
   to Drug Abuse and School
   Prevention Programs
New York, N.Y.

Judy Wenning
Co-Director, Center for
   Psychotherapy and Family Living
Brooklyn, N.Y.

Modular Workshops

DRUG ABUSE:

D3   Chemotherapeutic Treatment Approaches   *(Buckingham B)*

Melissa M. Freeman, M.D.—
   Moderator
Medical Director
New York City Methadone
   Maintenance Treatment Program
New York, N.Y.

Beny J. Primm, M.D.
Executive Director
Addiction Research and
   Treatment Corporation
Brooklyn, N.Y.

Richard A. Rawson, Ph.D.
Research Psychologist
New York Medical College
New York, N.Y.

D4   Prevention and Treatment of Prescription Drug Abuse   *(Biarritz)*

Phyllis Halpern—Moderator
Coordinator, Women's Programs
New Jersey State Department of
    Health
Division Alcohol, Narcotic
    and Drug Abuse Control

Tony Tommasello, R.Ph.
University of Maryland School of
    Pharmacy
Baltimore, Md.

Bruce H. Medd, M.D.
Director, Professional Services
Roche Laboratories, Division of
    Hoffmann-La Roche Inc.
Nutley, N.J.

D5   Research on Female Substance Abuse*   *(Malmaison 7)*

Dr. Walter Cuskey
President, Cuskey, Ipsen & McCall,
    Consultants, Inc.
Havertown, Penn.

Dr. Loretta Finnegan
Jefferson Medical College
Philadelphia, Penn.

Richard B. Wathey, Ph.D.—
    Moderator
Director of Research
Addiction Research and
    Treatment Corp.
Brooklyn, N.Y.

Kathleen M. Doyle
Assistant Director
Division of Social Medicine
New Jersey Medical School

ALCOHOL:

A4   Employee Assistance Programs   *(Vendome 11/12)*

Constance Boston, M.S.W.
Coordinator Alcoholism Services
Hartford Hospital
Hartford, Conn.

Fran Draft, C.S.W.—Moderator
Director, Personal Services Unit
District Council 37
New York, N.Y.

Peggy Carey, M.S.W.
Administrator, Social Service Unit
Employee Assistance Program
New England Telephone Co.
Boston, Mass.

Patricia B. Heubusch, MEd.
Coordinator, Alcoholism and
    Drug Abuse Program
Social Security Administration
Baltimore, Md.

*Previously listed as *Research on Substance Abuse*

A5   Pregnancy and Drinking   *(Chelsea A)*

Cheryl Gillen Rice—Moderator
Administrator, Department of
  Obstetrics and Gynecology
Columbia College of Physicians
  and Surgeons
Doctoral Candidate
Columbia School of Public Health
New York, N.Y.

Dr. Carrie Randall
Dept. of Psychiatry and
  Behavioral Sciences
Medical University of South Carolina

Lucy Barry Robe
Author, *Just So It's Healthy*

A6   Reshaping Programs to Better Serve Women: New developments
     (Versailles Ballroom)

Gwen Besson
Research Associate
Rutgers Center of Alcohol Studies
Former President, New Jersey
  Task Force on Women and Alcohol

Sheila Salcedo, R.N., M.A.
Program Administrator
Human Resource Group
New York, N.Y.

Marion Spratt
Director, Women's Projects
Drinking Driver Education
New York City Affiliate, National
  Council on Alcoholism
Special Advisor, Alcoholism
  Program, Marymount Manhattan
  College
New York, N.Y.

Brenda Haber Sutter, M.A.—
  Moderator
Director, Alcoholism Intensive
  Treatment Program
Western Massachusetts Hospital

MENTAL HEALTH:

MH5   Women and Stress   *(Regency Foyer)*

Elinor N. Polansky
Professor, School of Social Welfare
SUNY at Stony Brook

Lois Sigman, A.C.S.W.—Moderator
Clinical Coordinator,
Special Services
Coordinator, Alcoholism Services
The Wheeler Clinic
Plainville, Conn.

JUSTICE:

J3   Police Response: Women in policing; the treatment of the female victim
     and the female arrestee   *(Chelsea B)*

Catherine Milton, Special Assistant to
  Assistant Secretary (Enforcement &
  Operations) Department of the
  Treasury
Washington, D.C.

J4 Diversion: Do the standard pretrial intervention/ROR models still work?
(St. James A)

Sally Hillsman Baker
Assistant Director of Research
Vera Institute of Justice
New York, N.Y.

Sister Mary Nerney—Moderator
Executive Director
Project Green Hope: Services
    for Women, Inc.
New York, N.Y.

Delores Fitzgerald
Technical Assistance Associate
Pre-trial Services
    Resource Center

J5 Preparation for Justice Professionals: Current curricula and new approaches
(St. James B)

John Jay Douglass—Moderator
Dean, National College of
    District Attorneys
University of Houston
Houston, Tex.

Jess Maghan
Superintendent, State of Illinois
Correctional Training Academy

Albert H. Gross
Chief, Bronx Adult Supervision
NYC Department of Probation
Bronx, N.Y.

J6 Rape: The impact of public attention on victims, perpetrators, and
legislation   *(Chambord 14)*

Susan Halpern
Author & Consultant
Rape: Treating the Victim
New York, N.Y.

Flora Colao, C.S.W.
Coordinator, St. Vincent's Hospital
Rape Crisis Program
New York, N.Y.

Special Sessions

S2 A Model for Runaway Services   *(Chambord 15)*

Vondie M. Moore
Executive Director
Michigan Coalition of Runaway
    Services
East Lansing, Mich.

S3   Movement/Dance Therapy: A process of integrating body and mind into one total essence   *(Malmaison 6)*

Teresa Paredes
Acting Division Director—Women's
  Services
Project Return Foundation, Inc.
New York, N.Y.

S4   Abortion/Sterilization: The new attack on reproductive rights   *(Monte Carlo)*

Judy Norsigian
Co-Author, *Our Bodies, Ourselves*
Board Member, National Women's
  Health Network
Boston Women's Health Book
  Collective
Boston, Mass.

Karen Stamm
Member, Committee to End
  Sterilization Abuse
New York, N.Y.

Thurs 7:00 PM—Banquet

Introduction:

BETTY COMDEN, Lyricist and book writer: *Wonderful Town; On the Town; Bells are Ringing* and *On the Twentieth Century* among others. Among many movie credits, *Singing In The Rain.*

Presentation of Women In Crisis Conference Award to Marty Mann:

MARTY MANN, Founder, National Council on Alcoholism
Since her own recovery from the disease of alcoholism in 1939, Marty Mann has written effectively, lectured extensively at home and abroad, and today is considered a world authority in this major health field. Trained at the Yale School of Alcoholism in 1944 and became its Executive Director, a position she held until April 1968, when she became Founder-Consultant.

Speeches:

DR. GWEN MEAD, Professor of Political Science, University of Kentucky

THE HONORABLE BELLA S. ABZUG, Civil Rights and Civil Liberties Attorney, Former U.S. Representative, Founder of W.O.M.A.N.

Fri 9:00–10:30 AM—Integrated Panels

15   Client's Rights: The role of the service agency.   *(Malmaison 7)*

M. Ellen Moffett—Moderator
President/Executive Director
Gaudenzia Inc.
Philadelphia, Penn.

17   The Older Client   *(St. James B)*

Ronald J. Gaetano, R.Ph.—Moderator
Executive Director
Broome County Drug
  Awareness Center
Johnson City, N.Y.
Co-Chairman, National Task
  Force on Drugs and Alcohol

Eve Marsh
Program Consultant, Former
  Executive Director
Broward County Commission
  on Alcoholism
Ft. Lauderdale, Fla.

Kenneth Pommerenck
Director, Reality
  Orientation/Community Education
ICD Rehabilitation & Research
  Center
New York, N.Y.

18   Adolescent Intervention   *(Imperial Ballroom B)*

Kathryn Conroy, C.S.W.—Moderator
Director, Park Slope Programs
  Sisters of the Good Shepherd Res.
Brooklyn, N.Y.

Arthur Jaffee, Director of
  Spark, NYC Board of Education
  Division of High School
New York, N.Y.

Catharine B. Gilson
Juvenile Justice Consultant
Washington, D.C.

Carol E. Zimmerman
Executive Director, New Directions
  for Young Women
Tucson, Ariz.

19   The Use of Peers in Treatment   *(Monte Carlo)*

Peter P. Quinn-Moderator
Executive Director
Therapeutic Center at Fox Chase
Philadelphia, Penn.

Frances O'Leary
President, Fortune Society
New York, N.Y.

Patricia A. Joyner
Coordinator-Drug Education
Newark Board of Education

Dr. Lenore Powell
Psychotherapist

20   Multiple Substance Abuse—Treatment Approaches   *(Imperial Ballroom A)*

Dr. Stanley Gitlow
Clinical Professor of Medicine
Mount Sinai School of Medicine
Chairman, Committee on Alcoholism
Medical Society of the State of New
  York
New York, N.Y.

David Smith, M.D.
Medical Director
Haight-Ashbury Free
  Medical Clinic
San Francisco, Calif.

Modular Workshops

DRUG ABUSE:

D6   Treatment of Hispanic Women   *(Buckingham A)*

Omar Bordatto, Fiscal Officer
National Association of Puerto Rican
  Drug Abuse Programs
Washington, D.C.

Lillian Camejo, Director
The Center's Family
  Counseling Services
Bronx, N.Y.

D7   Women's Issues in Residential Treatment   *(Biarritz)*

Susan K. Fry—Moderator, Director
  of Women's Programming
Daytop Village, Inc.
New York, N.Y.

Donald Garnett
Gaudenzia, Inc.
32 East School House Lane
Philadelphia, Penn. 19144

D8   Female Sexuality—the Use of Drugs   *(Versailles Ballroom)*

Marie Broudy
Therapist, Mental Health Clinic
Lower East Side Service Center
New York, N.Y.
Consultant—Bureau of Training
  and Resource Development of
  Division of Substance Abuse
  Services

Stephen J. Levy, Ph.D.—Moderator
Director, Alcoholism Treatment
  Program
Beth Israel Medical Center
New York, N.Y.

Clary Jones
Women's Training & Support
  Program
1306 North 14th Street
Harrisburg, Penn. 17103

ALCOHOL:

A7   Innovative Programs for the Alcoholic Woman   *(Malmaison 6)*

Jean Dalton—Moderator
Clinical Supervisor
Family House of Eagleville Hospital
  and Rehabilitation Center
Norristown, Penn.

Sister Maurice Doody
Director, Office of New Directors
Bronx, N.Y.

Norma Finkelstein, M.S.W.
Director, The Women's Alcoholism
  Program of CASPAR, Inc.
Cambridge, Mass.

Luise K. Forseth
Executive Director
Chrysalis—Center for Women, Inc.
Minneapolis, Minn.

A8   The Role of the Family in the Treatment of the Alcoholic Woman
     (Buckingham B)

Anthony J. Panepinto, M.S.W.—
  Moderator
Executive Director
Community Mental Health
Organization
Englewood, N.J.
Member, Board of Trustees
Spring House (A Halfway House
  for Alcoholic Women)
Paramus, N.J.

Penny Pearlman, M.S.
Director, Family House
Norristown, Penn.

Sharon Wegscheider
Twin Town Training Center
St. Paul, Minn.

A9   Motivating the Alcoholic Woman to Seek Help   *(Chelsea A)*

Dorothy Phelan—Moderator
Sr. Consultant, New York State
  Division of
  Alcoholism and Alcohol Abuse

Anna D.
Recovered Alcoholic
New York, N.Y.

Nancy G.
Recovered Alcoholic
New York, N.Y.

Kathy S.
Recovered Alcoholic
Brooklyn, N.Y.

MENTAL HEALTH

MH7 Loss and Separation   *(Loire 2/3)*

Camille S. Tylden, A.C.S.W.—
  Moderator
Mental Hygiene Clinic
Veterans Administration
  Medical Center
Lebanon, Penn.

Judy Wenning
Co-Director, Center for
  Psychotherapy
  and Family Living
Brooklyn, N.Y.

MH8 Depression: Anger turned inwards.   *(Regency Foyer)*

Barbara Rothberg, M.S.W., A.C.S.W.
  —Moderator
Director, Family Services
Lutheran Community Services
Co-Director, Center for
  Psychotherapy and Family Living
Brooklyn, N.Y.

Bobbi Tower, M.Ed.
Tower & Associates
Harrisburg, Penn

MH9 Conspiracy of Silence: The trauma of incest.   *(Loire 4/5)*

Ethel F. Green, R.N.
New York, N.Y.

Leslie Lanzillo
Co-Therapist Counselor
Sexual Abuse Group
Odyssey House, Inc.
New York, N.Y.

Florence Koniski, R.N.—Moderator
Co-Therapist Incest Group
Sexual Abuse Group
Odyssey House, Inc.
New York, N.Y.

JUSTICE:

J7 Prostitution and Justice Issues   *(Chelsea B)*

Margo St. James
Private Investigator
Publisher: *Coyote Howls*
San Francisco, Calif.

Jennifer James, Ph.D.
Associate Professor
Department of Psychiatry
University of Washington

Cecilia L. Gardner
Examining Attorney
NYC Dep't of Investigation
Member, NY Women's Bar
  Association
New York, N.Y.

Rosalind Lichter—Moderator
Director, Diversion & Presentence
  Programs
Legal Aid Society
New York, N.Y.

J8   Discretionary versus Mandatory Sentencing   *(St. James A)*

Dr. David Fogel
Professor and Director
  of Graduate Studies
Dept. of Criminal Justice
University of Illinois

Honorable Jane B. Trichter—
  Moderator
Member, New York City Council
New York, N.Y.

J9   Establishing Comprehensive Community Networks   *(Chambord 14)*

Harriet Dronska
Ass't Deputy Administrator
Human Resources Administration
New York, N.Y.

Marianna Page Glidden
Associate Director
National Juvenile Justice
  Program Collaboration
National Assembly of
  National Voluntary Health
  and Social Welfare Organ., Inc.
New York, N.Y.

Laurel L. Rans
PA Board of Pardons
National Assoc. of
  Women in Criminal Justice
Partner, Entropy Limited
Pittsburg, Penn.

Hildy Simmons—Moderator
Office of the Deputy Mayor
  for Criminal Justice
New York, N.Y.

J10   Programs within Prisons   *(Versailles Terrace)*

Arlene M. Becker
Deputy Director
California Dept. of Corrections

Jane Roberts Chapman
Co-Director
Center for Women's Policy Studies
Washington, D.C.

Sally B. Johnson
Superintendent
Parkside Correctional Facility
New York, N.Y.

Sylvia McCollum—Moderator
Director of Education
Federal Bureau of Prisons
Washington, D.C.

Special Session

S15   The Drinking Driver   *(Chambord 15)*

Marion Spratt
Director Women's Projects and
  Drinking Driver Education
NYC Affiliate, National Council on
  Alcoholism
Special Advisor, Alcoholism Program
Marymount Manhattan College
New York, N.Y.

Fri 10:45 AM-12:15 PM—Integrated Panels

22   The Unwanted Client   *(Chambord 15)*

Lee D. Hanes, M.D.
Director, St. Lawrence
  Psychiatric Center
Ogdensburg, N.Y.

Olive M. Jacob—Moderator
Deputy Director, NYS Division
  of Alcoholism and Alcohol Abuse

Audrey McCoy, M.S.W.
Beth Israel Medical Center
Alcoholism Treatment Program
New York, N.Y.

Cookie Ridolfi
Director, Women's Self-Defense Law
  Project
Center for Constitutional Rights
New York, N.Y.

23   Services in Rural Areas   *(Buckingham B)*

William A. Clark
Project Director
Youth Services Program
Tuskegee Institute, AL

Andrew Evans, M.S.—Moderator
Treatment Director
Aide House, Inc.
Lafayette, La.
Rural Chairman - NDAC

Joan Weitzel, Coordinator
Maple Manor, Residential Treatment
  Facility
Coudersport, Penn.

24   Reaching the Middle Class Client   *(Loire 2/3)*

Nikki N. Duffié, Director
Women's Prescription Drug
  Misuse Program
Together, Glassboro State College
Glassboro, N.J.

Consultant From
  Women's Psychotherapy
  Referral Services, Inc.
New York, N.Y.

Judith Seixas
Alcoholism Services
Hastings-on-Hudson, N.Y.

Hildy Simmons—Moderator
Office of the Deputy Major
  for Criminal Justice
New York, N.Y.

25   The Mother Removed   *(Loire 4/5)*

Mary Bighorse, Coordinator
Social Services Program
American Indian Community House
New York, N.Y.

Zelma W. Henriques
Doctoral Candidate
Department of Applied Human
    Development
Teachers College
Columbia University
New York, N.Y.

Velma LaPoint, Ph.D.—Moderator
Laboratory of Developmental Psych.
National Institute of Mental Health
Bethesda, Md.

26   Vocational Rehabilitation: Options for women   *(Malmaison 7)*

Sandra Brandt
Area Representative
Human Resources Development
    Institute, AFL-CIO
Norfolk, Va.

Denise Capelli, M.S.
Certified Rehabilitation Counselor
NC Dept. Drug and Alcohol
    Addiction
New York, N.Y.

Robert L. Hubbard, Ph.D.
Research Triangle Institute, NC

Eileen Wolkstein, M.A.—Moderator
Career Consultant to Individuals,
    Groups, Business and Industry
Elizabeth, N.J.

27   Alone and Coping: Single parents.   *(Imperial Ballroom A)*

Terry S. Davis, Ph.D.—Moderator
Director, Family Rehabilitation
    Coordinator Project
UCLA Extension
Culver City, Calif.

Dr. Arlyn Miller, Psychologist
Independent Practice
Faculty, Temple Univ.
Philadelphia, Penn.

Katie Portis
Executive Director
Women, Inc.
Dorchester, Mass.

Frances O'Leary, President
Fortune Society
New York, N.Y.

28   The Family as a Potential Tool   *(Versailles Ballroom)*

Dr. Frances Brisbane, Director
Alcohol Abuse & Alcoholism Speciali-
    ization, School of Social Welfare
SUNY at Stony Brook

Mary Green
Children's Television Workshop
Dallas, Tex.

Richard Clayton, Ph.D.—Moderator
Professor of Sociology
University of Kentucky

Blair Barrett
NYS Council on Children and
  Families
Albany, N.Y.

29   The Double Bind: Minority Women (I)   *(Biarritz)*

Marguerite T. Saunders—Moderator
Deputy Commissioner for
  Treatment and Rehabilitation
New York State Division of Drug
  Abuse Services

Mary Ann Walker, R.N., M.H.A.
Associate Commissioner
Office of Mental Health
Albany, N.Y.

Debra Little Parkeiz
Assistant Director
Community Support Services
Pilgrim Psychiatric Center
Albany, N.Y.

29   The Double Bind: Minority Women (II)   *(Malmaison 6)*

Marilyn Aguirre—Moderator
Standing Committee on
  Women's Rights of the
  American Public Health Assoc.
President-Elect, Latino Caucus APHA
Leonia, N.J.

Dr. Gwendolyn Randall Puryear
University Counseling Services
Howard University
Washington, D.C.

Judy Glass, Counselor
Fortune Society
New York, N.Y.

30   Women in Authority   *(Imperial Ballroom B)*

Carol A. Beauvais, Ph.D.
Director, Division on Women
  and Stress for Executive Health
  Examiners
StressControl Systems, Inc.
Researcher, The Family and The
  Work Group: Dilemmas For
  Women in Authority.
Psychotherapist in Private Practice

Deborah Salem
Consultant/Trainer
Women's Training and Support
  Program
Harrisburg, Penn.

Jerri L. Shaw—Moderator
President, Shaw & Associates
Maryland

Arlene M. Becker, Deputy Director
Department of Corrections
Sacramento, Calif.

31   The Stigmatized Woman   *(Chelsea A)*

Rose Leone, C.S.W., C.R.C.—
Moderator
Division Director - Youth Services
Project Return Foundation, Inc.
New York, N.Y.

Deborah M. Greenberg, Esq.
President and Director of Staff
Legal Action Center
New York, N.Y.

Dr. Rose Pinckney, Director
Lincoln-Eagleville
Master's Program
Lincoln University
Lincoln, Penn.

Marion Spratt
Director, Women's Projects and
Drinking Driver Education
NYC Affiliate - National
Council on Alcoholism
Sp. Advisor—Alcoholism Program
Marymount Manhattan College

32   Institutional Violence   *(Buckingham A)*

Sue Bienemann, Director
PCADV
Harrisburg, Penn.

Jess Maghan, Superintendent
State of Illinois
Correctional Training Academy

Camille S. Tylden, A.C.S.W.—
Moderator
Mental Hygiene Clinic
Veterans Administration Medical
Center
Lebanon, Penn.

33   Federal Support: Understanding and utilizing the federal dollar.
(Chambord 14)

Ruth Sanchez-Dirks, Ph.D.—
Moderator
Special Assistant to Director
National Institute on Alcohol Abuse
and Alcoholism
Rockville, Md.

Marilee Grygelko
Senior Budget Examiner
New York State Division of the
Budget

Henry S. Dogin
Acting Administrator
Law Enforcement Assistance
Administration
Washington, D.C.

34   The Elusive Private Dollar   *(Monte Carlo)*

Dr. Sanford Kravitz, Dean
The School of Social Welfare
SUNY at Stony Brook

Claudia Rescigno
Foundation Center
New York, N.Y.

35   The Responsibility of Intervention   *(Chelsea B)*

Donald J. Ottenberg, M.D.—
  Moderator
Executive Director, Eagleville Hospt.
  & Rehabilitation Center
Clinical Associate Professor of
  Medicine
Temple University School of Medicine
Eagleville, Penn.

Pamela Skubick, M.S.W.
Mental Health Consultant
Detroit Central City
Community Mental Health Center
Detroit, Mich.

M. Sharon Smolick
Assistant Project Director
OAR/NYC
New York, N.Y.

Special Session

S6   Alcoholism: "Pills and Thrills"   *(Regency Foyer)*

Stanley Gitlow, M.D.
Clinical Professor of Medicine
Mount Sinai School of Medicine, NY
Formerly President of the American
  Medical Society on Alcoholism
Chairman, Committee on Alcoholism,
  Medical Society of the State of NY
New York, N.Y.

Fri 2:00–3:30 PM—Plenary: Postintervention/support systems

Chaney Allen
Author, *I'm Black & I'm Sober*
Lecturer, Counselor
San Diego, Calif.

Honorable Ruth W. Messinger
Member of the New York
  City Council
New York, N.Y.

Jacquelyn H. Hall, Ph.D.
Chief, Mental Health Ed. Branch
National Institute of Mental Health
Rockville, Md.

Jody Forman-Sher—Moderator
Special Ass't for Women's Affairs
National Institute of Drug Abuse
Rockville, Md.

Julio A. Martinez
Director, New York State Division of
  Substance
  Abuse Services

Fri 3:45–5:15 PM—Integrated Panels

36   The Revolving Door   *(Albert Hall I)*

Pauline Feingold
Assistant Commissioner
New York City Dept. of Correction
Chairwoman, New York Women
   in Criminal Justice
New York, N.Y.

Lee Koenigsberg—Moderator
Director, Community Treatment
   Foundation, Inc.
New York, N.Y.

Antoinette Mock
Women For Sobriety, Inc.
Quakertown, Penn.

Barbara McKeand-Stevenson, M.Ed.
Six Area Coalition, Community
   Mental Health Center -
   Women's Issues
Detroit, Mich.

37   The Risk of Post Treatment Substance Abuse   *(Chambord 14)*

Le Clair Bissell, M.D.
Chief, The Smithers Alcoholism
   Treatment & Training Center
The Roosevelt Hospital
New York, N.Y.

Christopher D'Amanda, M.D.
Chief Medical Officer
Coordinating Office for
   Drug & Alcohol Abuse Programs
Philadelphia, Penn.

38   Reintegration with the Family   *(Biarritz)*

Shirley Canty
Childcare Worker
Project Green Hope:
   Services for Women
New York, N.Y.

Dr. Avis Kristenson—Moderator
University of Wisconsin
School of Social Work
Madison, Wisc.

Genevra Ziegler-Driscoll, M.D.
Director, Psychiatry Department
Coordinator, Family Unit
Clinical Director, Family Resource
Center
Eagleville Hospital and Rehabilitation
Eagleville, Penn.

Beatriz Molina
Statewide Manager
California Commission on
   Alcoholism for the
   Spanish Speaking, Inc.

39   Employment: Teaching women to cope with vocational handicaps.
      (Monte Carlo)

Anne Kerrigan
Job Developer
Susquehanna Employment and
   Training Corporation
Harrisburg, Penn.

Mildred Kleiman, M.A.
Coordinator of Vocational
   Services
New York State Division of Substance
   Abuse Services

Claire Haaga
Associate Director
Vera Institute of Justice
New York, N.Y.

Barbara Taylor
American National Red Cross
Principal, Huggins-Taylor Association
New York, N.Y.

40   Post Treatment Support Systems   *(Chambord 15)*

Eileen Bergmann
Writer-Editor/Program Analyst
Washington, D.C.

Miriam Resnick, A.C.S.W.
Private Practice
Portland, Ore.

Sarah P.
Staff Member, General Service Office
Alcoholics Anonymous
New York, N.Y.

Jean Smith—Moderator
Outreach Counselor
Desire Outpatient Center
New Orleans, La.

41   The Forgotten Client: Reaching the women in need of treatment
     (Versailles Ballroom)

Edrys Woodroffe, C.S.W.
Senior Parole Officer
New York State Division of Parole

Billie Holliday
Commissioner
New York State Parole Board

42   Making the Break: Facilitating autonomy.   *(Albert Hall II)*

Jacqueline Cohen
M.S.W. Candidate
Hunter School of Social Work
New York, N.Y.

Steve Fried
Office of Criminal Justice Services
Columbus, Oh.

Sydney Goldfarb
Recovery, Inc.
Brooklyn, N.Y.

Lynne Hennecke—Moderator
Doctoral Candidate
Teachers College
Columbia University
New York, N.Y.

43   Post Treatment-Adolescent Issues   *(Malmaison 7)*

Robert E. Gould, M.D.—Moderator
Professor of Psychiatry
Associate Director, Family Life
Division
New York, Medical College
New York, N.Y.

Carol Peacock, M.S.W.
Assistant Commissioner for
   Girls Services
Department of Youth Services
Boston, Mass.

Ani Shahinian
Counselor, Teenage Alcohol Abuse
  Rehabilitation Program
Troy, N.Y.

Modular Workshops

DRUG ABUSE:

D9   Re-entry—Aftercare   *(St. James A)*

Roz Cohen—Moderator
Executive Assistant
Gaudenzia, Inc.
Philadelphia, Penn.

Patricia Spivack
Assistant Director of Women
Daytop Village, Inc.
New York, N.Y.

ALCOHOL:

A10   Support Systems for the Woman Alcoholic   *(Buckingham A)*

Paula H. Gould—Moderator
Managing Director
The Goddard Corporation
Consultant, Employee Program
  Development
Director, Staff Training Programs
New York, N.Y.

Kathleen M.
Alanon

Katherine Walker, M.S.W., C.S.W.
Personal Services
YWCA of the City of New York
New York, N.Y.

Dr. Jean Kirkpatrick
Women for Sobriety, Inc.
Quakertown, Penn.

A12   Helping Men to Help   *(Loire 4/5)*

Susan Deakins, M.D.
Department of Psychiatry
Roosevelt Hospital
New York, N.Y.

Edward Hayes
Senior Alcoholism Counselor
Family Services
Central Islip Alcoholism
  Rehabilitation Unit

Harrison M. Trice, Ph.D.—Moderator
Professor, Dept. of
  Organizational Behavior
New York State School of Industrial
  and Labor Relations
Cornell University

Alcoholism Counselor, South Oaks
  Alcoholism Program
Central Islip, N.Y.

MENTAL HEALTH:

MH11   Institutionalization: Does it differ for women?   *(Malmaison 6)*

Judi Chamberlin
Mental Patients' Liberation Front
Author, *On Our Own: Patient-*
Controlled Alternatives to the
Mental Health System
Cambridge, Mass.

Dr. Evelyn Boyden Darrell—
Moderator
Clinical Psychologist
Instructor in Psychology
Department of Psychiatry
New York University
Bellvue Medical Center
New York, N.Y.

Jan Van Zandt
Member, The Elizabeth Stone House
Jamaica Plain, Mass.

Brand Cotter
Member, The Elizabeth Stone House
Jamaica Plain, Mass.

MH12   Women and Health   *(St. James B)*

Gena Corea
Author, *The Hidden Malpractice: How*
American Medicine Mistreats
Women
Madison, N.J.

Irene Javors, M.A., M.Ed.
Co-Founder/Director of Research
The Feminist Center for Human
Growth and Development, Inc.
Psychotherapist in Private Practice
New York, N.Y.

Dr. Charlotte Schwab
Psychotherapist, Executive Director
The Feminist Center for Human
Growth and Development, Inc.
New York, N.Y.

Norma Swenson—Moderator
Co-Author, *Our Bodies, Ourselves*
Member, National Women's Health
Network
W. Somerville, Mass.

JUSTICE:

J11   The Neglected and Abused Child   *(Regency Foyer)*

Sharon Vogel
Social Worker, Juvenile Bureau
Paramus Police Department
Paramus, N.J.

J12 Runaways and Juvenile Prostitution   *(Loire 2/3)*

Jennifer James, Ph.D.—Moderator
Associate Professor
Department of Psychiatry
University of Washington

Vondie Moore
Executive Director
Michigan Coalition of Runaway
  Services

Judy Seckler
Technical Assistance Specialist
National Office for Social
  Responsibility
Arlington, Va.

Special Sessions

S8 The Displaced Homemaker   *(Buckingham B)*

Dr. N. Carol Eliason
Director, Center for Women's
  Opportunities
American Association of Community
  and Junior Colleges
Washington, D.C.

Cynthia Marano
Coordinator, Displaced Homemakers
  Network
Director, Maryland Center
  for Displaced Homemakers

S9 Implementing an Urban Rape Crisis Center   *(Chelsea A)*

L'Judie Simmons
Chairperson, Mayor's Task Force on
  Rape
New York, N.Y.

S10 Alternatives to Prison   *(Chelsea B)*

M. Sharon Smolick
Assistant Project Director
OAR/NYC
New York, N.Y.

S17 Family Life Theatre: A teenage improvisational theatre group.
  (Versailles Terrace)

New York Medical College
Metropolitan Hospital Center
Family Life Division
New York, N.Y.

Sat 9:00–10:30 AM—Integrated Panels

44   The Politics of Research—Design and Disclosure   *(Buckingham A)*

Jennifer James, Ph.D.—Moderator
Associate Professor
Department of Psychiatry and
   Behavioral Sciences
University of Washington

45   Program Evaluation and Accountability   *(Royal Ballroom)*

Virginia Borrok, DPA
Executive Director
Mental Health Board of HRS
   District IV, Inc.
Jacksonville, Fla.

Stephen Rosenberg
Consultant to
   Governments and Foundations
New York, N.Y.

Barbara McKeand-Stevenson, M.Ed.
   —Moderator
Six Area Coalition
Community Mental Health Center
   Women's Issues
Michigan

Maxine Womble
Assistant Commissioner for
   Alcoholism Services
New York City Department of Mental
   Health, Mental Retardation and
   Alcoholism Services
New York, N.Y.

46   Influencing Legislation—Section I   *(Princess)*

Judith Avner, Esq.
Staff Assistant to
   Rep. Elizabeth Holtzman
Brooklyn, N.Y.

Dr. Gwen Mead
Professor of Political Science
University of Kentucky

Luceille Fleming
Executive Director
Alcoholism & Addiction
   Association of Pennsylvania

47   Influencing Legislation—Section II   *(Regency Foyer)*

Hannah Achtenberg
Executive Director
The Coalition of Voluntary
   Mental Health, Mental Retardation
   and Alcoholism Agencies, Inc.
New York, N.Y.

Carol Whelan
Public Administration
Uniform Services
New York, N.Y.

Erica Spitz—Moderator
Director, New York Urban Coalition
  Resource Center
New York, N.Y.

Karen M. Zuckerman
Community Based Services Specialist
New York State Division of
  Alcoholism and Alcohol
  Abuse
Coordinator, New York State Alliance
  on Women, Alcoholism and
  Alcohol Abuse

48 The Role of the Media: Responsibility versus exploitation *(Regency Ballroom)*

Emma Bowen, President
Black Citizens for Media Affairs
New York, N.Y.

Geraldine R. Miller—Moderator
Partner, Creative Communications
Coudersport, Penn.

Carol Martin
Weekend Anchor-Correspondent
WCBS-TV News
New York, N.Y.

Alice Travis
Public Communications Consultant
  and Analyst
Partner, A&A Bedrosian, Inc.
New York, N.Y.

Dell Warner
Wayne County Dept. of Substance
  Abuse Services
Host, WXYZ-TV (ABC) "Woman to
  Woman"
Columnist, The Detroit News
  "Straight Dope"
Detroit, Mich.

49 Establishing Interdisciplinary Networks *(Versailles Terrace)*

Barbara Gibson, M.S.W.
Senior Administrative Associate to
  Executive Director
Addiction Research & Treatment
  Corporation
Brooklyn, N.Y.

Sylvia G. McCollum—Moderator
Education Administrator
Bureau of Prisons
Washington, D.C.

Stowe W. Hausner, M.S.W.
School of Social Welfare
SUNY at Stony Brook

Flora Koppel
Bedford Styvestant Alcoholism
  Treatment Program
Brooklyn, N.Y.

Modular Workshops

DRUG ABUSE:

D12   Credentialing: Licensing of the paraprofessional worker in the treatment
program   *(Biarritz)*

Martha Ottenberg—Moderator
Director, Outpatient Services
Interim House, Inc.
Philadelphia, Penn.

Sandra J. Robinson
Deputy Director
Western Regional Support Center
Salt Lake City, Utah

D13   Childcare—Role of Public Child Welfare Agencies   *(Loire 4/5)*

Ellen Hoffman
Director of Governmental Affairs
Children's Defense Fund
Washington, D.C.

ALCOHOL:

A13   The Politics of Planning and Funding Services for the Alcoholic Woman
(Albert Hall II)

Antonia D'Angelo, A.C.S.W.
Chair, Committee on Women
  and Alcoholism
National Council on
  Alcoholism, Inc.
New York, N.Y.

Clarice Staff—Moderator
Staff Services
Coordinator, Regional Coalition
  on the Special Needs of
  Women with Alcohol and
  Drug Abuse Problems
New York, N.Y.

Ann Baxter
Executive Director
California Women's Commission
  on Alcoholism
Chairwoman, Executive Advisory
  Council of the Congress of
  State Task Forces on
  Women and Alcohol
Inglewood, Calif.

MENTAL HEALTH:

MH13   Risk Taking, Creativity, and Self-Discovery   *(Malmaison 6)*

Janet Steele-Holloway, M.S.W.
Private Practice
Organizational Consultant in
  Applied Behavioral Sciences
New York, N.Y.

MH14   Lesbian Life Style   *(Albert Hall I)*

Rosemary Madl, R.N., B.S.N.—
   Moderator
Human Services Consultant
Trainer—Female Sexuality,
   Sexual Preference Choice,
   Co-Addiction, Pathophysiology
   of Addiction
Pittsburgh, Penn.

Pamela Ware
Member, Lesbian Mothers' Custody
   Center
New York, N.Y.

JUSTICE:

J14   Role of the Church, Private Business and Unions   *(Malmaison 7)*

Sandra Brandt
Area Representative
Human Resources Development
   Institute, AFL-CIO
Norfolk, Va.

John Ramsey
Community Worker
St. James' Church
New York, N.Y.

Rev. Virginia Mackey
Member, Advisory Committee
National Moratorium on Prison
   Construction
Chair, National Interreligious
   Task Force on Criminal Justice
New York, N.Y.

Cynthia Owen Philip—Moderator
Consultant

Special Session

S18   Operation Cork: Film—"If You Loved Me"   *(Loire 2/3)*

Gila Saks-Bobik
Educational Projects Director
Operation Cork
San Diego, Calif.

Sat 10:45 AM–12:15 PM—Integrated Panels

50   Use of Volunteers   *(Albert Hall I)*

Joseph Coviello
New York State Division of Substance
   Abuse Services
Bureau of Intervention
   and Volunteer Services

Gordon L. Steinhauer
St. Lawrence Hospital
Chairman, Board of Directors
National Council on Alcoholism
Vice President, St. Lawrence
   Hospital
Lansing, Mich.

Mary Farrar—Moderator
Assistant Manager
American Red Cross in
    Greater New York
New York, N.Y.

51   Strategies to Project Women into Leadership Roles   *(Versailles Terrace)*

Joy Fields, B.S., M.H.A.
Surveyor/Field Representative
Accreditation Council -
Psychiatric Facilities
Joint Commission on
    Accreditation of Hospitals
New York, N.Y.

Millie Jeffrey, Chair
National Women's Political Caucus
Washington, D.C.

Marlene Crosby Mainker
President, Womanpower Projects, Inc.
Chatham, N.J.

Anita Kurman Gulkin
Executive Director
Greenwich House
New York, N.Y.

Dr. Marcella Maxwell—Moderator
Chairperson, Commission on
    the Status of Women
City of New York
New York, N.Y.

52   Who Can Treat Whom for What   *(Albert Hall II)*

Marjorie Velimesis, Consultant
Berwyn, Pa

Eleanor R. Fisher, Ed.D.
Director, Alternatives to
    Alcohol Program
Marblehead Community Counseling
    Center
Psychotherapist, Private Practice
Swampscott, Mass.

53   Holistic Approaches for Women   *(Royal Ballroom)*

Marjorie Heller, M.S.
Women's Resource and
    Survival Center, Inc.
Keyport, N.J.

Lois Sigman, A.C.S.W.
Clinical Coordinator, Special
    Services
Coordinator, Alcoholism Services
The Wherler Clinic
Plainville, Conn.

Judi Chamberlin—Moderator
Mental Patients Liberation Front
Author, *On Our Own: Patient-*
    Controlled Alternatives to the
    Mental Health System
Chairperson, National Committee
    on Patients' Rights
Member, Task Panel on Legal
    and Ethical Issues, President's
    Commission on Mental Health

Gwen Ingram
National Council on Crime and
Delinquency
Hackensack, N.J.

Modular Workshops

DRUG ABUSE:

D14 Financing and Reimbursement: The determination of client population by
funding sources.   *(Malmaison 6)*

Norwig Debye-Saxinger
Assistant Director for Substance
Abuse, Contract Management
and Fund Allocation
New York State Division of Substance
Abuse Services

Carl Akins
Executive Director
National Association of State Alcohol
and Drug Abuse Directors
New York, N.Y.

D15 Teenage "Speak Out"   *(Loire 4/5)*

Denise Taylor—Moderator
Coordinator of Health
Advocacy Program
The Door—A Center of
Alternatives
New York, N.Y.

Carl Smith
New York, N.Y.

Denise Torres
New York, N.Y.

Chris Tomb
Eagleville, Penn.

Maritza Marin
New York, N.Y.

Jacqueline Bishop
New York, N.Y.

ALCOHOL:

A15 Obstacles to Implementing Services for Women   *(Regency Ballroom)*

Rozz Cole, M.S.W.
Consultant to Alcohol Programs
for women, minorities and
the aged
Sommerset, N.J.

Virginia S. Ryan, Ph.D.
Wayne County Dept. of
Substance Abuse Services
Detroit, Mich.

Dannie Rowell
Assistant Director
Bureau of Local Services
and Planning
Division of Alcoholism
Office of Substance Abuse
and Alcoholism
New York State

Rita A. Zimmer, M.A.—Moderator
Project Director
Lower Manhattan Sobering-Up
Station
New York, N.Y.

MENTAL HEALTH:

MH15 Authority-Communication Patterns *(Loire 2/3)*

Bobbi Tower
Tower & Associates
Harrisburg, Penn.

Anna Stern
Vice President
Project Return Foundation, Inc.

JUSTICE:

J15 Citizen Advocacy: The role played by private citizens in the criminal
justice process. *(Regency Foyer)*

Ann Dunbar
Ass't Commissioner
NYS-DOCS

Rev. Virginia Mackey
Member, Advisory Committee
National Moratorium on Prison
 Construction
Flora Rothman—Moderator
Chair, Justice for Children Task Force
National Council of Jewish Women
Chair, New York Coalition for
 Juvenile Justice and Youth Services
New York, N.Y.

National Interreligious
 Task Force on Criminal Justice
New York, N.Y.

Special Sessions

S12 It's a Family Affair—Alcoholism and Recovery *(Malmaison 7)*

Carole K.

Jack K.

S13 Compulsive Gambling *(Buckingham A)*

Herb S.
Gambler's Anonymous

S14 The Family Repertory Company—"Marriage Proposal" (a Play)
(Princess)

S19 Film: "Women Who Drink Too Much" *(Monte Carlo)*

Dell Warner
Project Coordinator, Department of
 Substance Abuse Services
Wayne County, Detroit, Mich.

Sat 2:00–3:30 PM—Plenary Session: Making Change

(Georgian B and C)

Violet Padayachi Cherry, A.C.S.W.—
Moderator
Director of Health Services
City of Englewood
Director of Alcohol Counseling
and Treatment Center
Englewood, N.J.

Jody Forman-Sher
Special Assistant for
Women's Affairs
National Institute on
Drug Abuse
Rockville, Md.

Wanda Frogg
President, National Indian Board on
Alcohol & Drug Abuse, Inc.
North American Indian Women's
Council on Chemical Dependency,
Inc.
Turtle Lake, Wisc.

Representative Lester Wolff
Chairman, Select Committee
on Narcotic Abuse Control

Conference Closing

INDEX